POETRY AS HEALER

POETRY AS HEALER

Mending the Troubled Mind

EDITED BY

JACK J. LEEDY, M.D.

NEW YORK
THE VANGUARD PRESS

616.89166 P745L

Poetry as healer

Copyright © 1985 by Jack J. Leedy, M.D.
Published by Vanguard Press, Inc., 424 Madison Avenue, New York, N.Y. 10017.
Published simultaneously in Canada by Book Center, Inc., Montreal, Quebec.
All rights reserved.
No part of this publication may be reproduced or transmitted in
any form or by any means, electronic or mechanical, including
photocopy, recording, or any information or retrieval system, or
otherwise, without the written permission of the publisher, except
by a reviewer who may wish to quote brief passages in connection
with a review for a newspaper, magazine, radio, or television.

Library of Congress Cataloging in Publication Data
Main entry under title:

Poetry as healer

  Includes bibliographies and index.
  1. Poetry — Therapeutic use. I. Leedy, Jack J.
1921–
RC489.P6P625   1985   616.89′166   85–6040
Cloth/ISBN 0–8149–0896–9   Paper/ISBN 0–8149–0911–6

Designer: Tom Bevans
Manufactured in the United States of America.

ACKNOWLEDGMENTS

The editor of POETRY AS HEALER gratefully acknowledges the kind permission of the following publishers and persons to reprint poems and prose:

The Belknapp Press of Harvard University Press and the Trustees of Amherst College for three poems from THE POEMS OF EMILY DICKINSON, edited by Thomas H. Johnson, Cambridge, Mass., copyright 1951 © 1955, 1979, 1983 by the President and Fellows of Harvard College.

Crown Publishers, Inc. for excerpts from A TREASURY OF MEXICAN FOLKWAYS by Frances Toor, copyright © 1947, 1975 by Crown Publishers, Inc.

The John Dewey Society for the Study of Education and Culture for a sentence from LITERATURE AS EXPLORATION by Louise M. Rosenblatt, 1938.

Farrar, Straus and Giroux, Inc. for a brief passage from ON POETRY AND POETS by T. S. Eliot, copyright 1957.

The Free Press, a Division of Macmillan, Inc. for excerpts from FAITH AND HEALING: STUDIES IN PRIMITIVE PSYCHIATRY edited by Ari Kiev, copyright © 1964 by The Free Press of Glencoe.

Harcourt Brace Jovanovich, Inc. for 30 lines from THE COCKTAIL PARTY by T. S. Eliot, copyright 1950 by T. S. Eliot, renewed 1978 by Esme Valerie Eliot.

Harvard University Press for excerpts from THE NAVAJO DOOR: AN INTRODUCTION TO NAVAJO LIFE by A. H. Leighton and D. C. Leighton, published by Harvard University Press, 1944; reprinted New York, Russell and Russell, 1967.

Holt, Rinehart and Winston for "The Road Not Taken" and "The Secret" from THE POETRY OF ROBERT FROST edited by Edward Connery Lathem, copyright 1916, © 1969 by Holt, Rinehart and Winston; 1942 and 1944 by Robert Frost; © 1970 by Lesley Frost Ballantine.

Holt, Rinehart and Winston for "Theme alone ... stay against confusion" from SELECTED PROSE OF ROBERT FROST edited by Hyde Cox and Edward Connery Lathem, copyright © 1939 by Holt, Rinehart and Winston.

Alfred A. Knopf, Inc. for excerpts from THE PROPHET by Kahlil Gibran, copyright 1923 by Kahlil Gibran and renewed 1951 by Administrators C.T.A. of Kahlil Gibran Estate, and Mary G. Gibran.

The Liveright Publishing Corporation for lines from "Hunger and Thirst" from THE EVERLASTING MINUTE by Louis Ginsberg, copyright 1937 by Liveright Publishing Corporation, copyright renewed 1964 by Louis Ginsberg.

The New York Review of Books for a poem, "Dream," from TEACHING THE UNTEACHABLE, copyright © 1967 by Herbert Kohl.

Clarkson N. Potter, Inc. for four limericks from THE LURE OF THE LIMERICK edited by William S. Baring-Gould, copyright © 1967 by William S. Baring-Gould.

The Princeton University Press for short quotations from SHAMANISM: ARCHAIC TECHNIQUES OF ECSTASY by Mircea Eliade, translated by William R. Trask, Bollingen Series LXXVI, copyright © 1964 by Princeton University Press.

Random House, Inc. for an excerpt from W. H. AUDEN: COLLECTED POEMS edited by Edward Mendelson, copyright 1940 and renewed 1968 by W. H. Auden.

Routledge & Kegan Paul Ltd. for translation of Maylay Chant 'Ho, Lord of the World!...' from MAYLAY MAGICIAN by R. Winstedt, published in London by Routledge & Kegan Paul PLC, 1961.

Rutledge Books for several selections from THE NONSENSE BOOK OF NONSENSE edited by J. Heavilin, copyright © 1964 by Manuscript Press.

Scott, Foresman and Company for a passage by Paul Engle and W. Carrier from READING MODERN POETRY, Glenview, IL, Scott, Foresman and Company, 1955.

The University of Chicago Press for a Navajo chant from RED MAN'S RELIGION by R. Underhill, copyright © 1965 by The University of Chicago Press.

Viking Penguin Inc. for an excerpt from JOHN KEATS, THE MAKING OF A POET by Aileen Ward, copyright © 1963 by Aileen Ward.

*To
Norma Leedy
for her understanding help*

*Give sorrow words: the grief that does not speak
Whispers the o'er-fraught heart, and bids it break.*
—S<small>HAKESPEARE</small>

CONTENTS

INTRODUCTION xix

PART I WHY

The Universal Language of Rhythm 3
    JOOST A. M. MEERLOO, M.D.

Why Poetry? 17
    S. SUE ROBINSON, M.S.S., A.C.S.W.
    and JEAN K. MOWBRAY, M.S.

A Defense of Poetry Therapy 28
    MORRIS ROBERT MORRISON, Ph.D.

Shamans, Witch Doctors, Medicine Men and Poetry 40
    ABRAHAM A. BLINDERMAN, Ph.D.

PART II HOW

Exploring the Unconscious through Nonsense Poetry 57
    ANTHONY A. PIETROPINTO, M.D.

Principles of Poetry Therapy 82
    JACK J. LEEDY, M.D.

Poetry as Communication in Psychotherapy 89
    HAROLD GREENWALD, Ph.D.

Validation of Poetry Therapy
 as a Group Therapy Technique 102
   KENNETH F. EDGAR, Ph.D. and RICHARD HAZLEY, M.A.

The Psychodynamics of Poetry by Patients 115
   E. MANSELL PATTISON, M.D.

PART III WHERE

IN PRISON
Poetry in a Cage 135
   BILL J. BARKLEY, Ph.D.

IN A MENTAL HEALTH CENTER
Poetry Therapy for Psychoneurotics 151
   CHARLES CROOTOF, Ph.D.

IN THE THERAPIST'S OFFICE
Poetry as Therapy—and Therapy as Poetry 163
   MILTON M. BERGER, M.D.

IN THE HOSPITAL
Treatment of a Psychotic Patient by Poetry Therapy 175
   ROBERT E. JONES, M.D.

Poetry Therapy with Hospitalized Schizophrenics 184
   KENNETH F. EDGAR, Ph.D., RICHARD HAZLEY, M.A.,
   and HERBERT I. LEVIT, Ed.D.

The Double Door 193
   ROBERT E. JONES, M.D.

The Use of Poetry in a Private Mental Hospital 201
   AARON KRAMER, Ph.D.

IN THE APARTMENTS OF HOME-BOUND PUPILS
Poetry Therapy with Disturbed Adolescents 212
   MORRIS ROBERT MORRISON, Ph.D.

IN PUBLIC SCHOOLS
Self-Discovery
    for Teacher and Youngster through Poetry   228
        ART BERGER, Ph.D.

Poetry Therapy in
    a "600" School and in a Counseling Center   249
        DOROTHY KOBAK, Ph.D.

IN A SCHOOL FOR DEAF CHILDREN, A COMMUNITY GUIDANCE CENTER, AND A SCHOOL FOR EMOTIONALLY DISTURBED CHILDREN
Opening New Worlds to the Deaf and the Disturbed   257
    LUCIEN BUCK, Ph.D. and AARON KRAMER, Ph.D.

IN A DRUG REHABILITATION CENTER
Poetry: A Therapeutic Tool
    with Treatment of Drug Abuse   287
        RUTH LISA SCHECHTER, C.P.T.

A LIST OF POEMS   294

INDEX   299

CONTRIBUTORS

BILL J. BARKLEY, Ph.D. (deceased)
*Chief Staff Clinical Psychologist, Psychiatric Service,
California Men's Colony—East A E, San Luis Obispo, California*

ART BERGER, Ed.D.
*Expressive Therapist, Institute of Mental Health, Cranston, Rhode Island;
C.P.T. (Certified Poetry Therapist); Widely published poet*

MILTON M. BERGER, M.D.
*Clinical Associate Professor of Psychiatry,
Downstate Medical Center, State University of New York;
Lecturer in Psychiatry, College of Physicians and Surgeons,
Columbia University, New York;
Director, Education and Training, South Beach Psychiatric Center,
Staten Island, New York;
Life Fellow, American Psychiatric Association;
Fellow, New York Academy of Medicine; American Academy
of Psychoanalysis; American Group Psychotherapy Association*

ABRAHAM A. BLINDERMAN, Ph.D.
*Professor Emeritus, S.U.N.Y., Farmingdale, New York;
Adjunct Professor of English, C. W. Post Center, Long Island University;
Contributor to many journals and newspapers, including*
The New York State Journal of Medicine, Newsday,
and The New York Times

LUCIEN BUCK, Ph.D.
Professor of Psychology, Dowling College, Oakdale, California

CHARLES CROOTOF, Ph.D.
*Private practice, Manhasset Hills, New York; Member,
Postgraduate Psychoanalytic Society, American Psychological Association,
and National Register of Health Service Providers in Psychology*

KENNETH F. EDGAR, Ph.D.
*Professor of Psychology, Indiana University of Pennsylvania,
Indiana, Pennsylvania; Clinical Psychologist, Indiana Guidance Center;
Member, American Psychological Association*

HAROLD GREENWALD, Ph.D.
*Director, Direct Decision Therapy Institute, San Diego, California;
President, Professional School of Psychological Studies;
Fellow, American Psychological Association, American Society of
Clinical Hypnosis, and American Psychotherapy Association;
Past President, National Psychological Association for Psychoanalysis,
Academy of Psychologists in Family Therapy, Association for
Applied Psychoanalysis*

RICHARD HAZELY, M.A.
*Professor, English Department, Indiana University of Pennsylvania,
Indiana, Pennsylvania; Co-therapist in poetry therapy groups;
Advisor at I.U.P. to poetry therapy interns*

ROBERT E. JONES, M.D.
*Professor of Psychiatry, Jefferson Medical College, Philadelphia,
Pennsylvania*

DOROTHY KOBAK, Ph.D.
*Executive Director, The Edu-Caring Foundation,
Resources for Human Development, Ardmore, Pennsylvania;
Visiting Professor, Temple University, and Thomas Jefferson University;
Associate Director and Psychotherapist,
Mid-Way Counseling Center, New York, New York;
Poetry Therapy in Special Education,
Alternative School at Bronx Regional High School*

AARON KRAMER, Ph.D.
*Professor of English, Dowling College, Oakdale, New York;
Distinguished poet and translator. Many of his poems have been
set to music, choreographed, and dramatized. Oblomov, a musical
play for which he wrote the lyrics was selected for development
and performance at The Eugene O'Neill Theatre Center;
Co-editor, West Hills Review:* A Whitman Journal

JACK J. LEEDY, M.D.
*Private practice, Manhattan and Brooklyn, New York,
Psychiatrist, Veterans Administration Outpatient Clinic,
Brooklyn, New York;
Member, Faculty, New School for Social Research, New York, New York;
Courtesy Staff, Department of Psychiatry, The Brooklyn Hospital—
Caledonian Hospital;
Founder and President Emeritus, National Association for Poetry Therapy;
Life Member, American Psychiatric Association*

HERBERT I. LEVIT, Ed.D.
*President, Dr. Herbert I. Levitt, P.C.,
Consulting Child Clinical Psychologist, Laughlin Children's Center,
Sewickly, Pennsylvania;
Member, Medical Staff, Allegheny General Hospital,
Pittsburgh, Pennsylvania;
Member, Medical Staff, Suburban General Hospital,
Pittsburgh, Pennsylvania;
Member, Board of Directors, United Mental Health, Inc.,
Pittsburgh, Pennsylvania;
Member, Board of Directors, Academy for Education in
Professional Psychology (Western Pennsylvania);
Member, Academy of Forensic Psychologists;
Private practice in Clinical and Forensic Psychology*

JOOST A.M. MEERLOO, M.D. (deceased)
Associate Professor of Psychiatry, New York School of Psychiatry

MORRIS ROBERT MORRISON, M.D.
*Founder and President, The American Academy for Poetry Therapy;
President Emeritus, National Association for Poetry Therapy;
Faculty, Department of Psychology, St. Edward's University,
Austin, Texas;
Fellow, American Association for Social Psychology;
Member, Faculty, Institute for Life to Learning, Austin Community College,
Austin, Texas;
Poetry Therapist,* Who's Who in America

JEAN K. MOWBRAY, M.S.
Freelance writer;
Retired as Full Professor of Psychology,
Harcum Junior College,
Bryn Mawr, Pennsylvania

E. MANSELL PATTISON, M.D.
Professor and Chairman, Department of Psychiatry and Health Behavior,
Medical College of Georgia, Augusta, Georgia

ANTHONY PIETROPINTO, M.D.
Supervising Psychiatrist, Manhattan Psychiatric Center,
New York, New York;
Associate Attending Psychiatrist, St. Vincent's Hospital and
Medical Center, New York, New York

S. SUE ROBINSON, M.S.S., A.C.S.W. (deceased)
Director of Social Services,
The Institute of Pennsylvania Hospital, Philadelphia, Pennsylvania

RUTH LISA SCHECTER, C.P.T. (Certified Poetry Therapist)
Certified Poetry Therapist, Odyssey Institute of Psychiatry,
Phelps Memorial Hospital;
Consultant C.P.T., Purdue University;
Guest Lecturer, Guest Poet; MacDowell Fellow;
Poet, eighth collection of poems, Speedway;
Member, P.E.N. and Poetry Society of America;
Editor, Croton Review, *a N.E.A. recipient*

INTRODUCTION

The Stone Age shaman was the first to incorporate poetry into his healing rituals through his use of spells, exhortations, and the rites of exorcism. Poetry continued to play a core role in the medical programs of ancient societies, as discerned in Mesopotamia and Babylon and in Greek, Roman, Hebrew, Etruscan, Arabic, Teutonic, and Celtic cultures. Anthropological evidence bears witness to the surviving place of poetry in medical practice in disparate areas across the globe—in Siberia and the Orient, in Polynesia, Australia, Africa, and among the Amer-Indians and the Eskimos. The identification of poetry with healing is still in evidence among peasant and surviving primitive communities.

We also have the testimony of a long line of poets, philosophers, and physicians from the classical period in Greece and Rome and the intervening centuries to representatives of contemporary psychiatry (Theodor Reik, J. L. Moreno, Silvano Arieti, Jules Masserman, Alan Stone, Robert Gibson) favoring the historic therapeutic alliance between medicine and poetry.

Recent medical research in the biochemistry of the emotions (Harvard, Yale, the University of Rochester, Chicago University, the Health Science School of the University of Texas) continue to emphasize how attitudes and emotions act as significant determinants of health or disease. Freud has already documented the close relations between mind and body, between psychological predisposition and behavioral manifestation.

Robert Graves noted that "A well-chosen anthology of verse is a complete dispensary for the more common mental disorders and may be used as much for prevention as cure." In the light of today's findings, Norman Cousins, once editor of *The Saturday Review of Literature* and currently one of the medical faculty of UCLA and Medical Advisory Board of the Veterans Administration, advises us that the human brain is "an apothecary capable of writing prescriptions for the human body" and that many of the patient's problems are "better comprehended through the realm bequeathed by art and literature than through the facts revealed by science." In a sense, he is echoing Masserman's advice to the psychotherapist to reflect on the plays of Euripedes, Aeschylus, and Aristophanes as writings that best explore and epitomize basic human relationships.

In 1928 my late friend, Eli Greifer, began a campaign to show that a poem's didactic message has a specific healing power in itself. Like Alexander Pope, he castigated those for whom poetry is mere sound or esthetic experience, those "tuneful fools"

> Who haunt Parnassus but to please their ear,
> Not mend their minds, as some to Church repair
> Not for the doctrine, but the music there.

Eli organized the Village Arts Center and the Messagists Club at 37 West Eighth Street, and then the Remedy Rhyme Gallery, at one Charles Street, New York City. In 1958 Eli joined me at Cumberland Hospital, Mental Hygiene Clinic, Brooklyn, New York, to form the first Poetry Therapy Group. We tried new approaches for the use of poetry in or as therapy; we went on tours; we participated in meetings and conventions. Our aim was to stimulate members of the mental health professions, teachers and educators, the clergy and penologists, nurses and others, to explore the uses of poetry in the alleviation of mental suffering.

In the past thirty years, the use of poetry for the treatment of emotional and physical disorders has made encouraging progress. In 1969 I founded APT (the Association for Poetry Therapy), which became NAPT (the National Association for Poetry Therapy) in 1981. Annual conventions have been held each year and attended by people from many nations of the world.

In New York City, Dr. Morris R. Morrison was a brilliant pioneer in poetry therapy, and he initiated the first course in Poetry As Therapy at the New School for Social Research. He served as President of APT for seven years. In Austin, Texas, Dr. Morrison actively continues his work as Director, American Academy of Poetry Therapy, and teaches Poetry As Therapy at the University of Texas, St. Edwards University, and Austin Community College.

In Encino, California, Dr. Arthur Lerner founded the Poetry Therapy Institute in 1973. Dr. Lerner is now President of the National Association for Poetry Therapy. The Los Angeles City Council recently honored him with a Resolution for Distinguished Service on the occasion of his retirement from the faculty of Los Angeles City College, Department of Psychology and Humanities where he taught since 1957. He is Director of Poetry Therapy at Woodview-Calabassas Hospital. He conducted classes in Poetry Therapy and related courses at UCLA Extension long before the founding of the Institute. He is Editor of the book *Poetry in the Therapeutic Experience* (Pergamon Press).

At St. Elizabeth's Hospital, Washington, D.C., Arleen Hynes initiated Biblio-Poetry Therapy workshops and has been followed with distinction by Clara Lack, C.P.T. and Rosalie Brown, C.P.T. In 1976 the first federal bibliotherapy position was established through the efforts of Arleen Hynes, who also helped to establish the National Federation for Biblio-Poetry Therapy, Inc., in order to unite the related fields with uniform standards.

In Manhattan, Evelyn Neinken, C.P.T. has assisted me with our Poetry Therapy Groups, and has enhanced the healing process with her exploration of body movement while poems are read aloud.

Ruth Lisa Schechter, C.P.T. spent seven years as a poetry therapist at Odyssey House, a national rehabilitation agency for drug and child abuse. She is now active in poetry therapy in Westchester County, New York, and serves as editor of the *Croton Review*.

Ann White, C.P.T. in Ft. Lauderdale, Florida, has been active in developing programs in Poetry and the Creative Arts as Therapy. She has been assisted by Debbie Grayson, C.P.T. Also active in Poetry Therapy in Florida are Dr. Nicholas Mazza, Editor, *N.A.P.T. Newsletter*, and S. Gale Gilburt, retired school principal.

In Baldwin, New York, Beverly Bussolati, O.T.R., Secretary of NAPT for the past four years, has been innovative with new approaches developing links between poetry and occupational therapy.

In Columbus, Ohio, Jennifer Groce Welch founded the Ohio Poetry Therapy Center, and is the founder and Editor of *Pudding* magazine. Dr. George Bell of Huron, Ohio, is Executive Director of NAPT, and his books of poetry as *Pauses* have healed many.

In Louisville, Kentucky, Dr. Glenn Roosevelt is co-director of the Louisville Poetry Institute. Joy Shieman, C.P.T. has been busy planting the seeds of poetry therapy all over the West Coast. She established the Poetry Therapy Program at El Camino Hospital, Mountain View, California. She has worked tirelessly to alert the public and the professionals to the healing properties of poetry.

With the creative arts therapies receiving more and more enthusiastic reception, and young pioneers entering the field, my associate Sherry Reiter, M.A., C.P.T. has worked hard to establish higher standards of poetry therapy and training. This has resulted in standards of certification and the initiation of new courses on the college and graduate level such as the one offered at Hofstra University in the Counseling, Psychology, Research and Education Division entitled "Poetry Therapy for the Helping Professional." At the New School for Social Research, New York City, Sherry Reiter and I teach the course "Poetry Therapy: Toward Self-Knowledge."

There are many potential uses of the healing force of poetry. Poetry can help the people of one nation understand people of another nation because poetry expresses the heart of a people. Percy Bysshe Shelley said, "Poets are the unacknowledged legislators of the world." Poetry can help bridge the generation gap. Poetry can be a healing force when it gives a person a new way of life. One sings the same song to all of one's life's experiences. Although one sings as one lives, there is increasing evidence that one may live a new way if one sings a new song.

"Every poet," said T. S. Eliot, "would like to be able to think that he had some direct social utility... as things are, poetry is not a career." Eliot spoke fifty-five years too soon. Poets are now allied with workers of the healing professions. Poetry is a royal road to the unconscious and a natural vehicle to encouraging communication. Like medications, poems are now used as tranquilizers, anti-depressants, sedatives, and hypnotics. No one has ever died of an overdosage of poetry.

People are looking for new ways of self expression or ways out of established unsatisfactory living patterns. Poetry is a secret power and an untapped national resource for healing. Poetry is a guide to the hidden mind and to more creative and enriching life.

This book, *Poetry as Healer*, is a reprinting of chapters from two books that I edited for J. B. Lippincott Company: *Poetry Therapy* in 1969 and *Poetry the Healer* in 1973. In accordance with the wishes of the Contributing Authors, the chapters remain in their original form.

—JACK J. LEEDY, M.D.

POETRY
AS
HEALER

PART I

WHY

The Universal Language of Rhythm

JOOST A. M. MEERLOO, M.D.

*Once we have command of the rhythm
We have command of the world.*
                                NOVALIS

During the second world war, I had a personal encounter with the healing powers of a kind of poetry therapy. It was during one of the most trying times of my life. I remember how three prisoners lay crowded across the one dirty cot in the cell, on a thin layer of straw where fleas and bed bugs held their nightly feast. We were from different lands and understood only a few words of each other's tongues. To make matters more uncomfortable, we had no idea whether the morning would bring death or liberation.

The humid summer night was devoid of sleep. After a while, one of us made a feeble attempt to hum, and then began to intone some lyrics in his own language. Gradually, we took over in turn each other's chanting of intimate thoughts in measured cadences. That was how we managed to soothe ourselves with a kind of verbal hypnosis, which took the place of sleep. We were lucky to have discovered something ecstatic in our playful rhythmization of words.

No great poetry was spoken that night, or on many another similar occasion. But it was my repeated experience in those stressful years that people in extreme anxiety, frozen by the enemy into complete passivity while awaiting their fate, would suddenly find a rhythmic voice inside themselves—a voice that spoke for their essential "me." It is a pity that more of this war poetry by non-poets has not been gathered. Almost written in blood, these verses were smuggled out of prison or concentration camp, while the authors waited for an echo in their silent isolation. With the liberation, the emergency poets stopped writing their verses. But they had found the secret of communion through rhythm and poetry, a form of communication usually used by more creative talents.

On the assumption that there is a universal rhythmic communication with complex biological and psychological aspects—as I described more elaborately in my studies on *Mental Contagion*[11,13]—I will limit myself here to some clinical features of rhythmic interaction. In some people, such communication will break out into dance, in others into music and singing, in still others into poetry. Indeed, we find that rhythm is back of all great creative cultural achievements.

Therapeutically, all forms of communication may be used to expand the usual means of interaction and mutual relationship between patient and therapist. It may be too pretentious here to use the terms music therapy, dance therapy, or even poetry therapy. They are adjuncts to the totality of interactions and transactions in every human contact.

Rhythmic interaction is of great importance in any form of human communication. The moment there is rhythm, something is shared by the participants. The young child reacts more to the cadences of poetry than to the words: he claps his hands in time, mouths and recites the music of the words. At the other end of the life span, when many functions of the mind have broken down, senile patients repeat rhythmic whisperings of the music of words. When verbalization of the message is no longer possible, the meter remains.

Biologic Rhythms

At this moment, the investigation of a variety of rhythmic functions is in full swing. The ancient Greek physicians were already keenly interested in the manifold rhythms of man: "The body," said Hippocrates, "consumes time by its functions." Life is a conglomeration of many rhythmic events, known and unknown. Today's scientists are becoming more and more aware of man's built-in biologic clock.

Among animals, various instances are observed of actual and accurate instinctual measuring of cosmic time without benefit of outer clocks. Fish in an aquarium rise to the surface to await their dinner at exactly fixed times. Certain worms of the seashore dig themselves into the sand shortly before the beginning of floodtide. Many butterflies change their coloring with the coming of day and night. The rhythm of not only sunrise and sunset but also the moon awakens analogous phenomena in many animals. There are worms that come out of the beach sand only at full moon. And many's the woman whose passions rise to full height with the coming of the full moon.

Darwin reasoned that man, having come forth from the sea, must still have in him a tidal rhythm, and he felt that we must accept some interrelation between the lunar phase and the menstrual hormonal process, even though the direct links are unknown.[6,14] Moreover, the term lunacy for mental disturbances belongs to the realm of explorable concepts of continuous geophysical action on man.[10] Psychiatrists are quite familiar with the cyclic psychoses and neuroses dependent on the season of the year as well as the tides. Usually, we human beings are not aware consciously of being subjected to various cosmic and biologic rhythms. Only when a too fast jet flight changes our adaptation to the day and night cycle do we recognize our adaptational troubles.

Periodic events in man are under the control of the autonomic nervous system. Yet the moment we start to measure bodily functions, for instance temperature, we become aware of a cosmic rhythm. We observe hormonal rhythms, to which the menstrual cycle belongs. We recognize the variation in moods related to the seasons, and we find, for example, the periodic seasonal appearance of stomach ulcer.[19]

Pathologists tend to relate certain periodic diseases to unknown rhythms of life—cyclic neutropenia, periodic arthralgia, periodic paralysis. With the use of the electrocardiogram, the electroencephalogram, and the electrodermatogram, normal and pathologic rhythms can be detected. Breathing, of course, has its distinct rhythms, as do the intestines, the heart and the muscles, the molecules and even the intra-atomic particles.

Embryonic Rhythmic Behavior

From the eighth intrauterine week, the organism lives in an envelope of rhythm; rhythmic reactive and protective movements are noted. The fetus reacts to sounds from the outside world; it lives in a floating rhythmic sound world (the word *rhythm*, incidentally, is derived from *rheein*—to flow) filled with auditive impressions. There is the sound of the maternal heartbeat and vessels, with a mean frequency of 70, and superimposed upon this the different rhythm of the fetal heart, with a mean frequency of 140.

Observation of fetal movements as reaction to sounds, combined with the knowledge that amniotic fluid is a better sound conductor than air, makes the existence of a prenatal syncopated rhythmic sound world more than likely. We can imitate the whole physical uterine plant and reproduce the various sounds in this experimental setting by holding our head under water and hearing the prebirth world. This experiment makes it easier for us to understand why there is in later life such a strong universal spontaneous reaction to syncopated music. The fact is that an old mnemonic pattern has been invoked with all its unconscious associations with previous nirvanic joys.

Some of the nonsense verses recapture for us the archaic syncopated rhythm:

> The water it soon came in, it did,
> The water it soon came in;
> So to keep them dry they wrapped their feet
> In a purky paper all folded neat,
> And they fastened it down with a pin.[9]

"Rhythm," says Sister Paul Gabriel,[4] "has the earliest appeal and is likely the most lasting." She quotes the following poem for a child:

> 'Tis all the way to Toe-Town
> Beyond the knee-high Hill
> That Baby has to travel down,
> To watch the soldiers drill.
>
> One, two, three, four, five
> A row; a captain and his men
> And on the other side, you see
> Are six, seven, eight, nine, ten.

The pleasure of rhyme and rhythm comes long before baby knows that the poem deals with his toes.

Rhythmic rocking, dancing, and floating in the amniotic fluid belong to normal intrauterine movements.[15] The child in the womb yawns (intrauterine drinking), scratches, cringes and stretches in response to outer stimulation. From patients in psychotherapy we have learned that the ecstasy of jazz music, not to mention rock and roll, is brought on by various reminiscent feelings of a lost long ago and far away happiness.

Postnatal Rhythmic Interaction

In cultures not so mechanized and civilized as our own, we can observe a rhythmic motoric interaction between mothers and newborn babies. This interaction develops when the child is brought to the breast immediately after birth. Baby's tiny hands open and close in rhythm, pawing at the breast (the milk reflex so clearly visible in cats when they are stroked); baby's head moves back and forth from one nipple to the other, and both mother and child move to and fro in a tender swaying—a "milk dance"[12] reminiscent of the rhythm of coitus. This is as if the basic acts in the service of the continuity of life were governed by the same rhythmic interaction. At the same time, it tells us why these same rhythmic interactions are so often suppressed in a puritanical hospital setting: I have known obstetrical nurses to scold the new mothers for going through such "childish" paces.

The rhythmic interaction between mother and infant is probably phylogenetically derived from an adaptive nipple-seeking behavior seen in higher animals. The newborn lamb is rejected by mother and flock and has to die if it cannot reach the nipple within a specific time span. For by its weakness it would expose the waiting flock to dangerous predators.

Mothers who breast-feed their children, especially among so-called primitive people, unwittingly use the same rhythmic movements every time they give the baby the breast. Even the infant's suckling occurs in rhythmic design, like thumbsucking at a later age. Usually these rhythmic interactions disappear when the period of breast feeding is delayed (frustrated) from four to six hours after birth. In our technological age, many hospitals delay the first feeding and libidinal encounter between mother and baby for 24 hours.[13]

Abnormal Rhythmic Expressions

The study of intrauterine movements and early infantile adaptational responses is important for pathology. The early repressed rhythmic reflexes return in neurotic and psychotic children in whom, according to psychoanalytic experience, oral deprivation and the lack of motoric pleasure become overwhelming trauma. Also, we repeatedly observe in therapy that even in older patients, either in deep hypnosis or in deep regression, early infantile motoric interaction patterns return spontaneously. Various adults complain about these rhythmic contractions of legs and body in half sleep shortly before falling asleep. The uncontrollable movements wake them fully again.

The startle reaction in infants also shows a pattern of rhythmic defense movements slowly petering out. Such a startle can also break out into rhythmic jumping in either frightened or extremely happy older persons. A film of Hitler, made after the surrender of France was signed at Versailles, shows him making just such stamping movements.

Spontaneous rocking, jumping, bouncing, headbanging are often also seen in well-cared-for infants. Mittelman[16] calls them autoerotic movements. They usually appear in the first year of life and are residuals of the repressed early adaptational rhythms. These returning, repressed movements can persist and be used as a masochistic self-hurting reaction to some frustrating experience.

Incessant scratching, headbanging,[3] genital rubbing, early masturbation and rhythmic rocking may all be interpreted as manifestations of displaced appropriate innate rhythmic adaptational reflexes in the service of primary gratification.[11] Many children use headbanging as a means of exhausting themselves and putting themselves to sleep. Even when it hurts, it gives sweet rhythmic catharsis. Frightened mothers who dread this can be taught to recite nursery rhymes and folk songs to their children as a substitute for the potentially harmful headbanging.

> I'm a lean dog, a keen dog, a wild dog and lone;
> I'm a rough dog, a tough dog, hunting on my own;
> I'm a bad dog, a mad dog, teasing silly sheep;
> I love to sit and bay at the moon, to keep fat souls from sleep.[4]

Autistic children show a return of early adaptational rhythms, chiefly to and fro rocking. They can sit a whole day long in a chair and do nothing else. The pawing, milking movement is often used towards those whom they want to touch, or they direct the same movement towards their own genitals. Compulsive masturbation is often a displaced milk reflex.

Headbanging is more frequently seen in autistic than in neurotic children. Often they get head wounds as a result of these wild orgiastic movements and develop, besides, as a reaction to any outside frightening stimulus, a wild dancing stamping step, which often resembles the uterine dance. In a camp for schizophrenic children, I was able to observe these rhythmic movements at close hand. One boy who loved to float for hours on a diving board in the swimming pool showed all these rhythmic movements, interrupted from time to time by agitated masturbation. It is not yet widely known that we can make use of these rhythmic signals to break through the autism of the child and build up a rhythmic sign language through sound or touch or movement.

These rhythmic manifestations call for more thorough clinical investigation. This writer intends if possible to study the whole gamut of rhythms in a total rhythmic profile. Such movements may also be seen in neurotics during therapeutic sessions. Many bizarre motions can be explained as a return of early frustrated adaptations. Especially in deep regression, while producing early infantile memories, patients on the couch are apt to reenact various rhythmic movements, particularly of the feet. The same is true for patients in hypnosis. The frequency of such movements and signals is usually slower than the heart rate and depends on subjective experiences relating to very early reminiscences.

The Communicative Function of Rhythm

Most mothers know by instinct that rhythmic movements soothe and relax the baby. Maternal and infantile pulsations co-vibrate. Rocking the cradle, singing lullabies, carrying and cuddling the child, holding it "under her heart" (in the double sense), rhythmic stroking of the back—these serve to supply and guarantee feelings of security and protection. Masserman[10] explains this dependency on rhythm as one of the magic *ur* defenses of man, the miraculous transformation of chaos into pleasurable order. The outside rhythm is incorporated into a personal beat and order of time. As we noted previously, the rhyme and rhythm of poetry often have a much more compelling force than the actual meaning of the words. Through rhythm, old phylogenetic memories are aroused, and rhythm helps us memorize what formerly seemed chaotic.

Our cooscillation with biological rhythms and the rhythms of the outside world brings us back to the Never-never land of our youth. The rhythm of the waves of the sea has a lulling, sleep-inviting action. It is when people cannot live and move in unison with this rhythm that they become sick—seasick. The whole world is experienced then as one vast cauldron of danger.

At birth, the rhythm of maternal schedules begins to intrude upon the biologic rhythms of the infant, the measured meter of solemnity and duty. The first clock the infant hears is the maternal heartbeat as it lies at mother's left breast. Waiting for feeding in hungry expectancy creates the first mnemonic impression of boredom and empty time—feelings that play central roles in dreams of frustrated people.

Monkeys as well as human babies behave more quietly when resting near the maternal heart. An artificial reproduction of the same beat often has a quieting influence. Those familiar with the training of pets know that a yelping anxious puppy can be soothed by a ticking clock wrapped in a blanket. Above all, rhythm gives a sense of familiarity. Hypnosis starts with a rhythmic soothing of the subject, and the lulling of lullabies is as old as mankind.

Sometimes the intrusion of artificial schedules may lead to an educational eurhythmia, or a clash—a dysrhythmia. Here the child pits his own rhythm against someone else's. The manic-depressive vacillation of moods is often explained as such an early acquired dysrhythmia. Social schedules are the huge synchronizers intruding into biologic rhythms. Psychosomatic diseases often start as defense against the intrusion by outside schedules upon biologic patterns. In attempting to control the unpleasant routine, the counterroutine begins to control the young protester.

The Language of Rhythm

At this moment, we are not able to give an exact analysis of the complex symphony of rhythms in our organism. Clinically, we are aware that every individual has a personal profile of rhythms. Future analysts of these profiles will be better able to predict the interference and cooscillation between outward rhythmic profiles, such as music or poetry, and inward rhythmic profiles. Rigid habits are often broken down by more primordial rhythms; they can even free repressed primitive impulses. It was impressive to find a silent catatonic patient starting to talk again after dancing.

This subject of rhythmic communication has become more and more significant since we have become aware that rhythm in one person can be transferred directly to another. Rhythm represents the collective memory of mankind; there exists a compulsion to imitate and cooscillate. The unobtrusive rhythm that I tap out on a desk while giving a lecture is unwittingly taken up by some of the people in my audience. This inadvertent interplay and interaction can often be observed among children, the dance of one provoking a dance in the playmate.

> It's hopperty, skipperty, high and low
> Summer's the time for fun.[4]

All of us experience this compulsive reverberation and cooscillation in the group. Few can resist the seductive pull of the marchers in a parade. We all succumb to this magic effect of rhythm. A group that chants collectively "we are not afraid" mesmerizes itself into being brave. Most of the primitive rituals and revivals that make a solid deindividualized mass of the group do it by incessant and insistent rhythmic movements. The rhythmic taking over of sound and motion in dance and chant is token contact and facilitates mutual identification.

Such rhythm may serve as the vitalizing impulse that changes accumulated violence into creative discharge. Order suppresses crude instinct. But we members of the technologic era are unwittingly subjected to various contaminating rhythms. Public opinion engineers use jingles and rhythmic slogans to make their suggestions penetrate more readily into our minds, no matter how resistant we try to be. Television and movies resort to a variety of rhythms and tunes so that we may become that much more involved with the suggestive actions on the screen.

Political propaganda uses rhythmic slogans, such as the Nazi "Sieg Heil, Sieg Heil" or the Fascist "Duce, Duce," to sweep the masses into receptive and submissive identification with the leader. Certain tricky beats and tunes catch us. We repeat them and go over them in our minds time and again:

> "Beware the Jabberwock, my son!
> The jaws that bite, the claws that catch!
> Beware the Jubjub bird, and shun
> The frumious Bandersnatch!"[2]

Our need to cheer and sing, to scan and rhyme words is partly a conquest of the mechanical beats pounding in us, partly the need to covibrate and cooscillate with others and feel at home in a group. Our word *emotion* means moving away or moving together in cooscillation and com-motion with another being. Such rhythmic commotion in the group may be observed when taking home movies in various family settings. If the films are flashed on the screen at a faster than normal speed, we can detect a continual rhythmic moving to and fro in the conversational circle. Similarly, the interaction in group psychotherapy is always combined with subliminal contagious movements.

Rhythm and Mental Contagion

Mental contagion is by definition the subtle transmission of feelings, thoughts and attitudes from one person to another. This form of psychic contamination may usually be traced to a common regression, to infantile physiologic responses.[11] Rhythm provokes rhythm; laughter provokes laughter; fright provokes fright. The distress call by one induces feelings of distress in the other. Scratching in one brings on itching in another. These phenomena are all subject to the common rule of mental infection: *The more an expression evokes infantile archaic responses of the organism—the innate biologic signal code—the more infectious it is.*

Archaic communication may be described as a rudimentary remnant of biologic signals, originally used as a warning to fellow creatures to flee or hide. The important implication of this rule of mental contamination is that it is so much easier to transmit regressive forms of communication, such as chaos, fury, panic and revolt, than to infect people with good examples and restraint. In Northern Italy, collective singing of spontaneous poetry, the ristornelli, is used as a token duel between groups.

One group of youngsters going through the gyrations of the last phase of rock and roll induces another group to regress to the same form of rhythmic interaction. In the meantime, the energy output increases. I have witnessed positive rock and roll furies. In dancing, one surrenders to the rhythm of the music, a major surrender to the greater rhythmic occurrences in the world.[8] There are tribes that use their magic dances to bring on and promote the rhythmic contractions of the mother's womb while she is in the throes of giving birth. Others beat the tribal drums and dance to stimulate the temporary pugnacity of war.

Poetry makes use of an archaic rhythmic language through which the symphony of vocal rhythms is often more expressive than the semantic overtones of the words. A national anthem stirs up in every breast the patriotic yearning to belong to the group. There is a deep resonance in people when they hear or see archaic sign behavior. The inner resonance unwittingly fills them with phylogenetic and ontogenetic nostalgia. The Bushmen dance on and on to keep the moon alive. The shared regressive fantasy and experience lead to mutual imitation. Alas, regression is much more contagious than progression!

Future study will have to direct greater attention to the analysis of these phenomena. We will have to ask ourselves which rhythm does what? The compulsive patient, for instance, cannot step out of his own rhythms and obsessive repetitions without developing enormous anxiety. Psychodynamically, it is known that the compulsion to repeat rhythmically is often used as a defense against the shock of new adaptation.

In some cases, mental contamination is merely the result of an induction of the same rhythm. In others, certain rhythms may interfere with existing defensive rhythms and thereby open new roads of communication and new adaptations. Finally, all this wherewithal of rhythmic communication will have to be clinically measured and tested.

In music, the transfer of emotions is much more complicated, but it follows the same principles, the same rules of mental induction and cooscillation. There are soothing rhythms, exciting rhythms and ambivalence-provoking counterpoints.

In poetry, inner ambivalence is also expressed in a harmonizing rhythm, sadness and joy, assertion and submission, acceptance of fate alongside rebellion—as in Francis Thompson's

THE KINGDOM OF GOD

"In no Strange Land"

O world invisible, we view thee;
　O world intangible, we touch thee;
　O world unknowable, we know thee;
　　Inapprehensible, we clutch thee!

Yea, in the night, my Soul, my daughter,
　Cry,—clinging heaven by the hems:
And lo, Christ walking on the water,
　Not of Gennesareth, but Thames!

In general, rhythm means recognition and responding to something familiar. Such preoccupation with familiar messages can be used as a defense against feelings of pain. In olden days, quacks pulled teeth under the soothing rhythm of drum beats, and today some dentists still resort to music with a lively beat.

Last but not least, there is the rhythmic gestural language of wooing. In Oriental lands, the rhythm and cadence of breathing is used to ignite erotic feelings in the mate. Every flirtation makes spontaneous use of this intuitive knowledge of the effect of rapid breathing. A lover can tell from the inhaling rhythm at the other end of the telephone whether his distant beloved accepts him or not. In the Orient, rhythm and chanting are used to bring a group of believers into a collective hypnosis. All this, of course, can be explained by well-known physiological and chemical processes.

Catharsis and the Language of Rhythm

All through history we encounter dance epidemics in which the masses tried to reduce tension and anxiety in frenzied movements.

Music and dance, the rhythmic intercommunication of man, were once the first forms of magic medicine. Indeed, the common regression to a cluster of interacted movements gives delight and catharsis and revitalizes us. However, the same human beings may also be seduced by rhythm into giving up their integrity and self-awareness completely.

On the other hand, there are some people who, on the basis of early infantile rhythmic frustration, are unable to join in any dance movements and thus cannot experience this common joy that is as old as mankind. Some are not touched by poetry either. They are motorically frustrated and do not understand gestures and pantomime. A cold logic has taken over the vital rhythms of life. No matter how intelligent they may be, they are excluded from a vast field of human intercommunication.

Rhythm, in short, is life itself. The tune is the mind. Music reflects to us the symphony and total profile of rhythms that we ourselves comprise. In the rhythm and repetition of themes in music and poetry, emotional abreaction takes place. The handling of counterpoint by composers evokes in listeners their own contrasting feelings, and this new harmony of contrasts temporarily frees them from inner tension and ambivalence. Rhythm can completely revolutionize our body system. Poet or composer may first inhibit us and provoke frustration, but then, suddenly, with new rhythms, liberate us.

Rhythm is an energy-saving device. The girl may not feel like walking, but be sure she can dance. A moment ago she felt she could not move anymore, but now she speaks her own gestural language in the musical trance of rhythm. By the same token, a swift game of tennis, which is a dance in itself, refreshes the players, and systematic exercise redoubles the individual's energy.

Rhythm in any form expresses many feelings that were repressed formerly. It ties the unawareness of hidden things together so as not to cause confusion by too much sophistication and by what Burrow[1] calls the smugness of formulation. Rhythm is the integration of chaotic inner and outer events into one's own "musical" experience.

In each of us dwells a need to repeat old patterns of behavior. We imitate not only others but also ourselves. It is sometimes a great struggle in psychotherapy to liberate a patient from such compulsive self-imitations and repetitions; and without a therapeutic regression to the origin of his ancient language of rhythms, the patient will fail in his attempt at self-recollection. For this reason poetry, as a well-chosen form of communication, is a welcome adjunct to psychotherapy.

REFERENCES

1. Burrow, T., *Preconscious Foundations of Human Experience* (New York, Basic, 1964).
2. Carroll, L., *The Hunting of the Snark; and other Nonsense Verse* (New York, Peter Pauper Press, 1955).
3. FitzHerbert, J., "Some further observations on headbanging and allied behavior," *J. Ment Sci 98*:330, 1952.
4. Gabriel, Sister P., "Poetry—the child's heritage," *Child and Family 5*:29, 1966.
5. Hooker, D., *The Prenatal Origin of Behavior* (Lawrence, Kansas, Univ. Kansas Press, 1952).
6. Inman, W. S., "The moon, the seasons, and man," *Brit J Med Psychol 24*:267, 1951.
7. Klages, L., *Vom Wesen des Rhythmus* (Kampen auf Sylt, Kampman Verlag, 1934).
8. Langer, S. K., *Feeling and Form* (New York, Scribner's, 1953).
9. Lear, E., *The Complete Nonsense Verse* (New York, Dover, 1951).
10. Masserman, J. H., "Say id isn't so—with music," in *Science and Psychoanalysis* (New York, Grune, 1958).
11. Meerloo, J. A. M., "Archaic behavior and the communicative act," *Psychiat Quart 29*:60, 1955.
12. _____, *The Dance—from Ritual to Rock and Roll* (New York, Chilton, 1960).
13. _____, "Mental contagion," *Amer J Psychother 13*:66, 1959.
14. _____, "The time sense in psychiatry," in *The Voices of Time* (New York, Braziller, 1966).
15. Minkowski, M., "*Neurobiologischen Studien am Menschlichen Foetus*," *Handbuch Biol Arbeitsmethoden*, vol. 5 (Berlin, Springer, 1928).
16. Mittelman, B., "Intrauterine and early infantile motility," *Psychoanal Study Child 15*:104, 1960.
17. Read, Herbert, *Education Through Art* (New York, Pantheon, 1945).
18. _____, *Poetic Consciousness and Creative Experience* (Zurich, Eranos Yearbook, 1956).
19. Reiman, H. A., "Periodic disease," *JAMA 166*:141, 1951.
20. Solberger, A., *Biological Rhythm Research* (New York, Elsevier, 1965).
21. Van Der Post, L., *The Creative Pattern in Primitive Africa* (Zurich, Eranos Yearbook, 1956).

Why Poetry?

S. SUE ROBINSON, M.S.S., A.C.S.W.
and JEAN K. MOWBRAY, M.S.

A literary project, *The Tatler*, was initiated at The Institute of the Pennsylvania Hospital in 1960. The idea for it was hardly new to this private psychiatric hospital. As far back as 1843, *The Illuminator*, a hand-written literary journal, was published here during the administration of Doctor Thomas Kirkbride. Reflecting his enlightened approach to the treatment of mental illness, this small magazine contained poems and articles by patients.

Practicing his philosophy of "moral treatment," Doctor Kirkbride had a basic guideline for therapy: if you treat the patient as a human being, he will behave as a human being. Within the patient community, which simulated life outside the hospital, the focal point for therapy was participation in the activities of daily living. The patient was encouraged to do for himself, think for himself, be himself. His own capacities to give and to contribute, to lift his experience to a plane of creative fulfillment, were the springs that contained his recovery.

Geared to this philosophy of adjunctive therapy, the hospital program supported expression in art, music, and poetry. Not only the creative activity of writing, but the feat of turning out multiple copies of *The Illuminator* by hand might be called occupational therapy today. Whether creative writing was considered therapeutic is not recorded. History tells us only that a few years later the journal no longer existed.

A hundred and twenty five years later, patients again write poetry at The Institute. Although an outgrowth of the program of resocialization, the emergence of writing poetry was not the result of a plan contrived to yield certain outcomes. The project evolved out of a normal sequence of events. At a meeting of the patient government, the patients requested a newsletter of their own to announce time and plans of all hospital events open to patients, such as movies, sports events, card parties, and special activities featuring outside entertainment. Before this newsletter, information about the organized program of activities within the hospital community was announced to the patients by the nurses. In a psychiatric setting, where participation needs specific encouragement, the weekly printed record of hospital activities served as an added stimulus to the withdrawing patient. When the announcement of events came from the patients rather than from authority, attendance increased.

As psychiatric social worker, representing the staff at patient governmental meetings, I was asked to act as "counselor" for this new publication. An exciting and rewarding experience followed. At that time, none of us could have predicted the birth of a literary project. Informal weekly meetings took place with a representative from each ward of the hospital. Forming the editorial staff, the committee gathered schedules of those activities of the hospital that were of potential interest to patients. When the materials were assembled, the newspaper staff typed, mimeographed and distributed the newsletter to every patient. In this simple way, a newspaper began.

In the next few months, the project took on new dimensions. The newsletter was named *The Tatler* after the original Addison and Steele periodical (1709–1721). Other staff members—from occupational therapy, the recreation department, and the nursing department—were asked to join the committee. Most important from a therapeutic standpoint, a resident psychiatrist was added to the already augmented patient committee, with his skills and his own enthusiasm for the project. The character of the group changed with the introduction of each new member. *The Tatler* now represented the whole hospital community.

In the mechanics of publishing the newsletter, now six mimeographed pages, ideas for content burgeoned. Encouraged to use their own initiative, the patients introduced the ideas for content, weighed their merit, and accepted or rejected them. All patients and staff were asked to submit their contributions for publication. As *The Tatler* flourished, the patients who contributed items, as well as those who read them, became more involved with the activities of the hospital. Soon an editor was elected, and an editorial appeared. With this beginning, the evolution of the newspaper became apparent.

It was not long before a patient submitted a poem. The committee decided to print the verse, not so much for its value as for the pride and pleasure of the contributor. Not only had the patient used her own creative energies, but approbation, so much needed by psychiatric patients, was implicit in the publication of her work. Many contributions of poetry were submitted to *The Tatler* office during the next few days, and continued in the weeks that followed. Any type of literary work was accepted by *The Tatler*; however, the contributions were predominantly poetry. Rarely were short stories or essays submitted. Although a relatively small percentage of patients contributed poetry at any given time, the productions were not the offerings of a prolific few. Most hospitalizations here are of short duration, the average stay about six weeks. The turnover in patients made the contributors a varied, changing group. Success bred success, and the poetry production continued. With this new source of material, a literary supplement was added to the newspaper.

So *The Tatler* again changed character. A professional poet was invited to join the group. An acquaintance of the resident psychiatrist, this writer was willing to give his time and talent to promote the literary project. Available to offer criticism for the patient's work, he read poetry aloud, including his own, led discussions on techniques, and probed for deeper meanings in the materials discussed. The poet's natural sensitivities to the patients' feelings created an immediate rapport. Moreover, his professional guidance gave serious status and dignity to the project. With the "poet in residence," the patients' writing became more disciplined, more artistic, more mature. Poetry itself became therapy. Another weekly meeting was scheduled as a literary seminar for all patients who were interested.

The success of *The Tatler*, now a monthly journal of twenty to thirty pages, was evident in many ways. The hospital staff allocated to the publication a room of its own, the editor's office, and a meeting place for the seminars on poetry. A typewriter and mimeograph machine were contributed for the journal's own use. A small charge was made for each copy to help defray expenses; any profit was used to buy supplies needed for publication. The number of readers expanded, for the mailing list included not only patients but the medical staff, the Board of Directors of the hospital, members of the women's auxiliary, and other community organizations. Among others, a newspaper editor and an English professor became regular subscribers.

Reflecting the inner feelings of the patients, the poems opened a new source of understanding for the medical staff. The residents' orientation manual now contains a patient's poem, written during an acute phase of his illness, the brief lines revealing inner conflict more poignantly than an objective case history.

In the course of a year, a newsletter became a literary journal. Retaining the original purpose, *The Tatler* still published the news, but the literary section became its most prominent feature, evidence of the patients' growing enthusiasm for creative writing. The hospital staff, always alert to new therapeutic approaches, promoted an optimal atmosphere for the literary project and at every level supported and encouraged the patient's natural interest in writing poetry.

Although the significance of poetry as therapy was never formally discussed, its healthy effects were apparent. The opportunity to read and analyze poetry in a group setting and to discuss ideas at the weekly seminar provided a constructive experience for the patient. Important as this outcome was, however, group discussions of this kind have long been accepted as part of milieu therapy. Writing poetry seemed to have a deeper consequence. As a verbal and imaginative art form, poetry appeared to be uniquely suited to serve the psychotherapeutic goal.

Regardless of diagnosis, the patient hospitalized for mental illness has often slipped along the continuum from well to sick. In crucial areas of his development, ego functions are impaired. In all cases, the goal of psychotherapy is to bring about a more mature integration of personality. Poetry seems to be geared to this integrative purpose. The etiology of poetry and psychotherapy both involve unconscious and preconscious materials, including dreams, daydreams, and fantasies. Both employ the defense mechanisms of condensation, sublimation, displacement, and symbolization.

Basically, the production of a poem may be considered a problem-solving activity. The poet's motives are conscious and deliberate, his productions the result of a skillful use of his tools to express rather than to conceal. He uses fantasy to elicit meaning in a fresh context; he distorts in order to clarify; he symbolizes in an effort to illuminate. To translate feelings into a verbal unit suggests an awareness of self. To probe for insights requires experimentation with language and economy of words. To give form to thought represents a maturity of effort, a growth-producing experience compatible with therapeutic aims.

The therapeutic values of poetry, however, scarcely explain the appeal of this activity among so many patients. In order to develop into such propostions, the poetry project must have been inherently satisfying for those who participated. The patients at The Institute did not write poetry because it was prescribed as therapy. They expressed themselves in poetry because that seemed a natural thing to do. This creative outlet seemed to touch a need of contributing patients more sensitively than other media. Why? The answers are neither simple not conclusive. *The Tatler* and the seminar may have encouraged some patients to try to write. In trying, there was the interest and stimulation of writing a poem, receiving professional criticism, and seeing the finished work in print, a satisfying creative sequence. At another level, writing poetry may have provided ventilation, a helpful release for the lonely, the depressed, the hostile.

At a deeper level, writing poetry might have offered an even more intrinsic satisfaction. The patients' poetry in *The Tatler* seemed to confirm some of the theories of Freud and his successors on creative writing. Freud described the poet as a "professional daydreamer"[1] whose unconscious wishes are fulfilled by sublimation. Creativity or poetry is similar to neurosis but is not neurotic. Art may even be described as a substitute for neurosis. The poet has the sensitivity to be aware of his own and others' impulses, dreams and fantasies and the courage to express them verbally. Many psychiatric patients, both in and outside the hospital, have this same sort of sensitivity, as well as some degree of awareness of preconscious material.

In another comment on creativity, Freud observed that art (or poetry) is "an activity to allay ungratified wishes—in the first place in the creative artist himself and subsequently in his audience or spectators."[2] This may account for the therapeutic value for those who participated in the literary seminar but who did not write poetry themselves.

Neither Freud nor his immediate successors—such as Ernst Kris, who wrote about art and psychoanalysis—were suggesting that poetry might be used as therapy. Their stated purposes were to explore the mind and personality of the artist in an effort to understand the "special qualities"[3] that produce creative artists. To summarize briefly Freud's theories on the qualities necessary for creativity, the artists must have *1.* a strong instinctual drive; *2.* an extraordinary capacity for sublimation; and *3*. laxity of repression.[3] The poet, in addition, must be able to verbalize. Poetry, then, of all the arts, comes closest to the therapeutic hour in psychoanalytic terms. The similarity is striking. Both use preconscious and unconscious material to probe for inner meanings. Both employ words to express this material in conscious form. Both seek a solution to resolve inner conflict.

In addition to sublimation, the defense mechanisms most frequently used by poets are condensation, symbolization, and displacement, which turn the frightening unconscious into something acceptable. Metaphor is used by both poet and psychiatry in similar ways. Catharsis of emotion by both poetry and reader, a philosophical concept, Freud accepts and explains. When basic emotions are turned into aesthetic form, the sexual or aggressive impulses are gratified in a pleasant and satisfying way. Relief is obtained from tension. This may be an explanation for humor, another form the poet uses, as illustrated in contributions to *The Tatler*. Humor adds another dimension to poetry and to psychiatry, allowing the writer to see a situation in another perspective or from another view point.

To carry the analogy a step further, myths may be termed the collective unconscious fantasies of whole groups of people. Their universal acceptance must signify a universal need of wish-fulfillment in the acceptable terms of imagination. For another viewpoint—from a layman, not a psychiatrist—Glenn White, a freelance writer, attended a *Tatler* staff meeting. He read many of the patients' poems and wrote an article about his experience.[4] His apt title was "The Healing Muse."

> Some of the poems are of such excellence that it is obvious they are not the work of mental patients who just happened to express themselves poetically; they are the creation of persons of poetic talent who happen, for the moment, to be mentally ill.
> The themes which recur in these poems are loneliness, the search for love, the search for self and for self-understanding. This is a type of self-revelation generally characteristic of lyric verse, but as the expression of mental patients it has unusual poignancy and, often, surprising, incisive humor. I found much to be learned and enjoyed, and some of the experience of anguish, in these poems; a psychiatrist may see even more, and see it differently. But it is always best to let a poem speak for itself, so that psychiatrists and other mortals may hear what they can hear and see what they can see.[5]

ALONE

How can one bear the awful loneliness
That makes the child shriek in the darkness for
   his mother,
That forces the hollow laughter of adults at
   cocktail parties
And gnaws at the heart of the aged as they sit, sit,
   sit, and rock, rock, rock?

Oh, we may dress the fearful ghost in activity
And by disguising it, forget for a while that it
   haunts our busy footsteps
As we hurry and scurry, push and shove, race, pant,
   strain, work, work, work, keeping busy, busy, busy.

But when we return at night to our empty rooms,
There sits the unwelcome guest with its hollow eyes
   and gaping mouth, beckoning to us with a bony finger,
So that we run into the bedroom, slam the door,
   and fling ourselves upon a solitary bed
And weep, weep, weep, cold tears, tears, tears.

SOUL

There is a dark place where sometimes
   no one dwells;
It is called my soul.

It is lonely and cold there;
   and far away from the warmth of the sun.
It is a lonely place;
   and few come there to visit.

It is a quiet place,
   because no one talks above a whisper.
It is a place where one can think
   if one dares to face the fearsome things
that are conjured when one meets self.

CANTE FLAMENCO

I sank into a well
   Of deep despair.

> It was so deep, so icy
> Sunken there.
>
> There was no rope, just walls
> That gleamed with slime
> And echoed back the endless
> Screams of time.

The psychiatric staff were more aware of the therapeutic value of writing, while White noticed the literary excellence of some of the poems: "And here is light verse of a quality to rival Phyllis McGinley's or Ogden Nash's—written in One North, an open floor of the Pennsylvania Hospital for patients nearing discharge."[6]

BLUES IN THE NIGHT, OR WAITING FOR THAT DAMNED SEDATION TO WORK

> Environment, heredity,
> beast's nature and so forth...
> I lie and ponder on the whys
> that brought me to One North.
>
> Was I a docile little gem
> or an obnoxious sibling?
> Did I say yes and no on cue,
> or spend my time in quibbling?
>
> When falling in and out of love,
> did I avoid the pitfalls?
> Was I murmuring honeyed words,
> or were they really spitballs?
>
> What kind of complex have I got?
> There's quite a list to choose from—
> is my bête noir a sense of guilt,
> or do I get the blues from
>
> that C in Math that shot to hell
> my straight-A dream diploma?
> that time the Pullman bed collapsed
> did I sustain berth trauma?

Why Poetry?

> Environment, heredity,
> beast's nature and so forth...
> I lie and ponder on the whys
> that brought me to One North.

Here is a decription of the shattered state in which so many mental patients find themselves.

MALLEABLE AS YOU ARE

Move and change,
Sleep and wake,
Flex and bend,
Malleable as you are

You break—
Not as a dish,
In two or three pieces,
But as a goblet
Hurled upon the hearth
After a toast.

If you were to count
The tiny fragments,
You would contract a job
Equal to counting
The stars,

Or all the words of men,
Or all the second-long bits of time.

Me, who am I?
My one-way mirror-mask
Is shattered.
I can't see!
Someone fix my eye!

Move and change,
Sleep and wake,
Flex and bend;
Malleable as you are,
You break.

"Many of the patients displayed in their poems poetic craftsmanship of a high order; some showed the kind of sensitivity and insight that sometimes results in literary art. If a college professor of creative writing were handed poems of the quality of these two by B. C., he might feel he had discovered another Edna St. Vincent Millay":[7]

2:00 AM

Then sleep, your dark head warm
Against my heart,
Your fingers slack upon my own
Which move to trace
Lightly, with love, the eyebrows' curve
The line of cheek, the quiet mouth.

The record spun out long ago,
The glasses emptied, talk was done;
Time is the one sound left,
Each honed and delicate tick
Chiselling our flesh and bone to death's dimension.

My own, a stranger and beloved,
When have I known you, when have I found you?
Time like a torrent roars between us,
Death like a meadow grows between us,
The serried stars fling through the silent night
And we on our separate star;
We are lost in the lurch of stars.
Then sleep, my love:
And I will hold the pity and the wonder in my arms
And let me for a little have this breathing-space
That spans the meadow and the torrent;
Let me touch this silence with tentative fingers
And see in your lost and sleeping face
The heartbreak of a world.

SONNET

As petals open one by one, asserting
The perfect sudden purity of bloom,
Or as a child thrusts into light, deserting
The chaste, archaic haven of the womb,
The guarded spirit struggles, frets, travails
To open, leaf by leaf itself, unclose
And flower, quickened, fed by truth, assails

> Imponderable darkness; labouring, grows
> Toward some mighty knowledge and intent,
> Pursuit primeval as the blood's old surge,
> The balance of negation and consent
> That love at last may brilliantly emerge;
>> So phoenix-like the spirit moved through flame
>> To give itself a passage, home, and name.

"This is loveliness, but for those of us who are old-fashioned and like verse with a moral, here is a modern one, as old as time":

> God is Godot and God is time
> I am as much Godot as anyone.
>> We are all our own connection;
> Our own Man.
>> There is a spark in each of us
>> That if we would but kindle
>> Would burn eternally.

"Some of these verses seem to me to contain much of an age-old wisdom that enables all men and women who make it their own to endure and enjoy the day.

"Having read them, I feel stronger."[8]

In reading the patients' poetry, those of us from the professional staff could not help feeling that we too had learned from the *Tatler* project. It is not a coincidence that the patient publication is now named *Insight*.

REFERENCES

1. Freud, Sigmund, *Creative writers and day-dreaming*, The Standard Edition of the Complete Psychological Works of Sigmund Freud (London, Hogarth, 1953) p. 147.
2. _____, "The claims of psychoanalysis to scientific interest," *Gesammelte Werke*, VIII (London, Imgo Publishing, 1940–1942) p. 416.
3. _____, "Creative writers and day-dreaming," *op. cit.*, ref. 1 p. 156.
4. White, Glenn, "The healing muse," *Psychiatric Reporter* (Philadelphia, Smith Kline and French, May-June, 1964).
5. _____, *Ibid.*, p. 11.
6. _____, *Ibid.*, p. 11.
7. _____, *Ibid.*, p. 12.
8. _____, *Ibid.*, p. 13.

A Defense of Poetry Therapy

MORRIS ROBERT MORRISON, Ph.D.

The Downstate Medical Center in Brooklyn, New York, initiated a visiting scholars program in 1970, inviting notables outside the field of medicine to participate with the medical faculty and their students in discussions related to the arts. Discussants at different dates included Arnold S. Toynbee, the historian, and the poets, Archibald MacLeish and W. H. Auden. During conversation following one of these sessions, Auden was asked, "Is there such a thing as therapeutic poetry?" "No," he replied, "I don't think so at all." He followed this pronouncement with another, defining the goal of the writer. "The aim of writing," the poet stated, "is to enable people a little better to enjoy life or a little better to endure it."[1] Professor J. C. Coleman, quoted approvingly by Dr. Robert M. Goldenson in *The Encyclopedia of Human Behaviour*, lists among the aims of psychotherapy "the resolution of handicapping or disabling conflicts and the opening of a pathway to a more meaningful and fulfilling existence."[2] In his act of denial Auden had unwittingly reaffirmed how germane are the concerns of poet and therapist.

Indeed, Auden's interest in Freud and psychoanalysis dates back to the twenties. Stephen Spender, referring to those days, tells us that at the time of his first acquaintance with Auden in 1928, he found him deeply concerned with psychotherapy and medicine. "At this early age," we are told, "Auden had already an extensive knowledge of the theories of modern psychology, which he used as a means of understanding his friends."[3] His friends, and fellow poets, C. Day Lewis and Christopher Isherwood, testify to Auden's parallel interests in poetry and psychotherapy. C. Day Lewis writes, "Auden, while regarding so many of our neuroses as tragic, so many of our actions as self-deception, yet believes as I have already said, that neurosis is the cause of an individual's development. Such a psychological dialect reflects itself in the paradoxes and the tensions of his poems."[4]

Christopher Isherwood tells of the great influence exerted over Auden by the American psychologist, Homer Lane, whose teachings are reflected in Auden's *The Orators* and *The Journal of an Airman*. Auden and Isherwood collaborated on a play, *The Enemies of a Bishop*, in which the hero, who represents sanity, appears as an idealized portrait of Lane. Auden had elsewhere enshrined Homer Lane, along with D. H. Lawrence and Andre Gide, as his spiritual mentors. Isherwood reveals the extent and degree of Lane's impact on Auden. "Auden was particularly interested in Lane's theories regarding the psychological causes of disease. References to these theories can be found in many of the early poems."[5]

In 1963 the Oxford University Press published a study by Professor Monroe K. Spears on the life and work of Auden. Allen Tate, paying tribute to the scholarship and intellectual powers of the critic, praised it as "the best book by anybody about a living poet."[6] Auden served as a behind-the-scenes collaborator. The dust-jacket of the book tells us, "With Auden's cooperation the record is here set straight." Spears wrote, "I have taken some pains (and put Mr. Auden to some trouble) to make sure that I have the facts straight."[7] It must then have been with Auden's endorsement that the following statement made not too long ago had been set down. "The notion of the poet as clinically detached, diagnosing the sickness of society and its component individuals, and of poetry as a kind of therapy performing a function somehow analogous to the psychoanalytic, is a fundamental in Auden's writing."[8]

Donald Davie in *Remembering the Movement*, a critical study of the poets of the 50's, many of whom were strongly influenced by Auden, wrote, "We conceived of it [poetry] as an act of public and private therapy, the poet resolving his conflicts by expressing them and offering them to the reader so that he could vicariously do the same thing."[9]

A poet for whom Auden has publicly expressed great admiration is Robert Graves. Reviewing Graves's *Collected Poems* in 1961, Auden confided that he had first read Graves in the volume of Georgian poetry when he was a schoolboy and that "Graves remained one of the very few poets whose volumes he always bought the moment they appeared."[10] Robert Graves discussing his goal as a writer says,

"My poetry is, or should be, useful to me for one reason: it is the record of my individual struggle from darkness towards some measure of light.... My poetry is, or should be, useful to others for its individual recording of that same struggle with which they are necessarily acquainted... Poetry recording the stripping of the individual darkness, must inevitably cast light upon what has been hidden for too long, and by so doing, make clear the naked exposure." Continuing, he says, "Freud cast light on a little of the darkness he had exposed. Benefiting by the sight of the light and the knowledge of the hidden nakedness poetry must drag further into the clear nakedness of light more even of the hidden causes than Freud could realize."[11]

In *White Goddess*, which deals with the poetic process, Graves reports,

"The pathology of poetic composition is no secret. A poet finds himself caught in some baffling emotional problem which is of such urgency that it sends him into a sort of trance. And in this trance his mind works, with astonishing boldness and precision on several imaginative levels at once. The poem is either a practical answer to his problem or else it is a clear statement of it; and a problem clearly stated is half way to solution. Some poets are more plagued than others with emotional problems, and more conscientious in working out poems which arise from them—that is more attentive in their service to the Muse."[12]

Elsewhere, Graves wrote that poetry is formed by the supralogical reconciliation of conflicting emotional ideas during a trancelike suspension of normal habits of thought. The poet, he advises us, learns to induce the trance in self-protection whenever he feels unable to resolve an emotional conflict by simple logic.[13]

After he experienced an emotional breakdown during military service in World War I, Graves was treated by Dr. W. H. R. Rivers, a physician of exceptional, if controversial, talent. Dr. Rivers theorized that "every neurotic system, like dreams, was at once the product of a mental conflict and an attempt to resolve it." Poems, he believed, functioned similarly. Reviewing his own poetry Graves wrote, "My hope was to help the recovery of public health of mind as well as my own by the writing of therapeutic poems."[14]

Professor George Stade of Columbia University tells of Graves's way of serving his Muse while looking after his neurosis:

"...when he came to write in 1922 his first book of criticism, *On*

English Poetry based on 'evidence mainly subjective'.... Graves advertised poetry as a 'form of psychotherapy' for the neurosis of poets and the culture they express and address. He assured his readers that 'a well-chosen anthology is a complete dispensary for the more common mental disorders and may be used as much for prevention as for cure.' A poem's rhythm puts the reader in a hypnotic trance; he is confronted with an allegorical solution of the problem that has been troubling him; his unconscious accepts the allegory as applicable to his own condition; the emotional crisis is relieved."[15] Professor Stade discusses the twenty years during which Graves "brought his poetic self into being through poems of self-definition and extrication."[16] This brings to mind Coleman's stated purpose of therapy: a better delineation of one's own identity and the opening of a pathway to a more meaningful and fulfilling existence.[17] "Instruction to the Orphic Adept," we are advised by Dr. Stade, is one of the "truly good" poems of modern literature.[18] It is in part a translation from the Egyptian Book of the Dead, a text employed by the priests of ancient Egypt for the treatment of emotional disorders.

Professor Spears, with no objection from Auden, had referred to the poet as "spiritual physician" and "witch-doctor."[19] Would it be surprising if Auden had detected in Graves a disposition to play a similar role? Reviewing Graves's work, it would seem that the purport of his poetry and of his critical writing constitutes a clear-cut defense of poetry therapy.

Did not Auden compose the following lines, *In Memory of W. B. Yeats*, a tribute to poetry as a healing modality?

> Follow poet, follow right
> To the bottom of the night,
> With your unconstraining voice
> Still persuade us to rejoice
>
> With the farming of a verse
> Make a vineyard of the curse,
> Sing of human unsuccess
> In a rapture of distress;
>
> In the deserts of the heart
> Let the healing fountain start,
> In the prison of his days
> Teach the free man how to praise.[20]

Professor Harold J. Laski of the London School of Economics, in his introduction to a reprint of John Stuart Mill's *Autobiography*, describes the book as "a document of the first importance and the most imperishable of Mill's writings."[21] A section of the story, "A Crisis in My Mental History," covers the period 1826–1827 when Mill fell victim to a nervous disorder characterized by a state of deep depression. In this chapter, the celebrated political scientist, economist, philosopher, and logician presents a careful exposition of his breakdown, his efforts at self-treatment, and the means through which he effected a cure. Mill simultaneously provides us with a closely documented testimonial to the healing power of poetry.

At twenty he seemed to be pursuing a highly purposeful and fulfilling existence—intellectually rewarding, involved with humanitarian concerns—when all at once the bottom dropped out of his world. He continued with his normal routine, afflicted, however, by what Professor Packe terms "the fearful lassitude of accidie."[22] Mills describes his condition: "I was in a dull state of nerves, such as everybody is occasionally liable to; unsusceptable to enjoyment or pleasurable excitement; one of those moods when what is pleasure at other times becomes insipid or indifferent; I seemed to have nothing left to live for."[23]

The nature of this melancholia eluded easy diagnosis, but a fitting description could be found, as Mill later discovered, in these lines from Colderidge's ode, "Dejection."

> A grief without a pang, void, dark and drear
> A drowsy, stifled, unimpassioned grief
> Which finds no natural outlet or relief
> In word, or sigh, or tear.[24]

Devastated by his ailment, and wishing to discuss it with some other person, he discovered there was no one to whom he could turn for help.

His friends were fellow-disciples of Jeremy Bentham, the apostle of utilitarianism, who enshrined purposefulness and the intellect above all with little tolerance for anyone's emotional remission. His mother had always been unable to give him a sense of being loved; while he respected his father, he had grown up fearing him. "My education, which was always his word, had been conducted without regard to the possibility of its ending in this result; and I saw no use in giving him the pain of thinking that his plans had failed, when the failure was probably irremediable, and, at all events, beyond the power of his remedies.

"I became persuaded that my love of mankind, and of excellence for its own sake had worn out.... In vain I sought relief from my favorite books, from which I had hitherto drawn strength and animation. I read them now without feeling."[25]

He continues, "The effect of music I had often experienced; but like all my pleasurable susceptibilities it was suspended during the gloomy period. I had sought relief again and again from this quarter but found none."[27]

He believed that he had lost the capacity to feel but forced himself to carry on mechanically and purely from force of habit. "To know that a feeling would make me happy if I had it, did not give me the feeling."[28]

"At first I hoped that the cloud would pass away of itself but it did not." He turned to thoughts of release by suicide. "I frequently asked myself if I could, or if I was bound to go on living when life must be passed in this manner. I generally answered to myself that I did not think I could possibly bear it beyond a year."[29]

However, six months after the onset of his melancholia he chanced upon a sentimental story by a Frenchman which affected him profoundly, since it touched upon some deep-seated, possibly repressed hostility against his father.

"I was reading, accidentally, Marmontel's *Memoires* and came to the passage which relates his father's death, the distressed position of his family, and the sudden inspiration by which he, then a mere boy, felt and made them feel that he would be everything to them—would supply the place of all that they had lost. A vivid conception of the scene and its feelings came over me, and I was moved to tears. From this moment my burden grew lighter. The oppression of the thought that all feeling was dead within me was gone. I was no longer hopeless."[30]

It is to be noted that Marmontel had reached Mill not through the quality of his writing. The value of bibliotherapy in this instance was based on the special personal meaning which the scene and its characters had for Mill. The experience with this reading helped, but it was not until he opened a volume of Wordsworth's miscellaneous poems that he discovered a lasting cure for his illness.

His father along with his fellow Benthamites while concerned with the human condition greatly underrated poetry. As "reasoning machines,"[31] they decried "all poetry as misrepresentation."[32] Mill's father referring to a popular writer, said, "Mr. Moore is a poet and therefore is not a reasoner."[33] As for John Stuart Mill, "The correct statement would be, not that I disliked poetry, but that I was theoretically indifferent to it.... And I was wholly blind to its place in human culture, as a means of educating the feelings."[34]

In the autumn of 1828, two years after the first onset of his trauma he took up a collection of miscellaneous poems by William Wordsworth. This happened, as he writes, "out of curiosity, with no expectation of mental relief from it."[35] Yet it was here that he discovered the clue which conducted him out of the labyrinth of his hopelessness. Wordsworth, he tells us, was exactly what suited his condition.

"I had looked into the *Excursion* two or three years before, and found little in it; and I should probably have found as little had I read it this time. But the miscellaneous poems, in the two-volume edition of 1815... proved to be the precise thing for my mental wants at that particular juncture.

"In the first place these poems addressed themselves powerfully to one of the strongest of my pleasurable susceptibilities, the love of rural objects and natural scenery.... But Wordsworth would never have had any great effect upon me, if he had merely placed before me beautiful pictures of natural scenery.... What made Wordsworth's poems a medicine for my state of mind was that they expressed not mere outward beauty, but states of feeling, and of thought colored by feeling under the excitement of beauty.... I needed to be made to feel that there was real, permanent happiness in tranquil contemplation. Wordsworth taught me this, not only without turning away from, but with a greatly increased interest in the common feelings and common destiny of human beings. And the delight which these poems gave me proved that with culture of this sort, there was nothing to dread from the most confirmed habit of analysis."[36]

The reassurance and emotional enrichment derived from the poet supplied answers to Mill's previous doubts regarding his emotional capacity and the value of his intellectual strivings. It also disposed of his sense of estrangement.

"At the conclusion of the *Poems* came the famous ode, "Intimations of Immortality" in which... I found that he too had similar experiences to mine...that he had sought compensation and found it in the way he was teaching me to find it. The result was that I gradually but completely emerged from my habitual depression, and was never again subject to it."[37]

John Stuart Mill spoke of Wordsworth's poetry as medicine, not simply as metaphor but in the same sense that Graves referred to a well-chosen anthology of poems as "a complete dispensary for the more common mental disorders that may be used as much for prevention as for cure." Auden, in his appearance at the Downstate Medical Center, told of an unfulfilled ambition of his to serve as bishop in the Anglican Church. Interestingly enough, both Cardinal Newman, and John Keble, a highly placed cleric and professor of poetry at Oxford, wrote poetry and were leaders of the same Anglican Church where it was Auden's dream to officiate. Both had testified to the curative power of poetry. Cardinal Newman spoke of poetry as a means of "relieving the over-burdened mind"[38] and of affording the poet "a channel through which emotion finds expression and that a safe, regulated expression." It accomplishes "thus a *cleansing*, as Aristotle would word it, of the sick soul."[39] John Keble theorized at length on poetry's therapeutic impact, stating, "Here, no doubt, is one final cause of poetry: to innumerable persons it acts as a safety-valve tending to preserve them from mental disease."[40] How closely Keble's view coincides with that of Auden's early views as related by Isherwood! John Keble was in fact a proto-Freudian, anticipating in his discussions of poetry as psychotherapy much of Freud's exposition of the dynamics of repression and its pathogenic effects. Poetic form, according to Keble, provides the necessary veils and disguises that circumvent resistance to expression. By facilitating the expression of repressed emotion, the poem helps to secure therapeutic release and assists in the resolution of the poet's conflict.

Frederick C. Prescott's *The Poetic Mind*, a study of the workings of the poet's mind, is notable for its recognition of poetry as therapy. Professor Stanley Burnshaw, in his foreword to the 1959 reprinting of Prescott's seminal dissertation, writes that the latter "counts heavily on certain theories advanced by the Rev. John Keble. Indeed if *The Poetic Mind* was noteworthy for relating Freud to literature, it was even more remarkable for rescuing and emphasizing the radical ideas that Keble had ventured eighteen years before the birth of Freud."[41]

Keble had described literature as unconscious autobiography and disguised wish-fulfillment.[42] Prescott accepting Keble's theories develops them further by drawing on Freud and the testimony of a great number of poets.

In line with Keble's thinking, Prescott attributes poetry's therapeutic value first as a safety valve, satisfying "what Keble calls the instinctive wish to communicate."[43] Secondly it serves as a means of obtaining through the imagination what had been desired and denied in reality.

In respect to the first, Prescott quotes Byron as well. "Poetry," Byron says, "is the lava of the imagination whose eruption prevents the earthquake. They say poets never or rarely go mad,... but [they] are generally so near it that I cannot help thinking rhyme is so far useful in anticipating and preventing the disorder."[44]

As for the second reason why poetry secures relief, Prescott says, "For the desire, giving rise to passion, repression, and madness, the poetic vision and the poetry afford a fictional gratification which tends to allay the desire and the emotional tension.... A poet when his vision is over may still feel his desire, but... even the fictional gratification puts the desire on the way to its ultimate actual satisfaction; and at any rate is robbed of its noxious effect. To this the poets testify as we have seen. Poetry is therefore broadly a safeguard for the individual and for the race against mental disturbance and disease."[45]

Molly Harrower, professor of psychology, writes, "Poetry is therapy.... The very act of creating is a self-sustaining experience, and in the poetic moment the self becomes both the ministering 'therapist' and the comforted 'patient.'"[46] Rev. Keble had described poetry as a safety-value; Professor Harrower calls it "a built-in safeguard."

Poetry and insanity represent alternate forms of self expression; each provides a vehicle for dealing with censored feelings and interdicted desires; both are means for the management of overpowering anxieties. The hysterical imagination is indeed an insane poetic one, the distinction being that in insanity the pathological product is disordered; poetry, whatever its genesis, is essentially a controlled expression of the organism. Writing in *Illusion and Reality, A Study of the Sources of Poetry*, Christopher Caudwell says, "Although there is a correspondence between artistic and schizophrenic solutions,... the goal is in fact the opposite. As compared with existing normality, the mad road leads to greater illusion, unconsciousness, and privacy, the scientific or artistic road to greater reality, consciousness, and publicity."[47] The poet through his art may skirt madness while retaining his base in reality. How is the reader helped? Keble spoke of the *vis medica poetica*, the powerful medicine of poetry. It is through his identification with the poet and his dilemma that the reader discovers an outlet for his own repressions and inhibitions. Poetry operates as a "safe, regulated expression" as a counterphobic for events that might have been engineered into emotional disturbance. "In the creative act we witness neither dissociation nor mere bisociation but integration and synthesis."[48]

Poetry has been referred to as the "great universal hypnotic, the all-time great mind-altering drug,"[49] and "as a healing process based on self-analysis."[50] It is adept at hypnosis and illusion; its components are frequently made up of dream, play, fantasy, and fictional gratification. The following passage from Wordsworth's *Prelude*, illustrates how poetry provides an essential need that reorients the reader to reality: "Dumb yearnings, hidden appetites, are ours, and they must have their food."[54]

> The tales that charm away the wakeful night.
> In Araby, romances: legends penned
> For solace by dim light of monkish lamps;
> Fictions, for ladies of their love, devised
> By youthful squires; adventures endless, spun
> By the dismantled warrior in old age,
> Out of the bowels of those very schemes
> In which his youth did first extravagate;
> These spread like day, and something in the shape
> Of these will live till man shall be no more.
> Dumb yearnings, hidden appetites, are ours,
> And they must have their food. Our childhood sits,
> Our simple childhood, sits upon a throne
> That hath more power than all the elements.
> I guess not what this tells of Being past,
> Nor what it augurs of the life to come;
> But so it is; and, in that dubious hour,
> That twilight—when we first begin to see
> This dawning earth, to recognize, expect,
> And in the long probation that ensues,
> The time of trial, ere we learn to live
> In reconcilement with our stinted powers;
> To endure this state of meagre vassalage,
> Unwilling to forego, confess, submit,

> Uneasy and unsettled, yoke-fellows
> To custom, mettlesome, and not yet tamed
> And humbled down;—oh! then we feel, we feel,
> We know where we have friends. Ye dreamers, then,
> Forgers of daring tales! We bless you then,
> Imposters, drivellers, dotards, as the ape
> Philosophy will call you: then we feel
> With what, and how great might ye are in league,
> Who make our wish, our power, our thought a deed,
> An empire, a possession.[52]

Literature is a force, an act of human magic that alters the way we see our lives and so changes us. Prescott observed, "Poetry in general 'cleanses the sick soul' and in its various forms should be recognized as a hygienic and curative agent of the highest value. Apollo has for his province both poetry and healing—not only the healing of the body but the more important care of the mind."[53]

Writing, Auden told us, "helps us a little better to enjoy life or a little better to endure it."[54] This, the function of the poet, is the *raison d'etre* of the psychotherapist.

REFERENCES

1. New York Times, Dec. 16, 1970, Sec. O, p. 49.
2. R. M. Goldenson, *The Encyclopedia of Human Behavior* (Garden City, Doubleday, 1970), II, 1082.
3. Monroe K. Spears, *The Poetry of W. H. Auden* (Oxford, Oxford University, 1963), p. 62.
4. *Ibid.*, p. 5.
5. C. Isherwood "Some Notes on Auden's Early Poetry," Monroe K. Spears, ed., *Auden: A Collection of Critical Essays*, 1 ed. (Englewood Cliffs, Prentice Hall, 1964), p. 13.
6. Monroe K. Spears, *The Poetry of W. H. Auden*, quoted on dust jacket.
7. *Ibid.*, p. v.
8. *Ibid.*, p. 7.
9. Donald Davie, "Remembering the Movement," *Prospect* (Summer, 1959) p. 16.
10. Spears, *op. cit.*, p. 65.
11. George Stade, *Robert Graves* (New York, Columbia University, 1967) p. 9.
12. *Ibid.*, p. 42.
13. *Ibid.*, p. 11.
14. *Id.*
15. *Ibid.*, p. 12.
16. *Ibid.*, p. 48
17. Goldenson, *op. cit.*, p. 1082.
18. Stade, *op. cit.*, p. 42.
19. Spears, *op. cit.*, p. 7.

20. W. H. Auden, "In Memory of W. B. Yeats," in *The Collected Poetry of W. H. Auden* (New York, Random House, 1966) p. 143.
21. John Stuart Mill, *Autobiography* (London, Oxford University Press, 1949) pp. ix, xx.
22. Michael St. John Packe, *The Life of John Stuart Mill* (New York, MacMillan, 1900) p. 80.
23. Mill, *op. cit.*, p. 113
24. *Ibid.*, p. 114.
25. *Ibid.*, p. 115.
26. *Ibid.*, p. 114.
27. *Ibid.*, p. 122.
28. *Ibid.*, p. 117.
29. *Ibid.*, p. 113.
30. *Ibid.*, p. 119.
31. *Ibid.*, p. 92
32. *Ibid.*, p. 94.
33. *Ibid.*, p. 95.
34. *Id.*
35. *Ibid.*, p. 124.
36. *Ibid.*, p. 125.
37. *Ibid.*, p. 126.
38. Frederick Clarke Prescott, *The Poetic Mind* (Ithaca, Cornell University, 1959) p. 271.
39. *Ibid.*, p. 271.
40. *Id.*
41. *Ibid.*, p. vi.
42. *Id.*
43. *Ibid.*, p. 273.
44. *Ibid.*, p. 272.
45. *Ibid.*, p. 273–274.
46. Molly Harrower, *The Therapy of Poetry* (Springfield, Ill., Charles C Thomas, 1972) p. 3.
47. Christopher Caudwell, *Illusion and Reality, A Study of the Sources of Poetry* (International Publishers, 1970) p. 230.
48. Frank Barron, "The Creative Personality Akin to Madness" *Psychology Today*, July, 1972, p. 85.
49. William Brandon ed., *The Magic World, American Indian Songs and Poems* (New York, William Morrow, 1971) p. xi.
50. Prescott, *op. cit.*, p. 276.
51. *Ibid.*, p. 275.
52. *Id.*
53. *Ibid.*, p. 277
54. New York Times, *op. cit.*, p. 49.

Shamans, Witch Doctors, Medicine Men and Poetry

ABRAHAM A. BLINDERMAN, Ph.D.

Introduction

Since preliterate times poetry has been in use as a modality for dealing with pathogenic emotional states. Spells, invocations, and incantations were invariably in the form of poetry. Primitive societies in the 20th century still continue the tradition initiated by that earliest of psychiatrists, the shaman. The primitive is more poetical than his civilized brother. It is therefore not strange that the shaman should discover in poetry an important therapeutic tool.

Shamanism is still prevalent throughout the world; the shaman functions as physician or as partner to a physician. During my association with Dr. Denny Thong on the island of Bali, I enjoyed the privilege of observing this self-trained psychiatrist and his corps of village- and hospital-based "balians." They achieved astonishing results with their shamanistic techniques. Poetry created in the trances of the healer played a major role.

It is appropriate to note at this point that the National Institute of Mental Health now sponsors a program for the training of medicine men. The novitiate must learn by rote hundreds of chants and songs until he knows the words letter-perfect and has mastered the nuances of their healing symbolism.

Celsus of old did not disdain the use of poetry in his healing practice. My own investigations into shamanistic medicine confirm Professor Blinderman's discussion of its use as effective therapy. If the shaman's intuition is medically sound, his art and wisdom provide a valuable psychiatric resource.

—STANLEY R. DEAN, M.D.

> *To me alone there came a thought of grief:*
> *A timely utterance gave that thought relief,*
> *And I again am strong:*
>
> WILLIAM WORDSWORTH

The great romantic poet William Wordsworth, a fledgling poet at a prison school in New York City, and an old Eskimo maker of songs do not seem to have much in common, but in each case, their quest for balm in poetic composition—for, indeed, all three are poets—gave them a firm sense of kinship with their fellows from whom they had felt alienated. Of the three poets cited, perhaps Wordsworth alone will survive critical scrutiny, for M. J. B., the young prison poet "discovered" by Herbert R. Kohl, an inspiring teacher of ghetto children, may lose his ecstatic vision if he becomes "that notorious man of society" who appeals to so many frustrated ghetto dreamers. Encouraged by his teacher, M. J. B. wrote many "curative" poems in Youth House, poems of semi-despair epitomized by:

DREAM

In my sanity (when I possess it)
    no dreams are permitted.
I can coagulate my thoughts with
    the utmost precision
Coordination is perfect and my reflexes
    stream with a new-found adrenalin.

I despise dreams (fantasy that is)
    For children with their
Immense maturity dream.
    (People in society don't dream.)
I want to be important someday
    (similar to those in high society)

I wish I had the ability to
    Dream though—
(But people would say: there
    Goes that notorious man of society—
But he *dreams*.)[14]

An astute student of the poetic mind, Frederic Clark Prescott, postulates that primitive men were probably greater dreamers and poets than their civilized followers,[25] a hypothesis which may have to await validation by thorough studies of aboriginal verse and poetry, since translations offer little definitive knowledge of a language's structure, style and unique function.[2] Yet the art of contemporary primitive people offers ample evidence of their imaginative prowess, their creative passions, and a concern for values quite akin to our own concern. In the Polar North, an ailing Eskimo hunter lay despondently in his igloo, lamenting the passing of his youth and the indifference of his former companions of the hunt. Suddenly, he began to compose a song that brought visions to him of his happier hunting days. Imbued with hope, he rose from his bed, sang his song over and over, and returned to the hunt, a vigorous veteran of many pursuits of the swift-swimming seal.[5] Thus, poetry has been a healing boom to a civilized Englishman of letters, an obscure ghetto boy in a prison school, and an elderly Eskimo in silent Arctic waters.

To its creators and critics, poetry is a way of life, capable of representing the "imaginary fulfillment of our ungratified wishes or desires,"[25] calming us in adversity, enlivening us in solitude, and endowing us with passion, tenderness, feeling, and sympathy.[38] Eminent clergymen, John Keble and Cardinal Newman, found a safety-valve function in poetry, for in relieving the overburdened mind, poetry prevents mental disease.[25] But for the true role of song in healing we must go to the song of primitive man; since song is his chief means of expression, we see in it his actual being—one far removed from the distorted view we derive of him from his "murderous enemies or misguided well-wishers."[5]

In the introduction to his remarkable two-volume collection of aboriginal, unwritten song, Willard R. Trask notes that the poems are almost always sung, that many are sung to relieve personal grief, impotence, and tiredness, and that the poets may be professionals or anyone who has a desire to compose.[33] More important to his well-being than his religion, with its frequent nightmares, poetry consoles and sustains primitive man constantly.[5] The Eskimos thrive on song, and poetry has kept up the moral of individuals and groups among the natives of America.[2] Interestingly, healing and procreative songs are more numerous than all other songs of the American Indian,[2] and in India, the Atharvavedas, curing poems, heal the sick and protect the well against misfortune.[24] The Iranian branch of the Aryans, the Venidad, distinguishes three ways to overcome disease: surgery, medicine, and the spell, but their practitioners believe that the pure man healed by the "word" is more effectively cured than the man treated by either surgery or medicine, a view held almost universally by primitive healers.[17] So important are words to the music of primitive songs that a small alteration in the words affects the song's melody.[5] Since a primitive melody is always the musical expression of an idea, primitive man sings only when he has a specific idea to express, and because of his spontaneous expression of thought, his performance is often marked by a union of song and speech.[29] Sometimes the aboriginal poet employs similes in his incantations; the Yoruba tribe of Nigeria uses the concreteness of the simile to clarify a direct command: "As the river always flows forwards and never back, so your illness will never return."[26] C. M. Bowra sees enchantment in the words of primitive song, since the power of the words renews the singer's and hearer's will to resist the malevolent universe which is incessantly threatening his well-being.[5] The word pictures of perfect health and bodily strength chanted by the wizard in healing magic are strong psychological prescriptions for tribal health.[20] His formulas abound in mythological allusions, which, when pronounced, unleash the powers of the past and hurl them into the present.[20] Song is not used in Western healing, but the widespread use of the singing commercial by advertisers attests to the persuasive power of song.[26]

Felix Marti-Ibanez, a medical historian, did not disassociate himself from his primitive medical brethren. To him, magic medicine had some of the traits of the modern psychosomatic approach to disease. Shamans, wizards, witch-doctors, and medicine men believe that all disease has a psychic phase; consequently, they endeavor to remove the traumatizing cause from the patient's mind.[7] In Northeast Asia, the shaman employs psychotherapy constantly in treating illness; he uses songs best in conjunction with psychotherapy.[28] The songs of the American Indian shaman are rhythmically monotonous, but the repetition and monotonous melodies have a hypnotic effect upon the patient's mind.[24] Generally, in primitive music, the prevailing psychological tension of the singer determines the relation between the musical style and the words of the song; the witch-doctor uses calm music when imploring the spirit of disease to release the possessed patient, but he sings martial music when he fights the unfriendly spirit with a spear.[29] Ruth M. Underhill reports a frank statement made to her by an Indian medicine man regarding the relative values of singing and sucking out techniques in therapy: "We could cure without that [sucking therapy], just by singing and remembering the vision. But people need something to see."[35] Many patients who could not be cured by song have attested, nevertheless, to the sense of calm and relief from pain that the songs brought them. This respite from anxiety, they avowed, could not be given them in hospitals.[35] At least one expert in primitive music, Richard Wallaschek, questions the primitive physician's use of musical accompaniment in his therapy, yet he finds that regardless of the shaman's medical ethics, his technique may be no more than a naively expressed bit of well-thought-out humbug that his European colleague practices with more sophistication.[36]

Bronislaw Malinowski, less concerned with the shaman's intent than Wallaschek, views primitive magic with respect. Medical magic is not a branch of scientific learning; instead, it is "a primeval possession of man known only through tradition and affirming man's autonomous power of creating desired ends."[20] The shaman is a specialist in mysticism, magic, and religion who masters the techniques of ecstasy to cure himself and others.[7] His religious ecstasies help him create pure poetic art which reveals the "essence of things." Generally eccentric and neurasthenic,[7] he applies his self-cure learning to healing his patients.[2] Ibanez honors the shaman as a sincere predecessor of the medical doctor; furthermore the shaman is to be commended for shielding his patient from harm and for believing strongly in the psychic component of disease.[12]

The American Indian, the Navajo in particular, believes strongly in the curative power of song. Fear of illness is the dominant fear of the Navajo.[11] Although curing ceremonials are directed at one or more patients, the events have communal interest, for all attending the rituals may benefit from the proceedings.[15] The singer who officiates at the curing ceremony is a man of prestige.[13] The ceremonials may last from two to nine days. Each singer is a specialist who has mastered hundreds of old songs, and these he must sing in precise tone and sequence during a healing session.[15] The chants stress purification and clean thinking,[13] and they "submerge ill in the beauty and perfection of primeval creation."[2] The Ceremony of the Evening Way, for example, disperses evil and ignorance; knowledge has given the singer power to avoid evil.[2] To stop bad dreams or deter insanity, the singer performs the Big Star Chant,⁹ and to insure his well-being, the Navajo warrior sings the Blessed Way Songs before retiring and on arising in the morning.[32]

On the last night of a curing session, the singer emphasizes legendary songs. The patient and visitors participate in the antiphonal singing of the patterned songs. First, the sing-doctor pleads: "His feet restore for him, his mind restore for him, his voice restore for him." The patient responds: "My feet are getting better, my head is feeling better, I am better all over."[15]

The intent of this responsive singing is "compulsion through orderly repetition."[13] The hypnotic effect of the chants is obvious; the singer is positive and the communal consolation he elicits reinforces the patient's desire to get well. Perhaps these further examples of Navajo healing poetry illustrate the patterns they use:

> You will recover; you will walk again,
> It is I who say it; my power is great.
> Through our white shell
> I will enable you to walk again.[2]

> NAVAJO NIGHT SONG
>
> I have made your sacrifice.
> I have prepared a smoke for you.
> My feet restore for me.
> My legs restore for me.
> My body restore for me.
> My mind restore for me.
>
> Impervious to pain may I walk.
> Feeling light within, may I walk...
> With lively feeling, may I walk.[35]

The Apache shaman, unlike the Eskimo shaman, does not heal through fits or trances.[3] He uses cajolery and pleading instead, usually in the form of song and prayer. In a specific healing ceremony, a shaman sings a series of songs mixed with prayer which he has learned from his familiar spirit. He invokes the spirit, asking him to designate the disease of his patient and the specific therapy to be used to cure the sufferer. When he receives the spirit's diagnosis, the shaman may attempt to cure by prescription, by sucking foreign objects supposedly causing the illness from the patient's body, and by intensifying his chanting.[3] As with the Navajo, Apache healing is communal. Music is regarded as a direct cure, and as the shaman sings over the sick, the people join in songs and dances that benefit both the patient and themselves.[10]

The Cheyenne shaman sings a cycle of seven songs to initiate his curing ritual; he then smokes a sacred pipe, administers medicine, and sings nine more songs. Finally, he consecrates food, of which all present partake.[32] The Choctaws cure disease by animal magnetism, song, and mouth suction.[30] As the shaman sings, his assistants beat sticks in rhythm. In Minnesota, the Chippewa Indians have a Grand Medicine Lodge. Their doctors go through a rigid initiation into the mysteries of the Lodge. Goodness and the good life are taught by these doctors; they receive ritualistic formulas in dream revelations, and these they preserve as songs. Each spring the Lodge sponsors a song festival, and each initiate brings his songs to this important event. The songs endeavor to bring good health and long life to the people.[2]

The Creek Indians believe that their spirits inhabit rain-clouds, springs, crevices, and caverns. Therefore to isolate the spirit causing a particular disease, the shaman localizes the cave dwelling of the culprit spirit by examining the patient. Once he learns the name of the specific spirit, he shakes his rattle and sings abusive and mocking songs to entice the reluctant demon to exit from the recesses of the afflicted body. The spirit confesses his guilt, becomes a song, but demands a song in return for its sacrifice.[20]

Among the Pueblos of Sia, New Mexico, sickness is caused by loss of heart, but the heart's strength can be restored by singing proper heart songs:

> You, Arrow youth, why is it that you are going
> about throwing your heart away?
> Come back, whole, and sit down in front of the
> altar where the iraho are.[19]

The Dakota Indians esteemed their wakan-man or medicine man very highly. He is the representative of the deities, dictates chants, defines sin, and demands complete servility of the tribesmen. The wakan-man has been presented with remarkable vocal powers by the deities and his chants and prayers are the gift of inspiration. The wakan-man has remarkable powers:

> Flying god-like, I encircle the heavens:
> I enlighten the earth to its centre.
> The little ox lies struggling on the earth,
> I lay my arrow to the string.[31]

Quesalid, a Kwakiutl Indian from the Vancouver region of Canada, associated with shamans in order to expose them, but consented to learn their art since they offered to convert him to shamanism. The training was rigorous; the convert had to learn pantomime, prestidigitation, simulation of fainting and nervous fits, sacred songs, and self-mutilation in order to become duly accredited as a master shaman.[23] Song is the therapeutic specific for the ailing Wallawalla Indians of the Columbia River. Convalescents sing several songs daily in a ceremony led by a squaw physician who is accompanied by a dozen men.[8] In Tehuantepec, Mexico, the curandera, or medicine women, use both medicine and prayer to rid the patient's body of evil spirits; unhappily, part of the incantation begs the spirits to inhabit "another unfortunate":

> Timorous body, why get frightened?
> Cowardly body, don't be afraid.
> Return...to your house and stable,
> That you may pardon her.
> May she not die of childbirth,
> May she not die of fright,
> May she not die without confession.
> May that fright fall into the ocean,
> May it fall into the mountains,
> May it seize another unfortunate.[34]

The Moluches and Puelches of Patagonia have an unusual healing ceremony. Epileptic boys dressed as female sorcerers attempt to cure disease by chanting songs as drummers and rattlers add to the din.[8] In colder climates far to the north, the extreme cold, long nights, and lack of vitamins contribute to mental illness. Perhaps the Arctic deserts induce hysteria since loneliness in barren wastelands menaces mental equilibrium.[7] The shamans of the Buryat tribe in the Arctic are the chief trustees of their rich, heroic oral literature. A Yakut shaman has a poetic vocabulary of 12,000 words, three times as many words as are known by the rest of the community.[7] The Greenland Eskimos have a novel way of dispelling gloom and anger. Disputants transfer their venom to their poems, singing them out as they pound their drums. Eventually, their anger evaporates and they become amicable once again.[2] Western man may profit from their sane practice. Rock and roll music, may, indeed, be more salutary for the young man than their parents care to concede.

The polar Eskimo is very liberal in granting shamanships. Almost every family has its special shaman—male or female—who looks after the family's health. Since the shaman's principal duty is to cure disease, he must be an expert in restoring lost souls to the patients, for disease is caused by loss of the soul. As in our society, a shaman's income and prestige are relative to his success in healing his afflicted clients. Therefore, his skill in memorizing and composing curing songs, as well as his frenzied enactment of them, is essential to his well-being in the tribe.[3]

In Nigeria, the Yoruba tribe of 6,000,000 people practice an interesting ritual to discharge the evil spirits inhabiting a neurotic's mind. The Dove Ceremony involves ablution, sprinkling of the patient's body with the blood of a dove, upon which the patient stands as the following incantation from the "Eji Ogbe" is uttered:

> Perhaps a hunter or a farmer paid money for this evil,
> Or a sorcerer or a witch or any other cause of evil
>   upon her,
> As she drinks and bathes in water,
> Let water bear all evil things away.
> Let only peace and contentment follow her home.
> Water always flows forward—it never comes back.[26]

The Nuer of the upper Nile valley love to sing poetry, a trait they share with most pastoral people. The boy sings when he is happy, when he courts, when he works. Some of his songs are traditional; others he composes at whim.[32] Apparently, the communal singing of primitive people is an art that civilized man should imitate. Even taunt songs and challenge chants might be salubrious substitutes for much of the malice that allegedly civilized men bear one another.

The Wasambara of East Africa sing curing responses to their doctor's solos;[16] the Uganda tribesmen find song a purge for melancholy when death of their loved ones palls them;[29] and the Dahomey people find it therapeutically sound to cure neuroses in public expression of songs and dances.[22] The Azande witch doctor tries to soothe the sister of a dying chief with tender words: "Break away tears, oo wee, we will sit down with her and brush away tears."[27] The comfort given to the grieving woman is enhanced by the choral singing of the sympathetic tribe; primitive men seek company in crises.

An elaborate healing cult in Ethiopia, the Zar cult, sees the sign of possession in a victim's proneness to accidents, sterility, convulsive fits, and extreme apathy. The healer, himself Zar-possessed, has, however, come to terms with the spirit.[23] Therefore, he can practice his curing art while the Zar possesses him, the Zar using his possessed body as a medium. Meanwhile, the male reader-composer of the Zar liturgy intones new or old hymns as the onlookers clap their hands in rhythm. Now, as if before a jury, the patient is questioned about his behavior, his loyalty to the society, his devotion to his family, and his participation in the community's social functions.[23] The cure is effected when the medium's Zar lures the unknown Zar of the patient into public confession; the Zar is cajoled to reveal his identity, and is banished from the area.[23]

In his study of African tribes, W. Lloyd Warner describes the consolations of song for a dying warrior. Surrounded by his relatives who sing the garma water cycle songs of his clan, the doomed man listens, feels his soul made good, and dies in comfort. The songs relieve even the pains of the speared warrior and assure him of the safety of his soul.[37] Another tribe employs a combination of hydrotherapy and psychological suggestion to cure the ill. Placed in the totem well, the ill man listens to the songs of the male members of the clan as they dance around the well. The songs refer to the ancient creator women of the tribe—allusions to the pristine days of purity in the tribe's mythical past.[37]

The problems of healing in Ceylon are complicated because of the hundreds of thousands of yakku (evil spirits) in the pantheon of demons that the edura, or doctor, must contend with in his exorcisms. The mantras, songs of exorcism, have well-defined formulae, and they are sung at all healing ceremonies. The mantra below lists a formidable number of mental diseases that the edura must deal with, and illustrates the close alliance between religion and medicine in this particular region:

Om, honor to Buddha, honor to Shiva, the eighteen mental disorders, the eighteen convulsion diseases, the eighteen fevers caused by the godlike Korasanniya, the diseases Korasanniya produced for the first, the second, the third time, may they be put to an end by the help of the deities and of glorious Buddha.[40]

In nearby Malaya, the shaman falls into a trance, the musicians suddenly beat the drums, and they intone in a language of literary romance to invoke the spirit causing disease:[39]

> Ho, Lord of the World!
> Sultan, prince of miraculous power!
> Prince, divinity of clear vision!
> Prince of pools of heavenly brightness!
> Lord of the word of dark plains!
> Hearken, prince, to the words of thy slaves!
> Hearken, prince, to their wind-borne cry!
> Arise and come to our jewelled curtains,
> Come and enter the (shaman's) ear posy.[39]

A special form of hypnotherapy is practiced by the Negritos in Northern Luzon. The shaman casts the patient into a trance and encourages him to fight to vanquish the "demon" that is assailing him. The conquering patient demands a song and dance from his humbled spirit. At this point the shaman ends the trance, and instructs the patient to sing the song and perform the dance he has just learned from the spirit. Especially significant in this performance is the communal benefit that accrues to the viewing tribe, since all of its esthetic life is derived from the curing ceremony. The Negritos learn of all of their songs and dances during these therapeutic sessions.[23]

In Australia, the aboriginal of the Arnhem Reservation studies his Karma songs very carefully for he relies upon their healing virtues during troubled times;[21] the women use the same songs at times of emotional stress.[4] The women of the Western Kimberleys find songs helpful in easing the rigors of childbirth[4]—a practice which might have some value in western obstetrical practice.

During the war, Japanese Americans were arbitrarily relocated at the Tuli Lake Relocation Center. Life at the Center was drab and induced melancholy among many of the unfortunate displaced persons. To avoid depression, some of the people began to compose a form of haiku. To both composer and hearer, the Senryu poetry was a refuge and an instrument of community expression.[22]

Modern poets find it difficult to have their collected works published. Few publishers care to invest in unpromising commercial ventures, and so, the nation fails to hear many of its singers. Anthropology records the written and unwritten songs of primitive peoples, but few western men ever read these remarkable anthologies sequestered in the specialized researches of scholars. But how the heart of primitive man sings! To Bowra, the song of primitive man is the truest song. He need not adapt his verse to the standards of television's mores. He sings his exultations, his fears, his aspirations. Unscientific in healing, he has, nevertheless, earned the approbation of anthropologists, medical historians, and psychiatrists for his intense efforts to effect healing with his rudimentary resources. His songs, chants, incantations, and prayers have yet to be studied extensively by teams of specialists from many disciplines in the sciences and the humanities for the purpose of establishing a meaningful correlation between primitive poetry therapy and scientific poetry therapy. The data for this proposed study is abundant; Trask's anthology of unwritten aboriginal song points the way to similar anthologies which will stress healing songs and poems.

Modern man lives as fearfully as any primitive denizen of jungle, tundra, or desert waste. Ironically, it may be that civilized man will succumb to his unrestrained scientific adventuring, whereas the so-called savages dwelling in wastelands might survive. More than ever, the world needs poetry therapy—the therapy that soothes the savage breast but which sophisticated man spurns or patronizes.

REFERENCES

1. F. Alexander, and S. Silesnick, *The History of Psychiatry* (New York, Harper, 1966) p. 9. See also, F. Marti-Ibanez, *A Prelude to Medical History* (New York, MD Pub, 1961) p. 45.

2. M. Astrov, *American Indian Prose* (New York, Putnam, 1962) pp. 2–31.

3. R. Beals, and H. Hoijer, *Introduction to Anthropology* (New York, Macmillan, 1961) pp. 544–546, 594.

4. R. Berndt, *The World of the First Australians* (Chicago, University Press, 1964) pp. 125, 317.

5. C. Bowra, *Primitive Song* (Cleveland, World Pub, 1962) pp. 26, 52, 282–286.

6. J. Campbell, *The Masks of God* (New York, Viking, 1959) p. 6.

7. M. Eliade, *From Primitive to Zen* (New York, Harper, 1967) pp. xix, 24–25, 30.

8. C. Engle, *Musical Myths and Facts* (London, Novello, Ewer, 1876) pp. 89–91.
9. E. Ferguson, *Dancing Gods* (Albuquerque, University of New Mexico, 1957) p. 41.
10. C. Hofmann, *American Indians Sing* (New York, Day, 1967) p. 49.
11. W. Howells, *The Heathens* (Garden City, Doubleday, 1948) p. 87.
12. F. Ibanez, *A Prelude to Medical History* (New York, MD Pub, 1961) p. 36.
13. C. Kluckhohn, and D. Leighton, *The Navaho* (Cambridge, Mass., Harvard University, 1947) pp. 155, 164, 224.
14. H. Kohl, *Teaching the "Unteachables"* (New York, New York Review, 1967) p. 28.
15. A. Leighton and D. Leighton, *The Navaho Door* (Cambridge, Mass., Harvard University, 1944) pp. 24, 26–27, 34.
16. S. Licht, *Music in Medicine* (Boston, N. E. Conservatory of Music, 1946) p. 4.
17. J. Lippert, *The Evolution of Culture* (New York, Macmillan, 1931) p. 601.
18. D. Mcallester, "Apache Music" in F. Wallace, ed., *The Role of Music in Western Apache Culture* (Philadelphia, University of Pennsylvania, 1960) p. 469.
19. A. Malefijt, *Religion and Culture* (New York, Macmillan, 1968) p. 258.
20. B. Malinowski, *Magic, Science, and Religion* (Garden City, Doubleday, 1955) pp. 74, 76, 83.
21. W. Malm, *Music Cultures of the Pacific, the Near East, and Asia* (Englewood Cliffs, Prentice Hall, 1967) p. 2.
22. A. Merriam, *The Anthropology of Music* (Bloomington, Ill., Northwestern University, 1964) pp. 73, 202–204.
23. John Middleton ed., *Magic, Witchcraft, and Curing* (Garden City, Natural History Press, 1967) pp. 31, 256, 284–286, 290.
24. P. Oursel-Masson, et al. *Ancient India and Indian Civilization* (New York, Barnes and Noble, 1957) p. 257.
25. F. Prescott, *The Poetic Mind* (Ithaca, Great Seal, 1959) pp. 61, 128, 171.
26. R. Prince, "Indigenous Yoruba Psychiatry," in A. Kiev, ed., *Magic, Faith, and Healing* (New York, Free Press of Glencoe, 1964) pp. 102, 111–113.
27. E. Pritchard, *Witchcraft, Oracles and Magic among the Azande* (Oxford, Clarendon Press, n.d.) pp. 180–182.
28. P. Radin, "Music and medicine among primitive peoples," in M. Schullian and M. Schoen, eds., *Music and Medicine* (New York, H. Schuman, 1948) pp. 4, 18–22.
29. M. Schneider, "Primitive music," in E. Wellesz, ed., *Ancient and Oriental Music* (London, Oxford University, 1957) pp. 2, 4, 31, 44.
30. H. Schoolcraft, *Indian Tribes of the U.S.* (Philadelphia, Lippincott and Grambo, 1853) V, 440.
31. Schoolcraft, VI, 654.
32. E. Service, *A Profile of Primitive Culture* (New York, Harper, 1958) pp. 127–128, 152, 179.
33. W. Trask, *The Unwritten Song* (New York, Macmillan, 1966) pp. x–xiii.
34. F. Toor, *A Treasury of Mexican Folkways* (New York, Crown, 1947) p. 148.
35. R. Underhill, *Red Man's Religion* (Chicago, University of Chicago, 1965) pp. 84–230.
36. R. Wallascheck, *Primitive Music* (London, Longman's Green, 1893) pp. 167–168.
37. L. Warner, *A Black Civilization* (New York, Harper, 1958) pp. 227, 413.

38. J. Hemming Webb, *An Essay on the Influence of Poetry on the Mind* (London, Hastings, 1839) p. 85.

39. R. Winstedt, *The Malay Magician* (London, Routledge and Paul, 1961) pp. 58–59.

40. Wirz, P.: *Exorcism and the Art of Healing in Ceylon* (Leiden, E. J. Brill, 1954), pp. 21–61. Buddha himself opposed prayer, chant, and conjuration in healing, although commentators to the Bhuddist scriptures note that he was asked to ward off pestilence by sermons. Legend has it that he rid Visālā of the plague by uttering a conjuring prayer. The common people apparently do not take Bhudda's proscriptions against incantation seriously for they employ his name in many rituals. (Wirz, pp. 235–237).

41. W. Wordsworth, "Intimations of Immortality From Recollections of Early Childhood," in A. Jackson (ed.), *The Complete Poetical Works of William Wordsworth* (Boston, Houghton Mifflin, 1904) p. 352.

PART II
HOW

Exploring the Unconscious through Nonsense Poetry

ANTHONY PIETROPINTO, M.D.

JABBERWOCKY

'Twas brillig, and the slithy toves
    Did gyre and gimble in the wabe:
All mimsy were the borogoves,
    And the mome raths outgrabe.

"Beware the Jabberwock, my son!
    The jaws that bite, the claws that catch!
Beware the Jubjub bird, and shun
    The frumious Bandersnatch!"

He took his vorpal sword in hand:
    Long time the manxome foe he sought—
So rested he by the Tumtum tree,
    And stood awhile in thought.

And, as in uffish thought he stood,
    The Jabberwock, with eyes of flame,
Came whiffling through the tulgey wood,
    And burbled as it came!

One, two! One, two! And through and through
    The vorpal blade went snicker-snack!
He left it dead, and with its head
    He went galumphing back.

"And hast thou slain the Jabberwock?
    Come to my arms, my beamish boy!
O frabjous day! Callooh! Callay!"
    He chortled in his joy.

> 'Twas brillig and the slithy toves
>   Did gyre and gimble in the wabe:
> All mimsy were the borogoves,
>   And the mome raths outgrabe.
>
>   —LEWIS CARROLL[1]

Nonsense is serious Stuff—or at least stuff to be taken seriously. Much has been written about the healing power of poetry, but the subject of nonsense poetry has largely been ignored in such discussions. Like a bottle of Dr. Pepper, the "misunderstood" soft drink, much of the problem lies in its name, since anything referred to as nonsense can hardly be considered a topic for serious consideration. Yet, nonsense poetry is by no means poetry that makes no sense. In literary terminology, nonsense poetry is that which deals in a humorous or whimsical way with odd or grotesque themes, characters, or actions, often employing coined words that are evocative but have no generally accepted meaning. In content and style, nonsense poems are similar to dreams.

It is generally agreed by psychotherapists that dreams are basically therapeutic. While we sleep, unresolved conflicts suppressed by the conscious mind during the day are played out, as on a stage or movie screen, by our unconscious minds. Because many of these dream topics are associated with unpleasant or forbidden feelings and are more apt to be expressed in an emotional, rather than a logical, frame of reference, the unconscious mind unfolds the dream matter in the bizarre form so familiar to every dreamer. Dream objects and people are often displaced by other objects and other people, with symbols replacing the actual subject matter. Personalities and images may become condensed and merged. When the dream-work is complete, the final dream has often become virtually unrecognizable from its source material, and painful conflicts and realities have been made thereby more acceptable to the subconscious.[2] A skilled psychoanalyst can often unravel the riddle posed by the dream; perhaps no single statement of Sigmund Freud's is quoted more often than "The interpretation of dreams is the royal road to a knowledge of the unconscious activities of the mind."[3]

Poetry therapists have noted that the poetic process is much like dream work. For poetry, too, uses symbol (or metaphor), free association of words and images, condensation and merging of concepts, and deliberate distortion of reality to evoke strong emotional feelings.[4] Thus, poetry is to prose as dreaming is to thinking. Poetry reaches close to the subconscious minds of both poet and reader. If the dream provides the "royal road" to be traveled by night, poetry may be said to provide a similar highway by day.

Psychiatrists and other practitioners in the rapidly expanding field of poetry therapy are aware that patients tormented by conflict and ambivalence welcome the opportunity to express such contradictory emotions, some of which they feel forbidden to reveal, in complex and secret language.[5] Yet, nonsense poetry is invariably shunned by the therapist in favor of poems that offer clear images and discrete messages, leaving nonsense poetry, which may be the poetic highway most parallel to the "royal road" of dreams, to suffer the fate of Robert Frost's *Road Not taken*. This is unfortunate, because nonsense poetry shares one major attribute with dreams that "serious" poetry lacks— the element of wit. Freud realized early in his exploration of the dream phenomenon that dreams and jokes are closely related. "In waking reality," he wrote, "I have little claim to be regarded as a wit. If my dreams seem amusing, that is not on my account, but on account of the peculiar psychological conditions under which dreams are constructed; and the fact is intimately connected with the theory of jokes and the comic. Dreams become ingenious and amusing because the direct and easiest pathway to the expression of their thoughts is barred: they are forced into being so."[6]

Most wit and humor can be recognized as cleverly disguised aggression, against either people or social institutions. Wit permits us to express aggression in a socially acceptable manner under an amiable guise.[7] Conscious wit is not easy to master, but wit in the dream-work comes naturally to everyone. And so does the process of nonsense.

Despite its shadowy ambiguities, nonsense is an old, familiar pathway for all. No sooner does a child begin to master speech than he begins to experiment with words and discover enjoyment in verbal play and double meanings. The age of speech development in the child, from approximately 15 to 30 months, corresponds to the period when complete dependence on the omnipotent parent is giving way to an awareness of autonomy. With walking and talking, processes of conceptual thinking, memory and awareness of time come into being.

The child, still bewildered and overwhelmed at times, uses nonsense language to ridicule intelligence, logic, and the limits of time and space, thereby reducing adults to his level of impotence.[8]

Nonsense is more than the antithesis of logic. Phyllis Greenacre writes, "Nonsense is not only the lack of reason or loss of expected order, but it is the defiance of reason which men value most, and it is achieved by apparent isolation, inconsequence, and generally heedless disconnection. There is a quality of (generally quiet) explosive destructiveness about sheer nonsense—an unannounced nihilism—which is never absolutely achieved to be sure, but is felt in its subtle implications." Nonsense is, therefore, regressive and aggressive, but not without purpose, for it enables one to ventilate his unconscious without getting into trouble. The further removed is the symbol from the reality, the safer the release of the unconscious drive.[9]

Nonsense is not logical, but logic is a notoriously ineffective tool for communicating with the unconscious. Martin Grotjahn says, "The natural brilliance of the unspoiled child stands in shocking contrast to the stupidity of the average adult, who has invented the term common sense as an excuse for his limitations.... The logical mind often makes man obtuse when dealing with himself and his fellow men; it becomes so difficult for him to read the minds of others that he must be considered psychologically illiterate.[10]

It is indeed difficult to establish true communication between minds, for, as Harry Stack Sullivan points out, "Language operations as thought are profoundly different, quite fundamentally different, from language operations as communication and as pure mechanisms used in dealing with others; the more completely one becomes self-centered, the more utterly he becomes cut off from integrations with other more or less real people, and the more utterly novel, perfectly magical, and wholly individual become the symbols which he uses as if they were language."[11]

"The psychologic and logical ways of thinking do not oppose each other—they ought to complement each other," Grotjahn writes. "Their combination will give us the tools to deal with the reality in which we live and which has two different aspects: a physical-material one and a psycho-symbolic one."[12]

It is probably the inherent aggressiveness, even violence, of nonsense that has influenced the poetry therapists to pass by nonsense poetry for that which apparently provides the patient with safer footing in bridging the logical and paralogical areas of the mind. They forget that, like the dream process, nonsense serves a defensive function by blunting the original raw emotional and ideational content in such a way as to make it unobjectionable, or even pleasurable.[13]

And so, convinced that nonsense poetry merited at least as much therapeutic consideration as its non-nonsensical counterparts, I embarked on the quest for the Jabberwock, attempting to explore what responses a nonsense poem might elicit from the minds of readers.

Why Jabberwocky?

In spite of the copious literature produced by distinguished psychoanalysts about nonsense, a psychiatrist still tends to feel a bit sheepish about using a creature as fantastic as the Jabberwock for any sort of serious study. He belongs to the realm of fairy tales; after all, did not Freud say that our collective intuitive knowledge of dream symbols, particularly sex symbols, was derived from fairy tales and myths, jokes and witticisms, and from folklore?[14]

A child's poem? Even our nursery rhymes have hidden meanings obscured by symbolism and the passage of time. *Mistress Mary, Quite Contrary* was a mocking criticism of Mary, Queen of Scots, and her Francophile ladies-in-waiting. Little Jack Horner was actually a steward who stole a deed to an estate from a pie in which it had been hidden on its way to Henry VIII. And *Ring-A-Ring-A-Roses* has been said to refer to the rosy rash of bubonic plague, the flowers carried by the victims to mask the odor of putrefying flesh, their sneezes, and their falling down dead.[15] You see how nonsense has a way of softening things.

Having, I hope, justified an attempt to explore the unconscious through nonsense poetry, it remains only to explain why I chose *Jabberwocky*, from Lewis Carroll's *Through the Looking Glass and What Alice Found There*, as the vehicle for the quest. *Jabberwocky* is possibly the most famous nonsense poem in the English language, and perhaps, as Martin Gardner believes,[16] the greatest of all nonsense poems in the English language. But beyond its literary merits, the Jabberwock is a veritable psychoanalyst's dream—or nightmare, if you prefer.

First, the Jabberwock is a child's monster of the "bogey-man" type that young minds take a terrified delight in fabricating. "Many children have some fabled ogre, often in animal form," writes Phyllis Greenacre, "or some 'secret' with which they scare each other and themselves. Psychoanalysis reveals that it is generally some representation of the primal scene, in which the sexual images of the parents are fused into a frightening or awe-inspiring single figure."[17] Freud maintained that "creative" fantasy can invent nothing new but can only regroup elements from different sources; hence, for instance, centaurs and other mythological beasts (such as griffins and unicorns). Dreamers frequently condense two or more unpleasant images or memories into one symbolic element, the disguise of which renders it less distressing.[18]

One might be more eager to challenge Greenacre's assumption that Carroll's *Jabberwocky* has primal scene implications if Carroll had not, three years later, published *The Hunting of the Snark*, a nonsense poem in which a crew of childish explorers compulsively pursue a fascinating monster. To look at a snark, however, may cause the observer to disappear into thin air immediately, and, indeed, the explorer who does set eyes on the monster suffers this very annihilation. The hero who dares to look seems to reenact, before his disappearance, the primal scene he is witnessing[19]:

> Erect and sublime, for one moment of time,
> In the next, that wild figure they saw
> (As if stung by a spasm) plunge into a chasm
> While they waited and listened in awe.

Jabberwocky is not only a monster story, but also the retelling of an ancient tale common to many cultures, that of the slaying of the dragon. It recalls Hercules, Jason, Perseus, Beowulf, Orlando Furioso, St. George, the Knights of the Round Table, and Frodo Baggins. There are three classic elements of the dragon story, not all of which appear in every tale, and only two of which appear in *Jabberwocky*. The first element is the killing of a powerful, evil monster by a virtuous young man. It is the triumph of virtue over vice, and, psychoanalytically, the dominance of superego over id.

The second element is the devotion of the dragon-slayer to his king, a noble older man to whom the young hero pledges his arms. Beowulf has his Hrothgar, Lancelot his Arthur, and it is to his father that the Jabberwock-slayer proudly bears the head of the monster.

Symbolically it is the resolution of the Oedipal period, in which the boy subjugates his incentuous drives and identifies with the father after undergoing a psychological auto-castration.

The third element in the dragon tale is the maiden, held captive by the dragon and rescued by the youth, such as Perseus's Andromeda or Orlando Furioso's Olimpia. According to Martin Grotjahn, the maiden is a symbol of the mother, whom the son prefers to think of as bound unwillingly to the father and yielding to the father's bestial assaults against her will.[20] In some versions of this myth, it is the dragon that drops out, leaving us with powerful Oedipal triangles (king-queen-knight), such as Arthur-Guinivere-Lancelot or Mark-Iseult-Tristan. The closest Carroll came to tackling this delicate element was the trial of the Knave of Hearts, who is punished by the King for stealing the Queen's tarts.[21]

The Quest

In order to explore what effect "Jabberwocky" might have on the imagination of others, I devised a simple questionnaire, which included the poem for the subject to read. The questionnaire asked subjects whether they had read the poem previously, where, what it meant to them, whether they liked it and why, and how it made them feel. They were asked to describe or draw a Jabberwock and to tell what images or thoughts the first (most ambiguous) stanza suggested. Finally, they were given a list of 15 of the nonsense words that appear in the poem and asked to select a meaning that seemed to fit each word best.

Fifty subjects answered the questionnaire, 32 of them male and 18 female. Thirty-one of the subjects were high school students, aged 15 to 17, from Fordham Prep and Marymount in New York City. Six were adolescent patients, aged 13 to 15, in therapy with me in a child psychiatry clinic. Eight were miscellaneous adults, ranging in age from 19 to 46. The remaining five questionnaires were completed by the director, three cast members and the stage manager of the Manhattan Project production of *Alice in Wonderland*, a play that opens with the cast huddled under an umbrella, reciting *Jabberwocky*. This show, cited by *Time* magazine as one of the year's ten best off-Broadway plays, and winner of the 1970 Obie award as the best off-Broadway show, was in rehearsal for two years while the cast members explored the "Alice" books for new insights.[22]

Not counting the "Alice" cast, 55 per cent of the subjects had read the poem before, most in high school English classes. Only three volunteered the source of the poem. All subjects were able to offer some meaning for it. ("*Somebody* killed *something*; that's clear at any rate," said Alice, the book's 7½-year-old heroine.) Some compared it with "the chivalry ballads," St. George, Beowulf, and even David and Goliath. Many expressed its meaning in general terms:

"It's just a situation that can be applied to any place today where someone overcomes a greater force."

"Suggests that people should be aware of their surroundings and should beware of evil."

"It shows man's desire to conquer or achieve; his desire to challenge the unchallenged."

"It definitely shows how good overcomes evil."

Some focused on the hero's defiance of the father's warning, as did the actress who portrays Alice: "If you don't dare to go against the set pattern set up by your ancestors and society, you will never achieve anything unique.... The Jabberwock is the embodiment of the monsters or fears within each one of us that make us take the conventional path because it is known and safe." An actor said, "It's about age's inability to recognize the dreams of youth."

A 16-year-old girl summarized the six stanzas as follows: "1st—People who close their eyes to the injustice of people today; 2nd—Beware of the people who cut you down; 3rd—The youth revolting against society; 4th—The youth comes in contact with society; 5th—Moment of truth; 6th—The other youth congratulating him; 7th—The people still unaware of society's injustice and prejudice today." Note that this young rebel saw "another youth" congratulating the hero, not the father. She also interpreted the repetition of the first stanza at the end of the poem as indicating a lack of change. Several subjects saw this repetition as symbolizing a return to peace, but one saw "the continuing return of more but different Jabberwocks," and another said, "The boy seems to have been able to overcome it, yet it still remains as a threat to him and to others." One of the actors said, "It's the life cycle of setting out, conquering, and beginning all over again."

The director of the play viewed the poem in terms that the analyst might describe as sublimating the drives of the id via the creative process: "I reached a brick wall in my life when monsters of the unconscious tried to destroy me, but I harnessed the monster instead, used his energy, and created something wild with it. Then back to business as usual."

A high school boy translated the story into more contemporary terms: "To me, the poem is about surfing and the speaker would be a father talking to his son, who is about to ride a wave."

A 14-year-old female patient who had made several suicide attempts and had been abandoned by her father said: "The Jabberwock could be a thing about life. Beware of life. The jaws that bite are bad things. He thought about what the Jabberwock told him. [Interestingly enough, she associated the name "Jabberwock" with the father, not the monster.] The sword might be a symbol of understanding what he said. The sword is wisdom. He went through life and came to his father's arms."

Seventy per cent of the subjects liked the poem, 17 per cent disliked it, and the rest expressed no strong opinion; only 52 per cent reported only positive emotions; 28 per cent reported chiefly unpleasant feelings, such as confusion, fear or sadness; and 12 per cent reported mixed or no emotions.

While a few objected to the poem's ambiguities, most welcomed this aspect enthusiastically. A 16-year-old boy said, "It gives you a chance to use your imagination and the opportunity to make the words mean what you want them to mean and, therefore, a chance to almost write a poem yourself by interpreting the words." (Compare the first part of his statement with Humpty Dumpty's "When *I* use a word, it means just what I choose it to mean—neither more nor less.... The question is which is to be master—that's all.") A 21-year-old student wrote, "It suggests a story, but allows the individual to project his ideas and imagination."

Phyllis Greenacre wrote, "The *Jabberwocky* contains many arresting words, neologisms, which sound as though we should know their meanings, yet leave us groping, and a little tickled at our own stupidity."[23] A 17-year-old boy said almost as eloquently, "It makes you feel unsure of yourself, like you don't know very much. You feel like the poem is very sensible and you are the nut." A 16-year-old girl called it "oddly ordered nonsense with wonderful pseudowords—the illusion of reality in an actual unreality; and the reminder of inability, sometimes, to tell one from the other."

Some reveled unashamedly in its regressive joys. "It holds my attention, which poems rarely do," said a 16-year-old boy, "It makes me feel as though I was seven years old." He added "Good," lest there be any misunderstanding. "It makes me feel childishly satisfied and happy," said a 16-year-old girl. The theatrical director said, "It's violent, childish, and like a muddy swamp on Mars."

The play's stage manager felt that the death of the Jabberwock meant the end of childhood: "I think that most people at some point in their childhood are subjected to, or encounter some kind of central, basic experience that forces them to leave childhood behind. It is both a sad and happy, good and bad sort of thing." The poem made him feel "sad and old."

"The poem puzzles me as each time I read, a different meaning seems to be implied," wrote a 17-year-old boy. An actor said, "It depends on what I bring to it. If I'm looking for reassurance, it gives reassurance. It could also give violence, despair."

An adolescent boy wrote, "Phrases like 'gyre and gimble in the wabe' have a quality that just pacifies you almost." A classmate of his described his feelings as "relaxed."

A 17-year-old nonpatient with a history of drug overdose found it unsettling: "Too violent; images are cruel and fierce and frightening to encounter, particularly in such an ambiguous situation. I feel scared at the hate and violence that takes place in it; also afraid of the joy of death."

Emotional responses cascaded forth: "excited—amused—mildly contented — angry — triumphant — blah — elated — happy — and proud—turned on and wanting to go into battle." And one 16-year-old boy, completely caught up in the spirit of the poem, answered the question, How does the poem make you feel? with the single word "beamish."

John Tenniel's classic illustration of the Jabberwock shows it to be a huge dragon-type monster, hovering in the air on bat-like wings. For those who like to look for phallic symbols, it has a serpentine neck, a long tail, many facial antennae, and elongated claws. It wears a waistcoat and its face vaguely resembles that of an anguished old man.

Asked to describe the Jabberwock, most subjects saw it as a dragon, but seven saw it as a bird, three as man-like, and others as a bear, bat, cat, alligator, wolf, dog, lizard, or combinations of the above. One 17-year-old boy said it was "much like an average, everyday, fire-eating dragon."

Those subjects who volunteered drawings provided some fascinating creations. The most artistic offering featured a monster possessing teeth, claws, feathered wings, scales and hair, standing in an upright position, as though epochs of evolution had been incorporated into one creature.

A high school girl described the Jabberwock as an "ugly, ugly, ugly chicken with teeth," and drew what could pass as a parody of the domineering mother, an elegantly plumed bird with a long tongue, sharp teeth, enormous claws and a "shock-proof two-way wristwatch" like Dick Tracy's, perhaps to insure constant communication.

Eyes played a prominent role in the drawings, one bird-man had five eyes, and another man-monster had two balls of fire in his eye-sockets—literally, a "Jabberwock with eyes of flame." The theatrical director produced a protoplasmic blob with one central eye and seven hairlike projections, looking like a nerve cell waiting to be stimulated.

My favorite drawing came from an attractive, unmarried 28-year-old secretary, who produced a one-eyed, pig-snouted, fanged monster that abounded in phallic symbols. It had a single horn on its head, along with a thin neck and tubular legs attached to feet that I can only describe as scrotal. Its fingers, one on the right extremity and three on the left, were long and pointed; some had been lost in battle, the artist explained.

The classically phallic single horn was suggested verbally by a 16-year-old girl who noted that she "can't draw," but described the Jabberwock as "a cross between a dragon and a dinosaur with a trace of unicorn blood." A 20-year-old woman drew a vague, skull-toothed creature bearing an unidentified shaft-like object. And so much for "Alice" and phallus!

Some subjects used hostile humor. "It's L. B. J., former inept president," wrote the rebellious coed. A 17-year-old boy described the Jabberwock as "a big ugly animal with mean huge eyes and a green face, with long hair, probably a female animal."

"It is asexual," maintained the stage "Alice" in part of a long description. "It is very large, fat, and clumsy.... Unlike Tenniel's drawing, it has no wings. It is very earth-bound. It has a large mouth and eats everything in sight.... It has great difficulty breathing." Her description reminds one of the omnivoristic, raging infant to which the subconscious id is often compared.

Some seemed to identify with the monster. A Fordham Prep student said, "A Jabberwock has maroon skin and has a large 'F' imprinted on its forehead." (Maroon is Fordham's school color.) "It's depressing," lamented a high school girl, "that the Jabberwock is so big and hulking, and then only burbles like a little kid. Everybody's so happy about the boy killing the Jabberwock, they don't think about the Jabberwock."

The boy who had found the poem "too violent" said, "He's mean-looking, big and thin, with lots of black hair, but if you didn't know he was so cruel, you might think his features were physically beautiful in a plastic, no-character way."

Subjects found the Jabberwock fascinating, but almost unbearable to encounter, like the expedition hunting the Snark, or like children approaching the parental bedroom. "I can mentally see it, but wouldn't dare try to describe or reproduce it," wrote a 16-year-old female fan of the "Alice" books. Asked to describe what a Jabberwock looks like, the stage manager responded, "I don't know. But I wouldn't if I could." One actor refused to answer any part of the questionnaire because his mental image of the Jabberwock was "too obscene" for depiction. "He looks like what you don't expect," said another actor, "and is always more fearful in the imagination than the reality."

When Carroll's Alice read the first stanza of the poem, she had said, "Somehow it seems to fill my head with ideas—only I don't exactly know what they are." A 16-year-old boy seemed to echo Alice's sentiments: "I have definite visual images, but I can't translate or articulate them." The theatrical director said the stanza suggested "uncontrollable impulses of a subterranean unconscious world."

Many subjects were able to recount vivid images that the nonsense stanza evoked. "I would set the scene in a meadow or glade. Very green and cool," wrote a 21-year-old student. "The atmosphere is very relaxed and restful. The animals seem to have no cares at all."

Some of the answers read like small poems in their own right. "The image of an ocean shore," wrote a 16-year-old boy, "with debris and seaweed being washed ashore with the rhythm of the waves. The sand and trees are being blown by a cold breeze." A high school girl wrote simply, "Moving waves, flashing lights, elusive shapes." A 46-

year-old woman with multiple sclerosis wrote: "Bright day. Sea/land creatures frolicking by the sea. Dark clouds cut up into little pieces as the sun rays cut up the darkness of the night." Again, a subject had produced the recurring theme of the primordial ocean, so akin to the subconscious.

The imagery was equally balanced between those who saw the scene as unequivocally peaceful and those who saw it as forbidding or mixed with unpleasantness. A 19-year-old girl who stammered wrote, "There is an image of this creature glowing in brilliance and slimy in appearance and of the life in the forest or swamp sensing something is approaching that may harm or kill them." A high school boy said, "It brings me inside the Jabberwock's lair, where all is slimy and dark and ancient."

A 14-year-old adopted boy whose foster parents were 79 and 69 years old said, "One setting would be a cemetery—gloomy, dark, some eerie things going on, fog lowering. 'Borogoves' could be graves."

Some juxtaposed the ugly and the beautiful, as did a 16-year-old girl: "A horrible mushy swamp full of toadlike animals making awful noises near flowers." A 17-year-old boy described: "Nature down by a river in a valley with mist and a biting air—the river is very choppy—there were dangerous caves and weird creatures lived in them. It was a bleak but interesting day."

The subconscious is filled with monsters and forbidding regions, but our conscious psyches find it fascinating despite, or because of, its half-known mysteries; hence, perhaps, the following scene, set by the stage manager: "Cold winter rain, marshland trees without leaves, broken branches, water animals (otters, muskrats, weasels) playing in a dank, foul, ugly place and loving it."

"Jabberwocky" contains 28 different nonsense words, comprising nearly half of the poem's nouns, adjectives and verbs. Ten of the nonsense words appear in the dictionary, two of them ("galumph" and "chortle") are attributed to Carroll,[24] but even the dictionary meanings are unfamiliar to the average reader and generally bear no relationship to the connotations Carroll ascribed to them.

Fifteen of the nonsense words were employed in the last part of the questionnaire, as the subjects were given a choice of three possible definition words from which to select that which best seemed to fit the nonsense word. In addition, the subjects were given the option of using a synonym of their own choosing. (Example—"SLITHY:

(   ) disgusting (   ) graceful (   ) oily (   )———.") Among the synonyms I suggested, I was careful to avoid words that might be unfamiliar to the average adolescent and words that were close in sound to the nonsense word. For example, "slithy" is defined by Carroll as a cross between "slimy" and "lithe," neither of which I used, substituting "oily" and "graceful" instead.

Thirty-six of the 50 subjects volunteered at least one original response to the 15 words, and 31 per cent of all responses to the nonsense words were original. Repetitions rarely occurred among original responses; slimy for slithy, galloping for galumphing, and fabulous for frabjous being the only ones to occur more than three times. (These particular synonyms had not been suggested because of their similarity in sound to the nonsense word.) Eighteen subjects offered 18 different meanings for "uffish," 20 subjects came up with 19 meanings (i.e., one repetition among the original responses) for "gyre," and 23 subjects offered 22 synonyms for "whiffling."

The possibilities for analyzing the responses to the nonsense words are endless. But, for example: five of the six psychiatric patients in the study defined "mimsy" as "unhappy," while only three of the remaining 44 subjects selected this definition. Four of the six patients saw the "whiffling" Jabberwock as "drifting," while 89 percent of the others used more aggressive adjectives. Half of the six patients interpreted "gyre" as "claw," while only one other subject selected this answer.

The males in the study seemed to identify more with the monster and to find the conflict more enervating—not surprising if the poem is viewed in oedipal terms. Nineteen per cent of the males dignified the "manxome foe" with the synonym noble, as opposed to six per cent of the females. Forty-one percent of the males viewed the "beamish boy" as brave, as opposed to only 17 per cent of the females. And 28 per cent of the females envisioned the "galumphing" hero as charging back, compared with 13 per cent of the males; while in almost identical but reversed proportions, 28 per cent of the males and 11 per cent of the females saw him "staggering" back, the men apparently having found the ordeal considerably more strenuous.

The meaningless words seemed to find meanings in the subjects' subconscious minds, and one lad defined "galumphing" and "burbled" simply as "galulmphing" and "burbled"; he could find no way to improve on their obvious clarity.

Perhaps among poetry therapists, galumphing hordes of uffish purists might burble their frumious indignation at the prospect of finding value in nonsense. I do not contend that the Jabberwock wrought any great psychic changes in the course of its march through my subjects' imaginations; but I was impressed by the enthusiasm with which most of them engaged the beast. Especially when dealing with adolescents who find poetry stern and obscure stuff, the therapist might find *Jabberwocky* an excellent ice-breaker. There are no right and wrong answers in nonsense interpretation—maybe no answers at all—but the patient can, like Humpty Dumpty, become a master of words for a while—"When *I* use a word, it means just what I choose it to mean—neither more nor less.... The question is which is to be master—that's all." And, in this mastery, the patient often becomes a poet.

The patient is invited into an acceptable, familiar, often therapeutic pathway of regression, where old conflicts may be re-encountered and mastered without the painful translation of thought language into word language. And if the tulgey wood of the unconscious becomes too threatening, one can retreat gracefully, for it was only nonsense, after all.

The most terrifying feature of the monsters of the mind, the fears and conflicts that nest in the unconscious, is that they have never been fully confronted. Hence, of Lewis Carroll's monsters, the Snark remains more terrible than the Jabberwock or the Bandersnatch or the Jubjub because no one has been able to look at it and survive.

The Unicorn (*Through the Looking Glass*) always thought children were fabulous monsters because he had never seen one. "Well, now that we *have* seen each other," he told Alice, "if you'll believe in me, I'll believe in you."

It's all nonsense, of course, but how pleasant to think of a world where children believe in unicorns. And unicorns believe in children.

MONSTERS AS HEALERS

No matter how grouchy you're feeling,
You'll find the smile more or less healing.
It grows in a wreath
All around the front teeth—
Thus preserving the face from congealing.[25]

The author of the above limerick probably never heard of poetry therapy, yet he offers an unequivocal testimonial to the healing powers of nonsense poetry, which may not always draw critical acclaim, but invariably invokes a smile. I have written in considerable detail about the Jabberwock and the poem that chronicles its demise; now, it remains to ask whether other nonsense poems, inferior in style and content, nevertheless possess some of the healing potential of *Jabberwocky*.

Ctesias, a Greek physician of the fifth century B.C., wrote that the horn of a unicorn, ground into a powder, was an infallible remedy against any kind of poison. Similar beliefs in the monster's healing powers persisted among physicians for fifteen hundred years.[26] Perhaps we may ask now whether there might be some intrinsic therapeutic quality in monsters, for nonsense poetry abound with ferocious beasts, from the classic limerick's famous tiger who devoured the smiling young lady of Niger[27] to the poetic monsters of Shel Silverstein, creator of the Sleepy-Eyed Skurk (who lets you sit in his mouth, but doesn't let you out), the Bald-Top Droan (who hides in ice cream cones) and the Squishy Squashy Staggitall (nine miles tall and standing behind you!)[28]

Beasts and monsters find a natural habitat in nonsense poetry, being as much at home there as in our nightmares. In the course of my experience with child patients, the following interchange has invariably occurred:

"Do you ever have bad dreams?"

"Sometimes."

"What are they about?"

"Monsters."

This revelation is made in an unemotional, matter-of-fact tone, for there is nothing extraordinary about encountering a monster where you would expect to find it, in the middle of a bad dream. Parents tend to be more concerned and less likely to leave monsters unmolested in their natural preserve, the nightmare, especially when these parents come to suspect that the creatures were spawned in the television movies and comic books that capture so much of their offsprings' attention. It should be noted that monsters antedate movies considerably; jackal- and hippo-headed deities abounded in the art and pictographs of ancient Egypt. In fact, the first monster may have been the caveman who donned the skin of the animal he had slain and danced about in it; perhaps he got the idea from a dream. Even the creator of the Jabberwock had some qualms about its possible adverse effects on the impressionable minds of children; Lewis Carroll conducted a private poll of about 30 mothers prior to the publication of the Jabberwock illustration, asking whether or not they felt the picture was "likely to alarm nervous and imaginative children."[29]

Frankenstein and Dracula are not the only film creations attacked by those who would defend our children. Walt Disney's *Snow White*, released in 1937, was deemed by many to be too frightening and too violent for children, and subsequent Disney films came under the same criticism because of the presence of witches (*Snow White*), whales (*Pinocchio*), storms (*Dumbo*), devils and demons (*Fantasia*) and fires (*Bambi*). When these monsters and calamities reappeared in children's nightmares, controversy flared. (In *Bambi*, incidentally, the creature that struck instant terror in the heart of every forest creature was called Man.) In the end, most psychological experts reached the conclusion that there was a great deal of pleasure for a child in experiencing the quick and simple resolution of a threatening element; that a child should be able to separate reality and fantasy at an early age, learning the difference between real danger and what is make-believe; that even children have to learn to deal with things that frighten them, and unless the "scare matter" touched on a child's particular phobia, no deep effect would occur, for the subject had no reference to the child's private tensions; and that monsters provide an early symbolic concept of the good-evil dichotomy and the necessity of overcoming evil.[30] The child who finds a particular movie monster too much to deal with will instinctively cover his eyes (or change the TV channel), just as the dreamer who cannot handle the dream tension will wake up.

Dr. Jean B. Rosenbaum is among the psychiatrists who find monsters a positive therapeutic factor: "Dream-provoking anxieties grow out of the intrinsic conflicts existing between small children and the adults around them. If anything, horror stories seem an effective way of confronting and mastering these very fears." (Dr. Rosenbaum, and all mankind, owe a special debt of gratitude to a monster, because Dr. Rosenbaum is credited with the invention of the artificial cardiac pacemaker, a device inspired by the doctor's memory of the movie "Frankenstein," in which electricity was used to stimulate the monster's body and give it life.[31])

The therapeutic value of monsters, like that of nonsense in general, is related to the regressive and aggressive elements they arouse in us. Regression is the psychological return of the ego to a more childlike state, a retreat to a period in our lives when we were more helpless, yet more secure, knowing our responsibilities were limited and our needs would be supplied by our parents. Monsters are plausible to a child's mind; to the adult's conscious mind, they become ludicrous, though the subconscious may still shudder at them. It is perhaps this duality of adult-child response that has given rise to that "camp" cult of adults who flock to see old horror movies and be overwhelmed by laughter and nostalgia.

Monsters are either enormous or hybrid, often both. Their enormity is quite plausible to a child, who must survive in a world of towering adults. Movie creatures such as King Kong and Godzilla are horrible by virtue of their size alone. Other monsters are no bigger than a tall adult, but are frightening because, like the griffin and the centaur, they possess elements of more than one creature in the same body. Dracula (man-bat), the Wolfman and the Creature from the Black Lagoon (man-amphibian) are such monsters, and Dr. Frankenstein's creature was patched together from the body parts of several different cadavers.

As for aggressive elements, they are never lacking in the monsters of the movies and nonsense poetry. While art and mythology may turn up an occasional benign unicorn or faun, the monsters that appeal to our imaginations are always hell-bent on mayhem. (Even Lewis Carroll's unicorn engaged in a noisy, though inept, battle with the lion for the crown.) Curiously, viewers or readers often feel a twinge of sympathy for the monster (as some of my subjects pitied the Jabberwock), because its aggressiveness proceeds from a blind instinct, not malice, and because it ultimately loses in the face of human (adult) logic and ingenuity. The monsters are kin to our ids, or subconscious drives, and whether our fascination for monsters stems from fantasies of the male-female sexual union or merely from the man-beast duality of our natures, there is an element of identification in our fascination.

Exploring the Unconscious through Nonsense Poetry

More Nonsense

Is all nonsense poetry aggressive? In most cases, yes. Some poems deal in a light manner with incredibly thorough annihilation, as does this old nursery poem:

> There once were two cats of Kilkenny.
> Each thought that was one cat too many;
> So they fought and they fit,
> And they scratched and they bit,
> Till—excepting their nails,
> And the tips of their tails—
> Instead of two cats, there weren't any.

Or:

> There was a young man of Herne Bay
> Who was making explosives one day:
> But he dropped his cigar
> In the gunpowder jar.
> There *was* a young man of Herne Bay.[32]

Mutilation is a frequent theme, as in two of Edward Lear's poems.[33] *The Pobble* tells how the Pobble lost his toes to unknown sea creatures, and *The Two Old Bachelors* describes the attempt of the heroes to chop a wise old sage into bits so they can make sage-and-onion dressing with which to stuff a mouse. The old bachelors fail and the mouse escapes, but it is, nevertheless, a gruesome device for a pun.

As for the Pobble, Lear concludes, "It's a fact the whole world knows/That Pobbles are happier without their toes," so again the aggression is blunted, after the fact.

Even the finality of death can be taken lightly:

> I had a dog, his name was Rover,
> When he rolled, he rolled in clover!
> When he died, he died all over.
> Good-by, Rover.[34]

In the nonsense poem, *A Chronicle*, not only death, but also a whole life is reduced to oblivion and absurdity. It reads in part:

> He lived—how many years
> I truly can't decide.
> But this one fact appears:
> He lived—until he died.

—and it concludes:

> I can't recall his name
> Or what he used to do.
> But then—well, such is fame,
> 'Twill so serve me and you![35]

Ironically, the author of this poem is unknown.

Often the aggression is expressed not in terms of annihilation, mutilation and death, but in terms of irreverance for the moral standards and values of polite, if hypocritical society, adding impetus to the constant struggle between personal wishes and environmental restrictions that begins with our introduction to the potty-seat.

The nonsense poems that so enhance Lewis Carroll's "Alice" books are irreverent and violent in their own right; however, their bite is sharpened by the realization that most of the poems are brutal burlesques of well-known (in Victorian England) poems and songs of a pious or sentimental nature.

Thus, compare this original poem...:

> "In the days of my youth," father William replied,
> "I remember'd that youth would fly fast,
> And abus'd not my health and my vigor at first,
> That I never might need them at last."[36]

...with Carroll's version:

> "In my youth," said his father, "I took to the law,
> And argued each case with my wife;
> And the muscular strength, which it gave to my jaw,
> Has lasted the rest of my life."

(Irreverence for age seems quite common in nonsense poetry, as witnessed by the innumerable "old men" that are the subjects of limericks.)

Carroll likewise took the following poem:

> Speak gently! It is better far
> To rule by love than fear;
> Speak gently; let no harsh words mar
> The good we might do here![37]

...and it became the Duchess' blood-curdling lullaby:

> Speak roughly to your little boy
> And beat him when he sneezes:
> He only does it to annoy,
> Because he knows it teases.

The Duchess does not actually beat the child, despite her violent threats. It is interesting to note that, in the course of Alice's journey through Wonderland, she is threatened many times: by the Queen and Duchess who demand her decapitation, by the giant puppy, by the plan to burn down the White Rabbit's house in which she is trapped, *ad infinitum*. Yet the only characters who actually suffer harm in the "Alice" books are those in the nonsense poems: the owl is eaten by the panther, the oysters by the Walrus and the Carpenter, and the little fishes by the little crocodile. There is Humpty Dumpty's fall, of course, but that was preordained by the nursery rhyme, another nonsense poem. Thus, actual harm is tolerated only within the protective shelter of nonsense poetry.

Educators, doctors, lawyers, rich men, famous men, artists, and members of virtually every respected profession have been subjected to the deflating barb of the limerick. Not even the clergy has been exempted:

> There once was a boring young Rev.
> Who preached till it seemed he would nev.
> His hearers, *en masse*,
> Got a pain in the ass
> And prayed for relief of their neth.[38]

The humor in this particular limerick arises from at least three sources, all to some degree aggressive. The first is the subject matter of a clergyman, a man usually entitled to respect, but deserving of less when he abuses his vocation. The second is the conjunction of a very base image (a painful posterior) with churches and preachers, and the congregation's use of prayer for its own ends. Laundered versions of this limerick are even funnier, since they avoid the vulgar rhyme that the fourth line practically demands, only to make the point anyway in the clever, euphemistic last line.

Finally, note the rhyming of "Rev.," "nev." and "neth." This device seduces the reader into taking outrageous liberties with the English language. If Rev. stands for Reverend, it follows that nev. would be "never end." That neth. should stand for nether end does not really follow at all, so if the naughty reader takes this liberty, he becomes partner to the poet's irreverence, which makes the poem that much more fun.

Much of nonsense poetry bases its humor on just such outrageous liberties with spellings, rhymes and abbreviations. As students, we were not only confronted with towns spelled "Leicester" and pronounced "Lester," but, on an even more elementary level, had to cope with such linguistic inanities as the words through, rough, cough, though, and bough, not one of which is pronounced like another despite an identical -ough ending. So, as children, we occasionally used nonsense talk to regain some mastery over these oppressive grammatical restrictions that sought to impede free expression of our thoughts. In the form of the limerick, we finally go the grammarians one better and beat them at their own game. Limericks have rhymed *Antigua* with *pigua* (pig you are), *Natchez* with *scratchez* and *Siouxs* with *shiouxs*. They have rhymed *pp.* with *ww.* (wages), *co.* with *do.* (dump any), *no.* with *cuco.* (cucumber), and *Ga.* with *Lucrezia Ba. Duquesne* has been rhymed with *champuesne*, *Dubuque* with *puque*, *Lincoln* with *stincoln* and *Worcester* with *sedorcester* (seduced her). And, if *M. A.* means *master of arts*, Cupid is a *C.D.* (caster of darts.)[39]

No discussion of the use of nonsense poetry to deal in an irreverent way with previously formidable and forbidden subjects would be complete without some mention of sex. As any regular reader of *Playboy* magazine knows, the limerick has been used to celebrate not only conventional sex, but also a wide variety of deviations, including nymphomania, homosexuality, exhibitionism, incest, and necrophilia. It will give my readers relief (or possibly dismay) when I state that the inclusion of specific examples is beyond the scope and propriety of this work. I will include one rather innocuous sex limerick for the sake of illustration, however:

> A young trapeze artist named Bract
> Is faced by a very sad fact.
> Imagine his pain
> When, again and again,
> He catches his wife in the act![40]

In this limerick, as in many, the humor may again be appreciated on several levels. There is the clever double entendre, redoubled, since it contains puns on both the word catch and the word act. There is the inherent pleasure in introducing the forbidden topic of sex and the painful topic of infidelity in a devious manner, plus the farcical irony of blending such serious subjects with frivolous, childish images of the circus. And, on a more subtle level, there is an easily overlooked aggressive element, for if the trapeze artist's dismay at catching his wife in the act refers to their circus routine, not their love life, it would imply strong homicidal feelings by Mr. Bract toward his wife. And, if we interpret the act in the amorous sense, we would again expect Mr. Bract to regret his sureness of hand on the trapeze where his unfaithful wife is involved. So, no matter which way we interpret the limerick, Mrs. Bract is in jeopardy.

And so, through wit, the nonsense poem, like the dream, serves a therapeutic function by allowing us to express aggressive and forbidden thoughts in a way acceptable to ourselves and others. "Our sincerest laughter with some pain is fraught," wrote Shelly.[41] We cannot banish the monsters of the mind that lurk in its subconscious depths, but laughter is the vorpal sword with which we can reduce them to impotence. Like the adults who haunt Saturday midnight movies to chuckle at Dracula and Frankenstein, we may find that some of these monsters are more enjoyable than terrifying.

The great secret, of course, in humor or in the dream, lies in finding the proper disguise for the forbidden material, a trick well learned by the hero of yet another limerick:

> There was a young man from Toledo
> Who traveled about incognito;
> The reason he did
> Was to bolster his id
> While appeasing his savage libido.[42]

REFERENCES

1. Lewis Carroll, *Through the Looking Glass and What Alice Found There* in Roger Lancelyn Green, ed., *The Works of Lewis Carroll* (London, Paul Hamlyn, 1965).
2. Sigmund Freud, *The Interpretation of Dreams* (New York, Avon, 1965) chap. 6.
3. *Ibid.*, p. 647.
4. Charles Crootof, "Poetry Therapy for Psychoneurotics in a Mental Health Center" in J. J. Leedy, ed., *Poetry Therapy* (Philadelphia, J. Lippincott, 1969) p. 46.
5. A. J. Ferreira, "The Semantics and the Context of the Schizophrenic's Language," *Arch. Gen. Psychia.*, III (1960) 128–138.
6. Freud, *op. cit.*, p. 332.
7. Martin Grotjahn, *Beyond Laughter* (New York, McGraw-Hill, 1966) p. 11.
8. Phyllis Greenacre, *Swift and Carroll* (New York, International Universities Press, 1955) p. 210.
9. *Ibid.*, p. 271.
10. Grotjahn, *op. cit.*, p. 236.
11. Harry Stack Sullivan, "The Language of Schizophrenia," in J. S. Kasanin, ed., *Language and Thought in Schizophrenia* (New York, W. W. Norton, 1964) p. 9.
12. Grotjahn, *op. cit.*, p. 237.
13. Warren J. Barker, "The Nonsense of Edward Lear," *Psychoanal. Quart.* XXXV (1966) 568–586.
14. Sigmund Freud, *A General Introduction to Psychoanalysis* (New York, Washington Square Press, 1966) p. 166.
15. William S. Baring-Gould, and Ceil Baring-Gould, *The Annotated Mother Goose* (New York, Bramhall House, 1962) pp. 31, 61, 253.
16. Martin Gardner, *The Annotated Alice* (New York, Clarkson N. Potter, 1960) p. 192.
17. Greenacre, *op. cit.*, p. 240.
18. Freud, *op. cit.*, p. 180.
19. Greenacre, *op. cit.*, p. 240.
20. Grotjahn, *op. cit.*, p. 106.
21. Greenacre, *op. cit.*, p. 214.
22. John Lahr, "Playing with Alice," *Evergreen Review 82*: LXXXII (1970) 59–64.
23. Greenacre, *op. cit.*, p. 234.
24. Gardner, *op. cit.*, pp. 194–197.
25. William S. Baring-Gould, *The Lure of the Limerick* (New York, Clarkson N. Potter, 1967) p. 84.
26. Richard Carrington, "The Natural History of the Unicorn" in John Hadfield, ed., *The Saturday Book*, vol. 20, (London, Hutchinson & Co., 1960) p. 274.
27. Baring-Gould, *op. cit.*, p. 106.
28. Shel Silverstein, "The Friendly Old Sleepy-Eyed Skurk, The Bald-Top Droan, and The Worst" in Jay Heavlin, ed., *The Nonsense Book of Nonsense* (New York, Random House, 1964) pp. 60–61.
29. Gardner, *op. cit.* p. 196.
30. Richard Schickel, *The Disney Version* (New York, Avon, 1969) pp. 185–187.
31. Jean B. Rosenbaum, "A Flash from the Flicks," *Med. Opin. & Rev.*, III (1967) 121.
32. Anon. in Heavlin, *op. cit.*, pp. 30, 52.

33. Edward Lear, "The Pobble, and The Two Old Bachelors," in Heavlin, *op. cit.*, pp. 20–21, 54–55.

34. Anon. "A Dog's Life," in Heavlin, *op. cit.*, p. 18.

35. Anon. "A Chronicle," in Heavlin, *op. cit.*, p. 66.

36. Robert Southey, "The Old Man's Comforts and How He Gained Them," in Gardner, *op. cit.*, p. 69.

37. David Bates, "Speak Gently," in Gardner, *op. cit.*, p. 85.

38. Baring-Gould, *op. cit.*, p. 210.

39. *Ibid.* p. 188.

40. *Ibid.* p. 126.

41. Percy Bysshe Shelley, "To a Skylark" *in* Kenneth N., Cameron, ed., *Percy Bysshe Shelley, Selected Poetry and Prose* (New York, Holt, Rinehart & Winston, 1963) p. 255.

42. Baring-Gould, *op. cit.*, p. 7.

Principles of Poetry Therapy

JACK J. LEEDY, M.D.

As poetry therapy continues to be explored and its values demonstrated, one hopes that this newest (and oldest?) of the ancillary therapies in psychiatry and psychotherapy will become an established part of the total treatment of the emotionally ill. For poetry therapy can play its adjunctive role in mental hygiene clinics, or in hospitals, or in private practice, with one patient or groups of patients. The principles that follow are based on my experience over the past ten years as psychiatric consultant to the poetry therapy groups of the Mental Hygiene Clinic of Cumberland Hospital and Project Teen Aid, OEO, in Brooklyn, conferences with other psychotherapists who utilize poetry in treating their patients, and many hours with my friend and associate, the late Eli Greifer.

1. The Isoprinciple

The isoprinciple, effective in music therapy, has proved important in the choice of poems for use in poetry therapy. As music that has the same feeling as the mood or mental tempo of the patient has proved a valuable tool, so poems that are close in feeling to the mood of the patient have been found helpful. Depressed patients, for example, are helped by poems sad and gloomy in tone yet having lines or stanzas that reflect hope and optimism, especially toward their conclusion. By reading, studying, memorizing, reciting or creating this kind of poem, depressed patients come to feel that they are not alone in their depressions, that others are also depressed, that others have been depressed and recovered from their depressions, and that no disgrace attaches to victims of extreme alterations of mood. For them, crying precipitated by a poem is often therapeutically helpful: the poem becomes symbolically an understanding someone with whom they can share their despair.

Because of the dangers of suicide and suicidal trends, gestures and ideas in the depressed, the therapist should not choose poems that *a.* offer no hope or that might increase the depth of the depression by implying that life has no meaning; *b.* increase guilt feelings; *c.* imply that God, father figures or mother figures forsake people, seek vengeance, and cannot be relied on in times of crisis; *d.* encourage, glorify, or even mention suicide; *e.* are confused, defeatist, homicidal, vulgar or debasing—Dryden[1] long ago remarked this sort of poetry:

> O gracious God! How far have we
> Profan'd thy Heav'nly Gift of Poesy?
> Made prostitute and profligate the Muse,
> Debas'd to each obscene and impious use,
> Whose Harmony was first ordain'd *Above*
> For Tongues of *Angels*, and for *Hymns* of *Love*?

—*f.* encourage silence and discourage vocalization, particularly of feelings of hostility; and *g.* are persistently pessimistic with self-destructive love and a fearful hatred of life, like, for example, some of the poems of Robinson Jeffers.

For depressed patients, poems like the following are suggested: Thomas Carlyle, "Today"; William Cowper, "Light Shining Out of Darkness"; Holmes, "The Chambered Nautilus"; Walter Savage Landor, "You Spoke, You Spoke, and I Believed"; Longfellow, "The Day is Done," "The Rainy Day"; Milton "On His Blindness"; Shelley, "Ode to the West Wind"; Robert Louis Stevenson, "The Celestial Surgeon"; Francis Thompson, "In No Strange Land"; Psalm 23: "The Lord is my Shepherd" (*Dominus regit me*); Whittier, "My Soul and I," "The Light that is Felt," and "The Eternal Goodness."

2. The Poetry Therapist

In the future—the near future, one hopes—poetry therapists will be registered in accordance with standards to be established by a yet unorganized National Association for Poetry Therapy, not unlike the registered occupational therapists or the music therapists. Professors K. F. Edgar and Richard Hazley, of the Indiana University of Pennsylvania, have proposed a curriculum for the training of poetry therapists, and trained therapists should increase in numbers and competence. Presently, psychotherapists, poets, teachers and social workers are assuming the roles of poetry therapists. Those occupational therapists who are interested and informed in poetry would greatly help as poetry therapists, also, because of the acute shortage of them.

Poetry therapists act as cotherapists in a poetry therapy group. They work with the psychotherapist in selecting the poems for the patients, in teaching them to read aloud and to cultivate their ability to listen to poetry, and in discussing in the group both the lives of the poets, where helpful, and the poetry itself. Reading poetry aloud enables the patients to respond more directly to its rhythms and patterns, and listening to it has a healing effect upon them.

3. Therapeutic Implications

Poetry therapy has guided patients to constructive adjustment after every approach known has been tried and failed. It helps some patients make their emotional disorders easier to bear, assists the process towards their recovery, and helps them to develop a philosophy of life that abets their adjustment to their misfortunes. Memorizing poems, enhanced by giving awards or prizes to those who memorize poems or even stanzas, has great value for the patients and should be encouraged. After memorizing a poem, the patients gain a feeling of mastery and think better of themselves.

Poetry encourages patients to explore their feelings, to feel more deeply, to extend their emotional range yet to discover patterns, also, of control and fulfillment. As Frost has written:

> Theme alone can steady us down. Just as the first mystery was how a poem could have a tune in such a straightness as meter, so the second mystery is how a poem can have wildness and at the same time a subject that shall be fulfilled.
>
> It should be the pleasure of a poem itself to tell how it can. The figure a poem makes. It begins in delight and ends in wisdom. The figure is the same as for love. No one can really hold that the ecstasy should be static and stand still in one place. It begins in delight, it inclines to the impulse, it assumes direction with the first line laid down, it runs a course of lucky events, and ends in a clarification of life—not necessarily a great clarification, such as sects and cults are founded on, but in a momentary stay against confusion.[2]

Poetry therapy helps patients to become more spontaneous and creative. Poetry is one of man's deepest expressions, and emotions are thereby released. A poem has been described as the shortest emotional distance between two points, the points representing the writer and the reader. This may explain why communication through poetry is established so readily, and why patients themselves are moved so frequently to attempt their own composition of poems. Psychotherapists are becoming increasingly aware that poetry can help their patients. For over forty years, Dr. Smiley Blanton used poetry in his practice as a psychiatrist. He writes, in *The Healing Power of Poetry*, that poetry can be of help with patients who need courage or feel overwhelmed; who suffer from insomnia; who are in love and must at times leave someone they love; who are angry or frustrated; who are depressed, anxious, or bereaved; and who are growing old.[3]

Certain poems, such as Coleridge's "Kubla Khan" and "The Ancient Mariner," Keats' "La Belle Dame Sans Merci," Longfellow's "Evageline," Poe's "Annabel Lee" and Byron's "Indian Serenade" have spellweaving, hypnoidal, or hypnotic effects on some patients. The decision to use these poems in a poetry therapy group should be made by the psychotherapist.

4. The Poetry Therapy Group

Members of the poetry therapy group are usually enthusiastic about group reading. It is pleasurable for them to read together. Group reciting of poems helps to increase ego strength, decreases the duration and intensity of anxieties, and decreases also tendencies toward introversion and paralyzing inhibitions. The diction of the members is often improved. In the poetry therapy group, all references to unconscious material, dreams, fantasies, and motivations as related to the poetry or to the associations stimulated by the poetry, are to be discussed at the discretion of the psychotherapist.

Poetry therapy groups may be structured with patients having the same diagnoses, like that for schizophrenics at Dixmont State Hospital, Pittsburgh; and that for mental defectives at the Staten Island Aid for Retarded Children, Inc. Or poetry therapy groups may include patients of different diagnoses.

Patients are encouraged to write their own poems. It has been noted that during periods of crisis, or when patterns of behavior or feelings are changing or have been recently changed, or when new insights are discovered, the patients often write poems, often in great quantity, and sometimes of considerable quality. The two poems that follow were written by patients in the poetry therapy group at Slippery Rock State College in Pennsylvania.

SNOWDRIFT
To walk the virgin snow alone.
To look back at your own footsteps
In the hissing stream of a ventilator
Swirling with fury into nothingness.
I feel guilty,
Destroying the perfect layer of white.
A thoughtless tramp destroyed beauty.
The ugliness of single tracks
not mated with another.
And no one to notice them.

NEW LOVE
She has new leaves
After her dead flowers,
Like the little almond tree
Which the frost hurt.

5. Therapeutic Poets and Poetry

With some patients, poems that are more regular in their thythmic scheme have proved more helpful than poems with less conventional patterns. Poems with regular rhythms, those that most nearly approximate the beat of the human heart, affect many patients deeply. This is to say that some masterpieces of poetry may not be therapeutic, whereas mediocre poems, never included in anthologies, may be extremely helpful or right for a patient, and may be his bridge to reality.

Before listing poets and their poems useful in poetry therapy, one needs to say a word about standards. A psychotherapist will choose verse that is useful to psychotherapy, however fine or poor it may appear to critics old or new. Some of it may be of the most inferior, some of the most superior order of poetry: for poetry therapy, the standard is not whether it is good or great poetry, but whether it will help heal the ill. For this purpose, Longfellow may be better than Shakespeare, Herrick than Milton, Greifer than Donne, or Holmes than Sophocles. And a happy meeting of "the time, the place and the loved one all together" may work a miracle.

THE DAY IS DONE[4]

Come, read to me some poem,
   Some simple and heartfelt lay,
That shall soothe this restless
     feeling,
   And banish the thoughts of day.

Not from the grand old masters,
   Not from the bards sublime,
Whose distant footsteps echo
   Through the corridors of Time.

Read from some humbler poet,
   Whose songs gushed from his
     heart,
As showers from the clouds of
     summer,
   Or tears from the eyelids start;

Such songs have power to quiet
   The restless pulse of care,
And come like the benediction
   That follows after prayer.

   Then read from the treasured volume
     The poem of thy choice,
   And lend to the rhyme of the poet
     The beauty of thy voice.

The poems given in the chapters of this book as used successfully may suggest a wider range of poetic than of therapeutic values, wide enough, in any case. So be it. As poetry therapy develops, as it is developing rapidly, and its practitioners learn more of our great English poetry, one can find no reason why the greatest poets may not prove of the greatest worth in psychotherapy, as they are in literature.

In addition to the poems earlier suggested for the depressed, the following poems have been useful in poetry therapy groups: Shakespeare's sonnets, especially 29 and 30, and "The Uses of Adversity" from *As You Like It*; Alfred Tennyson's "Sweet and Low"; Emily Bronte's "Last Lines"; Walt Whitman's "Song of Myself"; Arthur Hugh Clough's "Say Not the Struggle Naught Availeth"; Robert Frost's "Stopping by Woods on a Snowy Evening"; John Masefields's "Tomorrow"; Gerard Manley Hopkins' "God's Grandeur"; and William Ernest Henley's "Invictus."

Patients, particularly those who are in mental institutions, are encouraged when they learn that great poems have been written by poets who themselves were patients in mental hospitals. John Clare wrote "I Am" while in the Northampton County Asylum. Christopher Smart, who was also confined to an asylum, scratched "A Song to David"[5] with a key upon the wall of his room because he was not permitted the use of pen and paper. These verses are from his long, magnificent poem:

> O thou, that sit'st upon a throne,
> With harp of high majestic tone,
>   To praise the King of kings;
> And voice of heav'n-ascending swell,
> Which, while its deeper notes excel,
>   Clear, as a clarion, rings:
>
> To bless each valley, grove and coast,
> And charm the cherubs to the post
>   Of gratitude in throngs;
> To keep the days on Zion's mount,
> And send the year to his account,
>   With dances and with songs:
>
> O Servant of God's holiest charge,
> The minister of praise at large,
>   Which thou may'st now receive;
> From thy blest mansion hail and hear,
> From topmost eminence appear
>   To this the wreath I weave.

REFERENCES

1. Dryden, John, "To the Pious Memory of the Accomplisht Young Lady Mrs. Ann Killigrew. Excellent in the Two Sister-Arts of Poesie, and Painting. An Ode," in Crane, Ronald S., ed.: *A Collection of English Poems 1660–1800* (New York, Harper, 1932).

2. Frost, Robert, "The Figure a Poem Makes," in *Complete Poems of Robert Frost* (New York, Holt, 1939).

3. Blanton, Smiley, *The Healing Power of Poetry* (New York, Crowell, 1960).

4. Longfellow, Henry Wadsworth, *The Complete Poetical Works of Longfellow* (Boston, Houghton, 1922).

5. Smart, Christopher, "A Song to David," in Crane, R.S., ed.: *A Collection of English Poems 1660–1800* (New York, Harper, 1932).

Poetry as Communication in Psychotherapy

HAROLD GREENWALD, PH.D.

For many years, my patients have been writing poems—concerning their sessions and their feelings about themselves and others—and bringing them to me. At first, I did not realize what significant communications they were. I believe that most patients can tell their therapist how to treat them if he will listen carefully. But only recently did I see the value of their poems and begin to use them therapeutically. I have encouraged them to use poetry as communication, and have asked some of them to write a poem between every session.

Poetry is of value in group therapy, for some patients, although they find the group emotionally involving, find expressing themselves in it difficult. It is of value because many of its functions are the functions of therapy. Both "increase our awareness of one's own inner reactions,"[2] make a portion of the unconscious conscious, lead to "an expanded understanding of the nature of other people's behavior and of the messages they send, and also greater awareness of one's own behavior and of the impact this has on other people."[2] As T. S. Eliot has written[1]:

> Beyond any specific intention which poetry may have, there is always the communication of some new experience, or some fresh understanding of the familiar, or the expression of something we have experienced but have no words for, which enlarges our consciousness or refines our sensibility.

A patient has achieved emotional insight when his behavior changes.[3] Actually to do something oneself makes it possible to experience it more fully and therefore more nearly to integrate it into one's behavior. Poetry brings emotional insight more readily because it requires the patient's doing rather than reading or being told. More striking than any report of mine of the value of poetry for therapy are examples of poems written by three of my patients.

Sybil

Sybil came for therapy because she was unhappy about her marriage and unable to work constructively. Very able, she yet limited herself to part-time clerical jobs because she would not discipline herself to work steadily towards a career. She had a long history of homosexuality. After earlier therapy, she had made a heterosexual adaptation and married a passive and ineffectual young man, who did not consider supporting her and their child one of his duties. At about the time she wrote this poem, she was considering leaving her husband, and she was attracted by a young woman whom she had met.

WE WHO ARE AFRAID OF NIGHT

Like the child waiting in the night
For warm hands and arms to wrap
Themselves around his loneliness—
To spend himself in tears of sudden safety
And of love,
We too, in the dark aloneness of a self unloved,
Unanchored, abandoned and denied,
Still summon with silent child cries
The ancient hope—
The old sure magic of sweet wantedness.

The child still lives in us
With that eager hurt of innocence bewildered—and betrayed
Ah, painful paradox.
To sense the rescue
And know there is none.
But driven by old dreams, pale and powerful
Remembrances of the soft dear touch of love
We wait.

One waits. One always waits.
It is forgotten that nameless need
The years have beaten from our tired hearts.
But like some unshaped, primeval force, it beckons
Crowds out reality, blunts stiff reason
And we are grotesque with helpless wanting
Turning our minds inwards—backwards

> Dull too, is pain with young memories,
> That weaken and defy
> Submit and die.
> We do not live who wait in such unhope.

Here she expressed her reaction to her husband's imminent departure, the betrayal she experienced in his interest in another woman, and the regression to a longing for a mother's warmth. "Like the child waiting in the night/ For warm hands and arms to wrap/ Themselves around his loneliness." It is no accident that she became interested in a woman, as she had always regarded homosexual sex as a mother-daughter relationship, although she played mother oftener than daughter. This is no unusual paradox: the neurotic often takes the part that she would like someone to assume to her. Although she was desperately searching for a mother to relieve her pain, loneliness, desertion and sorrow, she yet gave someone what she herself could not find. Prose limps after the poignancy of Sybil's poetry.

Eventually, she broke up with this woman with whom she lived after divorcing her husband, and became involved with another woman. I pointed out that because the second woman was a companion much better suited to her, the danger and pain might be worse than before. She denied it, and wrote the poem that follows.

> To mine own executioner
> Be true.
> Lie still in trembled ecstasy,
> (Oh, ardent pain,
> Fear-pleasured, wish-wondered over
> In passion's sweet disguise)
> Throat-naked to the knife's caress.
>
> Beguiling destroyer,
> Unwitting abettor
> In this long preserved conspiracy,
> Take me with your kiss.
>
> Warm my chilled and frightened heart
> With woolen words of love.
> Comfort me with appetites,
> Taste of this tenderized spirit-flesh
> (Spiced with artful self-deceit)
> Explode my reason

> With deft confusion
> Rip away the muscled logic
> Slow crush the contentious bones of survival.
> Madness is numbing
> If it is total
> and death by loving
> Is a skillful way to die.
> (A most desirable consequence
> for natural prey)
>
> Your lips, your words, your needs
> Of the moment
> Are welded into a terrible truth.
> But they are only the instruments.
> I die by my own hand.

How clearly she sees the pain that awaits her—her need for the woman, the excitement she brought, the destruction. Many authors have pointed out the essential masochism of the homosexual relationship. "And death by loving/ Is a skillful way to die." These two poems may tell us more about the mechanics and dynamics of female homosexuality than many learned papers. The wish to return to the arms of a comforting mother, the search for pain and the suspension of reason, these are in them.

Lewis

Lewis is a brilliant scientist, who came for therapy because he felt unable to proceed in his professional life. He suffered from depression, despite his ability to mask it usually with a glittering sense of humor. The first poem here gives his presenting symptoms better than an entire battery of projective tests could.

> **GRAVE BIRD/INERTIA'S LAMENT**
>
> Of wounded times the grave bird wails
> Reveling in secret pockets of pride
> That he does nothing.
>
> Over the lost horizon, Shangri-la
> Beckons with shiny burdens of delight
> But he does nothing.

In the vacant morning of his brain
Enters the perverse imp of his despair
And he does nothing.

Downbeating shafts of pain disturb
The dusty surface of his softened nerve
Yet he does nothing.

Whittling the bark of hours
From the tragic tree of time
He does nothing. He weeps
As he does nothing. He dreams
As he does nothing. He mourns
As he does nothing.
Nothing.

As Lewis' first poem gives his presenting problem, so his second presents his life history.

EVOCATION

How came such poisoned pap from so excellent an udder?
The infinite promise and sweet grace of all the
    many rounded shapes of childhood,
Charming, long-ago time when, without conscience or wit,
But with much pleasure,
I followed the song of myself.

And later, in the way it went—
The great Boy time:
Oatmeal and airplanes and skin-the-cat
And mumblety-peg and territory
And double-dutch when the fat-legged girls were by.

And rainy days. Inside at last
With chins on window seats, atop no warming hearth
But great steamy iron beasts fastened to the floor
That sputtered and spat and covered the
    icy windows with vapor
That saw fine use to write my own name in.

I write my name today with no such pride,
    nor recognize the boy who did it once.

Memory is a conjurer,
Preparing tricks alien to nature and
    confounding simple truth;
The boy is not the man, nor ever was, but only this:
That once there was a boy.

Whence his sweet nature came, like new corn on
    a slender stalk,
Mulling the wine of life with gentle spice,
    tasted out the earth—
That herb is lost.
Tall, rapid man, raised from a broken spell, am I;
The boy is gone.

It shows forth one of the problems that many suffer from who use an intellectual defense. "Tall, rapid man, raised from a broken spell, am I;/ The boy is gone." Among many others, Eric Berne[4] has pointed out that the child should be retained within the adult; it is the child remaining within us who makes possible the joy and creativity of living. The adult within us is too busy coping with the world's reality; to make creativity possible, we need the imaginative qualities of the child. By eliminating the child from his life, Lewis eliminated the pleasure from his work, and it is no wonder that having done so, he was depressed.

And the third poem of Lewis' given here depicts his transference, on many levels.

MY ANALYST

Short sleek and witty sits this gravid owl
And with Boswellian calm
Surveys the shavings in an empty glass.

The pieces wend, blend, mend—
the shards are curried, combed and glued
and burnished to a lustrous milk.

The eunuch turns in grim, beseeching grief
To Jupiter and Moses, his right hand
to set the bone that hid the stars away.

And tells the story of his life, the bitter truth
In words of cool deception, Mother-fed;
To synthesize the Ego from the Dead.

> As love whose purple tongue denies the flame
> Of passion and defiles its name
> Gives up its ghost, recruited to the game
> And anger stalks the country hungrily.
>
> Into this night the great scythe cuts its swath
> In furrows deep with light. In its cold train
> A cicatrix of crystal hue
> Burns like a fire in a dismal rain.
>
> And lo! The satyrs weight of wine and nymphs
> Bursts like a sack of hair and rusted nails
> Gorged with Himself—Narcissus pallid sun—
> Spills in the ditch as from a running sore.
>
> Something to fill the blasted, feral void—
> Something of value, redolent of life;
> A day of striving, loving without pain,
> Rutting with Pan's delight, scorning the Devil's wife.
>
> Puckish he sits and pulls the tightening string
> Hovering the puppet higher from his ground
> Testing his wings in new, sweet-scented air
> Dry-eyed he laughs—and cries—and turns his chair.

One of this patient's problems was his dependency needs; in the second stanza, he writes of material "burnished to a lustrous milk." The feeling of impotence, of inability to do anything, causes him to transform himself into a "eunuch." In the transference, one must expect a reliving of some major problems of the individual. This makes it possible for the analyst to work through or deal with the problems, because the patient presents them in relationships with the analyst as he has with people significant in his past. Notice that the "eunuch turns in grim, beseeching grief/ To Jupiter and Moses" and, in the next stanza, "And tells the story of his life, the bitter truth/ In words of cool deception, Mother-fed." The relationship between the search to have his dependency needs met by the analyst and the fostering of dependency by the mother is made poetically if not explicitly. As in all dependent people, behind the dependency is great anger, and so—"And anger stalks the country hungrily."

Lewis was essentially passive-aggressive, and such a man has as his outstanding characteristic the wish to be dependent but the refusal to be controlled. This dependency he expressed in the earlier references to milk and the grim beseeching grief. The refusal to be controlled and the anger at experiencing control by the analyst he expressed by allusion, "Puckish he sits and pulls the tightening string/ Hovering the puppet higher from his ground."

Glenda

The poetry of Glenda has always been an integral part of her therapy. When Glenda first entered the group—I have seen her only there—she said little for months, although clearly she was following everything with greatest interest. An early poem was:

> We sat in a room
> Selma, Jean, Jessie, Jack
> Some others
> And me
>
> We played the game
> I feel, I feel, I feel
> I feel anxious—
> You do?
> I do, too.
>
> And how can I tell you
> What it was like,
> I don't know.
>
> But I'll go and I'll go
> And I'll go and I'll go,
> And so, so, so, so
> What.

These verses depict much of Glenda, how she experienced the group: hopelessness, meaningless, futility—but not quite. For she permitted me to read this poem to the group, and the next one. It expresses her hostility, again, and something of the grandiose wishes that most of us experience in a group situation, when we hope that others will recognize our brilliance and intelligence.

> If the world were my oyster,
> And my cup of tea,
> I'd make those shitheads
> Bow down to me.

During the following group sessions, she began to speak more freely.

One of the members of the group did all the things suggested in Glenda's poem "Joan." Though Glenda was annoyed, she said not a word; she did write this verse, useful to her in understanding her own behavior.

> JOAN
>
> I bounce in late
> For my Tuesday date
> My hair is long
> My skirt's up high
> So you can
> *See me, see me*
> Make me
> Be.

Glenda was separated from her husband, had a small child, and suffered loneliness. So strong was her determination not to spill over orally that she held all her complaints in, but had her say in this poem:

> My universe is small, you see
> There's only me—and me and me.
>
> No one to touch,
> No one to hold,
> No one to keep me from the cold.
>
> Oh, yes, there is a gentleman
> Who comes and quickly goes again.
>
> And though I say that's not enough.
> Maybe there's nothing more.

In this as in previous poems, her feeling of hoplessness is clearly expressed. But in contrast to the others, her next poem reveals a new insight concerning the neurotic's desperate search for happiness.

> No man is an island,
> Is he a sea?
> No, he's a personality.
>
> A coddled self
> Who wants to pick
> The pimples of his inmost quick
> Traveling endless psychic paths
> To find—true happiness at last.
>
> *Happiness:*
> Our endless quest
> Our heart's desire.
> Our egos, ids, and selves conspire,
> To flush him out
> To catch him quick
> To make Hap-Happy stick and stick.
>
> But his elusiveness outruns
> Our analysts on fatted bums.
> It makes them rich,
> While we go round
> Seeking what cannot be found.

Glenda here succeeded in verbalizing an important but rarely stated truth about neurosis and therapy: that of a promise, too often implied by therapists, that happiness is what they have to offer. Freud's answer to a neurotic patient's question whether he could promise that therapy would result in happiness was negative. He held forth the promise not of happiness, but of a sharing in the general unhappiness of humanity rather than in the special unhappiness of the neurotic. Seeking to recapture the Lost Eden days of infancy, the neurotic is searching for a kind of happiness that does not exist for the adult. Glenda's phrase, "seeking what cannot be found," is a clear statement that neurotic methods lead not to happiness but to an increase in pain and suffering.

As most patients do, Glenda also refers to the problem of transference—this in her gallows humor:

> Harold—
> Your heart is as big
> As the borough of Brooklyn,

> Yet I find that your tactic,
> Flamboyant didactic,
> Is not too attractive
> To me, poor me.

That I did, in fact, live in Brooklyn is readily discernible in my speech, hence the charming second and third lines. The rest of the poem is a criticism of my lack of sensitivity and a clear statement that I should change my tactics.

In one session, a younger woman had occupied much of the group's attention, describing what she labeled her severe depression. Glenda said nothing during the session, but went home and wrote the following:

> I wanted to ask Nancy
> Where's your hidden greatness,
> Your secret fancy?
>
> What are you underneath and inside,
> What is it you have to hide?
>
> I know my answer
> My hidden vice:
> Never to want, need, give,
> Or seek advice.
>
> Arrogance is the name,
> Denial—they tell me—is the game.
> No one will ever tell me what to do
> Not even you, bubby, not even you.
>
>   Underneath
>   Is not grief.

The next of Glenda's poems was written following my suggestion that she use poetry for her therapy. In it, she describes the reason she refrains from speaking in group.

> I never say
> What I want to say.
> It never sounds
> How I want it to.
> Talking to you,

> Talking to Stan,
> Talking to any other man,
> Or woman, too.
>
> I want to say
> What can I do?
> But I'm afraid
> You'll tell me.

She is indicating to the therapist that he should make no great effort to change her. If she were to ask: "What can I do, what can I do?" and the therapist were to tell her, the therapeutic relationship would be destroyed and her dependency become more pronounced. As she points out, letting her be is the better alternative.

Glenda's poem about Nancy indicates considerable identification with her and is expressive of many of her own feelings. Again referring to the therapist, she writes: "No one will ever tell me what to do/ Not even you, bubby, not even you." Although still concealed, the rage that has kept Glenda immobilized is clearly hinted at in, "Underneath/ Is not grief." The task is made much clearer for the therapist in these two poems. She seems to indicate that to try to help her would bottle up her rage and not permit its expression. Only grief, sorrow, and appeals for help would appear, when what has to be released is her aggression. It would seem then that Glenda sees in Nancy a kindred soul; that both of them are sitting as if paralyzed while hiding their grandiose fantasies, their omnipotence, from the world. They are in a fury because they have been deprived, and still the world does not bow down to them; therefore their determination to "turn off and drop out."

These examples from the poetry of patients may indicate how valuable poetry can be as a communicative device in the context of therapy. I think that readers will be able to understand a good deal more through reading the poetry cited here than I have had the temerity to venture.

The most important function of poetry as therapy consists in the opportunity given the patient to express his emotion in a socially acceptable form—that of a poem, which is not a direct unconscious expression as the dream is. Something more than a spurting forth of raw feeling is created through its transmutation into poetry. T. S. Eliot has said:

In expressing what other people feel, he (the poet) is also changing the feeling by making it more conscious; he is making people more aware of what they feel already, and therefore teaching them something about themselves. But he is not merely a more conscious person than the others; he is also individually different from other people, and from other poets too, and can make his readers share consciously in new feelings which they had not experienced before. That is the difference between the writer who is merely eccentric or mad and the genuine poet. The former may have feelings which are unique, which cannot be shared and are therefore useless; the latter discovers new variations of sensibility which can be appropriated by others.

Eliot's statement is particularly appropriate to group therapy, in which patients read their poetry to other group members. It contains an implication regarding the diagnostic value of poetry, i.e., unlike the writer who is eccentric or mad, the genuine poet can share his sensitivities with others. A wonderful goal for all of us: to share our sensitivities with others, so that they may make use of them.

REFERENCES

1. Eliot, T. S., *On Poetry and Poets* (New York, Farrar, Straus and Cudahy, 1957) pp. 7–9.
2. Hogan, P., and Alger, I. "The Impact of Videotape Recording on Insight in Group Psychotherapy," presented at the 24th Annual Conf Amer Group Psychotherapy Assn, New York, January 28, 1967.
3. Robbins, B.S., "Insight, activity and change," J Robbins Institute *1* (#4) 1956.
4. Berne, E., *Transactional Analysis in Psychotherapy* (New York, Grove, 1961).

Validation of Poetry Therapy as a Group Therapy Technique

KENNETH F. EDGAR, Ph.D.
and RICHARD HAZLEY, M.A.

When power narrows the areas of man's concern, poetry reminds him of the richness and diversity of his existence. When power corrupts, poetry cleanses. For art establishes the basic human truth which must serve as the touchstone of our judgment.
—JOHN R. KENNEDY

Although most colleges and universities offer some form of individual counseling to students with personal problems, few appear to offer group therapy within the campus clinic. Nor is it difficult to understand why. Students are reluctant to be "open" in the presence of peers who might recoil from revealed dependency, impoverished personality, sexual inversion and the like. Yet this openness may be the crucial variable, as Mowrer states[18]:

> Would it be too arbitrary an assumption to propose that people become clients because they do not disclose themselves in some optimal degree to the people in their life? I have come to believe that it is not communication per se which is fouled up in the mentally ill. Rather it is a foul-up in the process of knowing others, and in becoming known to others.

Considering group therapy at Slippery Rock State College, we became interested in poetry therapy, a technique in group psychotherapy being pioneered at Cumberland Hospital in Brooklyn by Jack Leedy, MD, psychiatrist, and Eli Greifer, poet therapist. It seemed possible that group discussion through poetry might provide a means by which members could know and become known by others. It was felt that by using a poem as a starting point and as an objectification of known but inarticulate feelings, the members of a group might be provided with the means to open themselves through the interpretation of poetry, however obliquely at first, that conventional group therapy did not offer.

The choice of poetic material, according to Leedy,[13] should be guided by the isoprinciple developed in music therapy: the material should express the same mood or emotional state that the patient is experiencing. Leedy suggests that depressed patients are helped by poems that are sad and gloomy; through them, they recognize that they are not alone in their depression. Eli Greifer[4] stresses memorization as cogent in the therapeutic process: "We have here no less than a psychograft-by-memorization in the inmost reaches of the brain, where the soul can allow the soul-stuff of stalwart poet-prophets to 'take' and to become one with the spirit of the patient." Greifer's thesis[5] on poetry therapy finds support from Reik,[20] who writes of the therapeutic potential of poetry.

The greatest actors do not enter into the personality of a tragic hero, but they become Hamlet, so to speak. They do not imitate his experience, they actually experience his destiny, with the help of the same psychical possibilities within themselves, and of memory-traces within their own experience. Poetry has touched upon a fragment of buried life, has stirred the actor's own hidden possibilities.

Observing the enthusiasm of patients at Cumberland Hospital's Mental Hygiene Clinic, the authors attempted an experiment to evaluate the effectiveness of poetry therapy as a group technique in the college counseling clinic.

Procedure

Sixteen students who had applied for individual counseling at the college clinic and had taken a battery of projective tests were asked whether they would be willing to participate in an experiment involving poetry as a tool in group psychotherapy. It was explained to the students that they had been invited to participate because they shared some common problems with each other. No further details were offered. All of the students, eight males and eight females, accepted. On the basis of a psychiatric interview and the evidence from the projective battery, it was believed that the common problem experienced by the group was inadequate psychosexual identification and failure to become weaned from the "family of orientation." All 16 were either juniors or seniors at the college; the IQ range was 108–135, the mean 120. By sex, the mean IQ was 127 for the girls and 113 for the boys. The group was then divided by sex and each of the members was asked to draw numbers, either one or two, from a hat. The eight boys and girls who had drawn the number one were assigned to the control group, and control group members were informed that, should they wish, they could be admitted into treatment or seek treatment outside the college at any time, and at the beginning of the second semester they could be admitted into the experimental group.

PRETEST

The pretest battery, administered in September, 1964, consisted of:

a. An MMPI profile[3,8]   c. Cards 6BM and 7BM of the TAT
b. The Draw-A-Person test[7,15]   d. Card #1 of the Rorschach

The MMPI, the DAP, and the TAT were evaluated as measures of dependency. Card #1 of the Rorschach was interpreted, as Ledwith's text[12] suggests, as "being indicative of either the parental figure with whom the child experiences the greatest conflict, the relationship of the child to his parents, and/or a condensed self-image."

METHOD

The experimental group met every Thursday, from 4:00 to about 6:00 PM, in a comfortable room designated for group therapy. Sessions were always informal. The participants sat around a large table; coffee was served and, on occasion, cakes or cookies. The only structuring was that of a simulated family setting with the cotherapists placed at opposite ends of the table. It was hoped that this setting would encourage transference and that the presence of two males would not preclude the feeling of family which the cotherapists desired to create. As Clark[2] has pointed out, a "patient may think of a male analyst as both a father and a mother figure, at once, for the therapist's anima is in the situation as well as his ego." Or, as described by Lundlin and Aronov[14]:

...a simulated family setting is created by the presence of two authority figures.... The physical characteristics of the therapists become less important than subtle psychological differences.... One therapist will be seen as more aggressive and masculine, the other as more protective and feminine.

Poems were selected that expressed feelings thought to be troubling members of the group. Menninger's[16] statement was considered an axiom: "Psychiatrists realize from clinical experience what poets have proclaimed in inspired verse, that to retreat permanently into the loneliness of one's own soul is to surrender one's claim upon life." Copies of poems that the therapists thought appropriate were made and distributed to group members, and the poems were read and discussed. Members were then encouraged to describe any feelings made manifest by the readings of the poems. A search was made for what Stekel[22] in dream analysis termed the "personification of the parapathy." Members were frequently encouraged to write additional stanzas of their own and read them to the group. These discussions were not concerned with the student's ability as a poet, but rather with the feelings being expressed. Jung's[10] evaluation of poetry and the poet was thought to be significant: "When a form of 'art' is primarily personal it deserves to be treated as if it were a neurosis."

The concern in the student's writing, therefore, was with the expression of his "parapathy" as found in the central theme of his poetry, or in his reactions to the poetry of others. This is what Gutheil[6] would call his "symbolic parallelism." For example, a poem expressing the despair of not having a "self" would be read. Individuals would react with their own feelings as a result of hearing the poem. Then, several at least, would try to add a stanza or even two. These stanzas would be analyzed somewhat as Bonime[1] would approach a patient's dream:

> The action of the dream...symbolizes part of the total living process of the patient. Although only fragments of a dream may be preserved, or although the dream may be no more than a flash, a tableau, a sensation, a sound, a word or a pain, process is implied.

The philosophy of this chapter is concerned with the belief that "process is implied," also, in the production of a poem or in the individual reaction to a poem. Reik[20] claims that it "is with the antennae of our own unconscious that we feel what is the essence of the thoughts and emotions of our patients, not with the tools of reasoning and logic." The purpose of the experiment with poetry therapy was to encourage each individual to respond with his feelings as he heard the reading of "inspired verse," or read what was, perhaps, not so inspired, his own verse. It was recognized, of course, that, as Reik[20] states, "to get hold of an unconscious thought or emotion is only one part of the analytical process. To follow it, to observe its consequences, reverberations and repercussions in the unconscious life of the person is the other part." A part of the group process in this experiment was to observe and react to the unconscious emotions manifested by various individuals as they responded to their own poetry and the poetry of others.

POSTTEST RESULTS

In January, 1965, the same projective tests that were administered earlier as the pretest were given for the purpose of comparison. The posttest interview involved an effort to determine whether the student had improved as a result of 26 hours of poetry therapy. The tests were administered to the eight original subjects designated as the experimental group. The control group had ceased to exist, since four of the eight subjects requested treatment before the 12th hour of the experiment had been completed.

There are two significant limitations to any attempt to generalize on the data gathered by this study. First, the failure to obtain data for a control group makes it difficult to answer the usual question regarding whether the members of this group might have changed over the period of four months due to factors other than poetry therapy. Second, eight subjects do not constitute a sufficient sample. The authors report their results, therefore, as interesting data that suggest that poetry therapy may be a profitable area for continued research.

The results of the projective tests were submitted to three psychologists, who served as an evaluation team. They were instructed to evaluate the data and to conclude simply on the basis of a dichotomy: improved or not improved. The unaminous conclusion was that seven subjects were improved and one was not improved as determined by a blind comparison of pre- and posttest responses to the four projective devices. This was with one exception consistent with the results of the posttest interview conducted by the psychologist member of the poetry therapy team. In addition, the seven students judged to be improved indicated that they believed that they had profited from poetry therapy. The student judged not improved stated that he had found the treatment "interesting but of little real value to him." In summary, then, seven of the eight students participating in 26 hours of poetry therapy were "improved" as determined by a psychiatric interview, a self analysis, and an evaluation of projective data by a team of psychologists. A sample of the data is reported below for student AJ, female, aged 20, IQ 128.

Discussion

The evaluation of the pre- and posttest data indicated that the female members of the group profited more than the males. This greater change in the females might be attributed to the higher mean IQ level, which would indicate that the type of poetry used in this experiment (geared to the college-level student) requires a certain level of intellectual functioning before it can exercise a therapeutic effect. For noncollege groups, then, less difficult poetry, even doggerel, might be advisable. It is also possible that, both therapists being male, the females were able to effect greater sex-linked transfer. The authors concluded, in agreement with Mintz,[17] that the study might have been improved by using male and female cotherapists to stimulate more concretely the "reproduction of the original family situation."

In reference to the conjecture that a certain level of intellectual functioning is required to make this method meaningful, it is necessary to report that the one individual whose tests failed to indicate change had the second highest IQ recorded for the group. But there were other factors. The student was an English major obsessed with the idea of being a poet. And although he did, in fact, make a greater contribution of his own poetry than any other member of the group, it appeared to the cotherapists that writing, for him, was part of what Horney[9] has called the idealized image. In this case, the individual appeared to be concerned primarily with securing an admiring audience for his poetry. He was frequently condescending when other poems, by either recognized authors or members of the group, were read. During the reading of poetry written by other members of the

MMPI T SCORE

Scale		Pretest	Posttest	Difference
2	(Depression)	80	71	−9
6	(Paranoia)	71	59	−12
7	(Psychasthenia)	75	64	−11
8	(Schizophrenia)	73	68	−5
10	(Social)	81	81	0

TAT

6BM

Pretest themata
Life is bitter, hopeless, unalterably lonely.

Posttest themata
One must make an effort not to be bitter in life, even if it means staying away from mother.

Difference
She feels not quite so hopeless.

7BM

Individuals can become so frightened in life that they lose confidence and beg for help.

One must make an effort to solve one's own problems.

Increased responsibility for herself.

DRAW-A-PERSON

Pretest
A bent, old man about 70 years of age (3 inches on the page). Heavy black lines, much shading. She broke her pencil under excessive pressure while making the drawing. Comments while drawing included: "He sure looks like he's carrying the world on his back, doesn't he?" "Poor old man. He looks like he ought to just go home and die."

Posttest
A sturdy college boy (7 inches on the page) with a feminine face. She was relaxed while making the drawing. Comments while drawing included: "I can't make boys look like boys." "Oh, he's almost too pretty to be a boy." "He looks like my brother."

Difference
Evidence manifest that she is abandoning the internalized father for whom she attempted to be a "boy" and is beginning the transition toward female identification.

RORSCHACH CARD #1

Pretest
A girl being swallowed up somehow by an angry old woman, a sort of witchy old woman; it just sort of seems like she's being absorbed into the woman.

Posttest
I see a girl tied to a stake. She's spread-eagled sort of and it looks like she's gotten one leg free and she's struggling to get loose.

Difference
She is in the process of breaking away from the bondage imposed by her disapproving and hostile mother.

group, he pretended to be pained and attempted to exchange "knowing" glances with the cotherapists. He was not interested in any discussion of latent meaning or "symbolic parallelism." It is suggested, therefore, that in forming a poetry therapy group, the psychologist might be wise to exclude that type of individual with literary ambitions cathected to the idealized image. Poetry therapy in this case would possibly increase the protecting arrogance and magnify the discrepancy between actual and idealized self.

A further observation in the technique of poetry therapy as it developed in this experiment concerns the importance of what Reik[20] has called the "psychological moment." After approximately 12 hours of treatment, one of the major goals of the experiment had been reached: the group had become cohesive; it was evident that the members had come to know and care for each other and were willing, via their interpretations of poems, to be relatively "open" with each other. From this point on, it became increasingly apparent to the cotherapists and to the members of the group that when one individual reacted very strongly to a particular poem, the time had come for the entire group to focus on that person and sometimes to spend the entire hour discussing just a few lines of poetry as they related to that individual. It became increasingly clear to the cotherapists that these times constituted a precise moment "to communicate the repressed meaning of a series of symptoms or the hidden sense of some attitude of mind...." The following example will illustrate.

During the 14th meeting, a poem was read that expressed the effort of the author to come to terms with his real self. The author expressed acceptance of the real self in terms of his effort to be satisfied with the house he had built. Though imperfect, out of plumb, out of joint, he had built it, and he would live in it. A particular student reacted with considerable distaste, stating that he did not "like that poem at all." The recorded dialogue is self-explanatory:

Therapist: What would you say if I told you that I feel like that?
Student: You mean like that house?
Therapist: Yes. What would you say if I told you that I feel that way sometimes? Out of joint. Imperfect.
Student: I wouldn't believe you.
Therapist: But if it was true?
Student: Then I would feel sorry for you, very sorry for you.

Although this student had the lowest IQ in the group (108), he affected an attitude of superiority and a marginal tolerance of the other members of the group. He was openly contemptuous, for example, of several students who claimed to prefer modern jazz to classical music; he protested that he could not find anyone at the college able to challenge him at chess; he stated that he did not go home between semesters because his mind had "outdistanced" his parents and that efforts at conversation were overwhelming chores. In reacting to the poem, he was in fact reacting to the threat to the idealized image employed in the service of protecting him from anxiety, from feelings of meaninglessness. His overreactions to the poem prompted the cotherapists to ask him to read the poem aloud, which he did, disdainfully. Then he suddenly snapped his fingers and stated: "Hey, I just remembered a dream I had last night. It just popped right into my mind." He reported the dream:

> I enter an elevator and press the button and it starts up. Pretty soon I realize that I'm really up too high and that I'm actually just on a platform. The sides of the elevator have disappeared. I'm frightened because I realize I've gone higher than is safe but I don't know how to stop the elevator.

He reacted to the request to simplify the dream with the statement: "Well, I'm in danger because I've gone too high and there's a real threat I might fall off the platform." To the request that he describe the affect in the dream, he said: "A feeling of absolute loneliness." No dream analysis was attempted. It was felt that too much probing into the meaning of the dream would take the student beyond his capacity to adjust at that time.

The poet therapist and his psychology colleague are encouraged to be aware of this "psychological moment," for it may come and go almost unnoticed.

Finally, the authors found that some of the members of the treatment group responded in a sequence that appeared consistent with Jung's[11] concept of emerging archetypes from the collective unconscious.

> The first manifestation of the "*child*" is, as a rule, a totally unconscious phenomenon. Here the patient identifies himself with his personal infantilism. Then, under the influence of therapy, we get a more or less gradual separation from and objectification of the "child," that is, the identity breaks down and

is accompanied by an intensification...of fantasy, with the result that archaic or mythological features become increasingly apparent. Further transformations run to the hero-myth. The theme of "mighty feats" is generally absent, but on the other hand the mythical dangers play all the greater part. At this stage, there is usually another identification, this time with the *hero*, whose role is attractive for a variety of reasons. The identification is often extremely stubborn and dangerous to the psychic equilibrium. If it can be broken down and if consciousness can be reduced to human proportions, the figure of the hero can gradually be differentiated into a symbol of the *self*. [Italics added.]

Two students in particular serve as good examples of psychological growth as observed in emerging archetypes. One of these, male, submitted a poem entitled "Mom and Dad." It dealt quite frankly with the desire to hold on to them. A later poem, written for the 13th session, was a fantasy dealing with the heroics of a soldier in WW II. The poem he presented during the last week of treatment was called "Wherever I Go, I Go." It described a preoccupation with the search for job, love, home, children. It was not childlike, not heroic, but rather a simple expression of his emerging concern for the developmental tasks ahead, in proper sequence and phenomenologically sound.

A second student, female, wrote an early poem that she entitled "Asleep at my Mother's Breast." A later poem (15th session) was frankly sexual:

>...the arching goddess,
> a silken lure,
> behold the hero
> entwined
> at the Gates of Eden.

Her final poem, presented during the last week of treatment and titled "Sad Ann," described the feelings of a girl who realized that she was not at all a goddess, that she was too skinny, but that hopefully her "lover" would see through to her soul which was "beauty enough for the rest of her." Again, it appeared that the student had projected the child, had, in short, objectified the child, then the hero (goddess), and was beginning, at the conclusion of the semester, to objectify and to attempt a differentiation of the goddess into a symbol of the self. The authors concluded:

Poetry therapy may offer the individual the opportunity to project the child, hero, and self through the medium of verse, each archetype in its natural sequence, and that therapy will of necessity be of at least four months duration to allow time for the objectification of the archetypes. A caution is presented here, specifically that the therapist, watching for the epiphany of the hero, be aware that failure to attenuate the inflation of identification at this point may result in the entrenchment of the idealized image with its corresponding impoverishment of real self.

It is conjectured that this is perhaps what happened with the student in this experiment who did not appear to change from pre- to post-test.

Summary

1. For treatment using a group technique called poetry therapy, eight students were accepted on the basis of data obtained from: 1. a psychiatric interview; 2. MMPI; 3. Draw-A-Person; 4. Card 6BM and Card 7BM of the TAT; and 5. Card #1 of the Rorschach. The students were all junior or senior rank in college, four were male, four female, and the range in IQ 108 to 135. By sex, the mean IQ was female 127, male 113.

2. The group met every Thursday from 4:00 to 6:00 PM in a large room with two cotherapists, one a psychologist and the other a poet and professor of English. In principle, the method of treatment consisted of the selection and reading of poems thought to convey symbolically feelings and attitudes being repressed by the members of the group. The students were encouraged to associate freely to the poem and to write their own poems. These free associations and the themata of poems were then subject to a conventional type of analysis employed in most group therapy.

3. After the completion of 26 hours of treatment over a four month period, a second psychiatric interview and the same projective battery was administered as the posttest. A panel of three clinical psychologists was asked to evaluate the data and to conclude simply whether, in their opinion, improvement had occurred. They agreed unanimously that seven students had "improved" and that one apparently had "not improved."

4. A discussion of the data called attention to four specific phenomena: a. The females improved more significantly than the males. The relevance of IQ was not determined to be significant in this study, but it may offer an avenue of fruitful research for another study, i.e. Does the individual with a high IQ tend to profit more from poetry therapy than the average or sub-average individual? Or would a different type of verse be equally profitable with a group with fewer cultural advantages?

b. "An individual with an idealized image feeding upon his competence as poet or writer may not be a suitable candidate for this form of therapy inasmuch as the sessions may enhance the image at the expense of the already deflated real self."

c. "The therapists should watch for the emergence of the 'psychological moment' in individual patients, that moment of special readiness to accept change sometimes signaled by an original poem or an especially strong reaction to the poem of another."

d. "There appears to be some tendency for the original poems of individuals in group therapy to resemble the projections of Jungian archetypes, the child, the hero, the self."

5. The experiment did not involve a control group and it is difficult to generalize upon data employing a small number. It is recommended, therefore, that the experiment be repeated and an attempt be made to employ a control group.

REFERENCES

1. Bonime, Walter, *The Clinical Use of Dreams* (New York, Basic, 1962).
2. Clark, Robert A., *Six Talks on Jung's Psychology* (Pittsburgh, Boxwood Press, 1953).
3. Dahlstrom, W. G. and Welsh, G. S., *An MMPI Handbook* (Minneapolis, Univ Minnesota Press, 1960).
4. Greifer, Eli, "Poetry therapy," *The Brooklyn Psychologist*, September, 1964.
5. ———, "Principles of Poetry Therapy" (New York, Poetry Therapy Center, 1963).
6. Gutheil, Emil A., *The Handbook of Dream Analysis* (New York, Grove Press, 1951).
7. Hammer, Emanuel F., *The Clinical Application of Projective Drawings* (Springfield, Ill, Thomas, 1958).
8. Hathaway, S., and Meehl, P., *An Atlas For the Clinical Use of the MMPI* (Minneapolis, Univ Minnesota Press, 1951).
9. Horney, Karen, *Our Inner Conflicts* (New York, Norton, 1945).
10. Jung, C. G., *Modern Man In Search of a Soul* (New York, Harcourt, 1933).
11. ———, *Psyche & Symbol* (New York, Doubleday, 1953).
12. Ledwith, Nettie H., *A Rorschach Study of Child Development* (Pittsburgh, Univ Pittsburgh Press, 1960).
13. Leedy, J. J., "Poetry and medicine," *MD*: Med Newsmagazine, 3, 1964.
14. Lundlin, W. H. and Aronov, B. M., "Use of co-therapists in group psychotherapy," *J Consult Psychol* 16:60–76, 1952.
15. Machover, Karen, *Personality Projection* (Springfield, Ill, Thomas, 1949).
16. Menninger, Karl, *Love Against Hate* (New York, Harcourt, 1942).
17. Mintz, Elizabeth E., "Transference in co-therapy groups," *J Consult Psychol* 27:34–39, 1963.
18. Mowrer, O. Hobart, "The loss and recovery of personal identity as clinical problems," unpublished manuscript, Univ of Illinois, 1963.
19. Murray, H. A., *Thematic Apperception Test* (Cambridge, Mass, Harvard Univ. 1943).

20. Reik, Theodor, *Listening With The Third Ear* (New York, Grove Press, 1948).
21. Rorschach, Hermann, *Psychodiagnostics* (New York, Grune, 1921).
22. Stekel, Wilhelm, *The Interpretation of Dreams* (New York, Grosset & Dunlap, 1943).

The Psychodynamics of Poetry by Patients

E. MANSELL PATTISON, M.D.

In this chapter I shall discuss the use of poetry in psychotherapy in terms of psychodynamic processes. More specifically, I shall focus on poetry written by patients in terms of the communicational and interactional aspects of psychotherapy.

Poetry and the Processes of Psychotherapy

For the purposes of discussion here, I shall define psychotherapy as a complex social interaction that is both an interaction, *per se*, and a reflection upon that interaction. As Wolstein[29] observes in his book, *Theory of Psychoanalytic Therapy*, the therapist and patient engage in a communicational experience with each other and then engage in reflection and interpretation of that experience. Communication is behavior and vice versa. Further, communication in the psychotherapeutic interaction includes four sets of data: (1) words, their configuration, and meanings; (2) the nonlinguistic verbal concomitants of language (i.e., para-linguistics); (3) nonverbal communication, including body language; and (4) the communication inherent in the context (for example, role-determined responses and expectations).

Studies on communication in psychotherapy began with the rich, psychoanalytically oriented investigation of words[13,17,23] followed by extension into para-linguistics,[9] then nonverbal communication,[2,7,19] and, finally, context and role.[3,4,25] Current investigations are now addressed to a synthetic analysis of the complex interaction of all these modes in psychotherapy; as for example, Watzlawick, *et al.*[26] in *Pragmatics of Human Communication*.

Nevertheless, much of our contemporary discussion of psychotherapy still focuses upon words alone, as if they were the only, or the major variable of communication in psychotherapy. This limited view of psychotherapeutic communication is wryly attacked by the sociologist Erving Goffman[8]:

> A second effect of the enlightened psychiatric approach which the sociologist might bewail is that a very special and limited version of communication has resulted from it. Psychiatrists... have tended to labor under the telephone-booth bias that what the patient was engaged in was somehow a type of talking, of information imparting, the problem being that the line was busy, the connection defective, the party at the other end shy, cagey, afraid to talk, or insistent that a code be used.

Now this view of psychotherapeutic communication, namely to exchange clear and precise verbal signals, is a reductionism of the rich complexity of communication. In this view, word communication is merely a mathematical exchange. Words are seen as *signs*, not *symbols*. This distinction is critical to our discussion, hence a brief definition must be made. Signs or signals *present* a specific substitute cue to the recipient. Signs present a one-to-one correlation with what they substitute for. Thus Pavlov's bell sound is a sign substitute for food; or semaphore flags are signs that present specific substitute messages. For this reason the analytic philosophers of language can present their discussion in mathematical signs as a substitute for our usual words. However a symbol is a very different thing. Symbols do not present, but *represent*. Symbols are a means of organizing and synthesizing experience and thought. Thus a white flag of truce is a symbol. A symbol is a creative product and cannot be reduced to the component parts which it synthetically presents. (cf. Werner and Kaplan[27] *Symbol Formation*.)

My point here is that there is a proclivity among psychotherapists to view communication in psychotherapy as a scientific language exchange—to view the language of psychotherapeutic communication as an exchange of *signs*, and to ignore the symbolic nature of psychotherapeutic communication.

This is perhaps understandable in that we do not ordinarily discriminate between several different modal uses of language that range from sign exchange to symbol exchange. To refer back to our definition of psychotherapy, communicational interaction in psychotherapy is primarily symbol exchange; whereas the reflection and interpretation of the interaction is primarily a sign exchange. Yet often neither therapist nor patient is aware of the fact that they have shifted their mode of communication.

Recently McGuire and Lorch[14] provided a useful classification of four types of natural language conversation modes:

1. Associational: Language is primarily used for the mutual display of experiences and thoughts related to each other through association(s).

2. Problem Solving: Language is primarily used to convey factual knowledge and/or ideas comprehensible to both participants which may be logically or experientially related to the agreed-upon goals of the conversation: the problem(s) to be solved.

3. Interrogation: The interrogator uses language either to obtain specific information or to see how the question itself is processed by the listener. The interrogated participant uses language either to comply, to appear to comply, or to evade the interrogator.

4. Clarification of Assumed or Actual Misunderstanding: Language is used by the participant who believes he has been misunderstood, either to clarify a logical or evidential point, or to change the listener's way of thinking. The misunderstanding participant uses language to indicate his state of knowledge and understanding during the attempted clarification.

Note that in these four types of communication, only Type 1 is primarily a symbolic exchange, while the other three modes are primarily sign exchanges. Now when the therapist is listening to the patient or interacting with the patient in the experiencing part of psychotherapy, the mode of communication is symbolic. The language is symbolic. Thus in the classic tradition, the therapist is admonished, à la Theodore Reik,[18] to *listen with the third ear.* Or as Shave[21] recently put it, the therapist must learn to "read" the metaphorical communication of the patient.

It is when the therapist and patient shift to the observational and interpretive task that the mode of communication utilizes the sign components of language. But the temptation is to hear and interact with the patient using only the sign modalities of communication.

This produces two major problems. First, the therapist has difficulty truly comprehending the nature of the patient. The understanding of the patient is a clinical case report—bare-boned and identical to those of innumerable other patients. In contrast, a metaphorical or symbolic understanding of the patient more likely leads to an understanding of him that is not precise, but certainly more human. A novelist more fully describes a patient than does a clinician.[22] It is no accident that the great clinicians, beginning with Freud, not only looked to literature to understand patients but also wrote great literature about their patients. The second problem is that the failure to comprehend and engage in symbolic communication leads to a failure of communication *between* therapist and patient, for they engage in dissimilar modes that do not communicate the same message although the same words are used. This is borne out in the research by Truax and Carkhuff,[24] who demonstrated that a major determinant of successful psychotherapy was the capacity of the therapist to respond to the patient within the framework of the patient's communicational mode.

Let us now go back to examine the nature of poetry as a mode of communication. I have already suggested that the associational style of communication is a symbolic one. Further I would suggest that a major portion of psychotherapy is devoted to an associational interaction wherein the therapist has the opportunity to come to know the patient as a fully embodied person. Now this knowing of the patient cannot be accomplished via the mere accumulation of sign-type data. Human beings are unique creatures owing to their capacity to symbolize. And it is the comprehension of a patient's symbols that provides comprehension of the patient. It is in the most symbolic activities of the patient that perhaps we most fully comprehend the patient. Thus it is when the patient moves away from signal language to symbolic language that he most fully communicates the essence of himself to us. (See Arieti[1] and Shapiro[20] for examples and discussion of the different patterns of symbolization as related to personality organization.)

Poetry, and prose that approaches a type of poetic communication, involves the greatest degree of symbolization of the self; that is, the greatest degree of representation, organization, and synthesis of what I am, what I feel, how I respond and react. Robert Krauss[12], a research psychologist writing on language as a symbolic process in communication, recently noted that "the poem...exploits the resources of language to bring booming into our awareness that which we had only sensed before."

The poet John Ciardi[6] describes the symbolic fulcrum of poetry to loosen, enlighten, and enrich as follows:

Esthetic joy, because it stirs forever toward new possibilities and new combinations of possibility, puts us into a mood to receive new impressions. It beguiles us to horizons of ourselves and beyond.... The esthetic action sees acclaim; it hearkens. It waits for possibility to sound toward insight, and it reaches to insight in a glad serendipity.

Poetry as Symbolic Representation of Self

My argument, then, is that in the most highly symbolic modes of communication, the patient is afforded the opportunities to represent himself most closely, and for the therapist to see him and understand him most adequately. The hallmark of poetry is its highly symbolic quality. Thus the poetic productions of patients may afford some of the most fundamental, far-reaching revelations of the self. The following examples are given to illustrate this proposition.

Example 1. Samuel, a lean lad of 21, was referred for therapy because of repeated failures in college despite a demonstrated capacity for high classroom performance. He gave stereotyped descriptions of himself and relations with others. Psychological tests revealed a high intellectual capacity but with extremely intense internal hostility, and hostility was capped by precarious defenses that allowed for no expression of feelings or any of his ego skills. Clinically this was revealed by a vacuous schizoid demeanor and an almost total inability to share verbally any thoughts or feelings. After four months of seemingly little progress he began to bring in poems regularly. I would have him read the poems, after which he would gingerly begin to explore the self revealed in his poetry.

The first poem reflects his isolation, his despair, his dawning hope, and his sense of actual engagement with the therapist in a relationship with promise:

> Dense clouds, nor rain from our eastern region,
> The wind arrives across heaven,
> The light has sunk into the earth.
> Not light but darkness.
> First he climbed to heaven.
> Then he plunged into the depth of the earth.
> Surrounded by difficulties in the midst of kin.
> Nonetheless keeping his will fixed on the right,

> He veils his light, yet still shines.
> The darkness wounds his thigh,
> But he lifts himself with the strength of a horse.
> The taming power of the small has success
> Perseverance furthers
> Good fortune.

A month later Samuel had acquired a sense of himself that he had not experienced for many years, a sense of being able to cope, at least in some measure, with himself and his world. He was ready to really work in therapy. Note the references to therapy in the following poem:

> It is not I who seek the young fool;
> The young fool seeks me.
> At the first oracle I inform him.
> If he asks two or three times, it is importunity.
> If he importunes, I give him no information.
> When after difficulties at the beginning,
> Things have just been born,
> They are always wrapped at birth in obtuseness.
> Entangled youthful folly is, of all things, furthest from
>   What is real. This leads to humiliation.
> Take not a maiden who, when she sees a man of bronze,
> Loses possesion of herself.
> Nothing furthers.
>
> A spring wells up at the foot of a mountain:
> Thus the superior man fosters his character
> By thoroughness in all that he does.
> Fire in heaven above:
> Thus the superior man curbs evil and furthers good,
> And thereby obeys the benevolent will of heaven.
> Youthful folly means confusion and subsequent
>   enlightenment.
>
> Possession in great measure—
> Supreme success.

Some months later, Samuel, still via the medium of poems came to the point at which he could express carefully guarded fantasies of annihilation of both himself and others. In this poem he indicates both his schizoid isolation, the struggle that had wounded him, producing fear and fright, and his hope for a more fully embodied self that could only be attained by refusal to hide in his schizoid desert self:

MING I

Electra
TKL
LKT
Elkstar
Cold composition for three clarinets
Thin voices calling one to another
Crying from the flames in the soul's night
Singing the song of the Elkstar
Woe to him who hides his desert!
Hot sand shall petrify his flesh
That he may neither laugh nor dance.
Though I fled from the blood smeared door posts
I am covered with blood
Though I bathe in blood
Though I drink blood
I lie wounded among the rocks
Upon the evil mountain
Where Earth has risen up to drink
The thin light of cold, dry stars

The vast, dense darkness sips their ancient glow
Imported from heaven's brink
Sips out remains dark and cold and dry
Sinking to its center—heavy, thick, hard—
Weighted down, pressed down, pulled down from below
To the dark center untouched by any ray
Where no way
Is up—
Woe to him who hides his desert!
Hot sand shall petrify his flesh
That he may neither laugh nor dance.

Note that the content of the poem shifts thematically with the therapy. Nevertheless, the style of the poem remains an austere, intellectual, obtuse representation that indeed was the image of this isolated, frightened young man.

Example 2. Roger, a bright, blond, crinkly-haired boy, was referred for therapy by a college counselor because of increasing attacks of depression. Roger was verbal and facile. He was intellectual and delighted in playing the game of psychodynamics. He always had copious notes on relevant topics that he wanted to discuss in therapy. When I observed that he never really discussed his notes in therapy he was able to pick up the challenge to produce writing that really reflected his personal concerns. The following free verse composition reflects his vigorous style and his late adolescent search for identity. (Again, note the allusions to his therapy.)

Graffitti Found Near the First Entrance to the Gate of Freedom

I

F———you world! F———your bloody ass, "Everything"!
"faith in the universe"
that is where it either begins or ends.
We start with *me*.
Like it, honey, or f———you.
ME. This is where we start on this little transcript. We start here
    and either dig or
refuse to. But we start here, friends and we pursue...
My mind-being, on our Magnificant Assumption, as good as that of
    Jesus (for starters)
or Krishnamurti or mr. (MISTER!) Henry Miller (he being up first
    for execution, being the
nearest of kin, or perhaps the most/least understood of the most recent
    master of
this Roger's life).
Ah yes, but here we begin.

II

Up popped Roger
From the womb (no matter whose—who's nearest?)
Up—as we said—popped Roger from her vagina and surveyed the hairy
    (spell: beautiful)
surroundings
"and they *are* beautiful"
he loves it!
Vaginal odours—not so pleasant to some.
But to this boy, why they'd beat the pines of Rainier.
Does the boy tire of this smell and move on?
Perhaps to manure

perhaps to Chanel #5
perhaps to Gethsemane AD 29
perhaps to Buchenwald
perhaps to Vesuvius
perhaps to the smell of Mister Kennedy's blood on the pavement
or perhaps to the smell of leather arm rests on the fifth floor of Foggy
    Bottom
or those of Mister Nixon's situation room
or perhaps the boy would desire the smell of sweaty watchband
    scratching fanatical
radical wrists in the labyrinth of an SDS shouting match
or that or mr. ———'s sweaty shirt as he picks flies out of the eyes
    of dying children
of Algeria
or (perhaps) the exquisite smell of Billy Graham's oily eyeballs
Both raising shade of Hades in the eyes of the gathered
And holding up the possibility of immediate Redemption on the cross
or (since we are by necessity in this arena in Houston)
at the end of a short aisle in camera range of the folks from NBC:

Well you see what one must put up with
the Boy can take a deep breath of those vaginal odors and
        A) smile *yes* affirmation style
        B) vomit

in the vomiting dies everything.

But vomit he may
(choruses of people summoning Dr. Freud to free associate the boy's
    neurotic
front lobes back to life)
(choruses of fellow freaks shouting "welcome aboard this flaming
    raft!")
(choruses of parents—and their entourage—murmuring what's become
    of our (OUR) Roger?
and what, dear Lord up above, can we do to bring him back to Thee
    (read: us/security/
Buicks/good glances from the neighbors/de-caffeinated coffee).
(choruses of... but F———the choruses)
F——— *All* of the choruses
        including those of the
        angels
        the nihilists
        the American Legion

The Friends Society of Reconciliation
even the chorus of *his* friends
    John
    Bill
    Sue
    Norm
    Ron
    Letha
and on, and on, and on, and on.

III

Do we stop with f_____ing?
    or
   do we
    shout *yes* to all these choruses

ALL the choruses
All the choruses of the Universe
Yes being the thing of which friends are made.
Roger ("There is but one truly serious philosophical problem, and
    that is suicide")
does say yes
(did I hear say?)
shouts yes
(did I hear shout?)
sings yes
(did I hear sing?)
BREATHES—from the core of his gut—
Yes, Yes, Yes,
YES!!!!!

IV

But how, if one may be anticlimactic enough to ask—
HOW does Roger breathe yes?
How does Roger breathe yes in the face of Saigon
—where we teach the Vietnamese children how to suck

in the face of Czechoslovakia
—where dreams die, rekindle, and die again

in the face of Biafra
—where dreams in the form of little children lie bloated, choking

for the lack of the very same substance that forms muscle
nay fat, nay cholesterol
in the bodies
and minds
of American males
in the face of white racism
in the face of—
well take a glass
and look at your own face, honey
how does he say yes
nay BREATHE yes

(there being but one truly serious philosophical problem)
in the face of *that*
    ?????
you wait, no doubt (f——— you), for an answer
but that very answer is currently unwinding
(if you don't see it, it ain't for your eyes, honeybun)
in the (auto, —very very auto) biography
of Roger John Smith's
    living.
Oh the pretense of the above letters!
(Oh the plight, but is it just a plight?
of having by default—
to turn to oneself
for the hero one has always sought.)

  By way of comment, I should add that Roger was at first dismayed and appalled by the spontaneous outpouring when he allowed himself to put down on paper the panoply of thought, impulse, and reaction that seethed within himself. However, the fact that he had himself down on paper was in a sense irrevocable. This then provided an avenue past his defenses, provided an avenue for observation and interpretation of the self.

  Example 3. Mary, a 30-ish housewife, was a talented painter but a frustrated housewife. The product of a Puritan family she presented herself with complaints of anxiety and depression that turned out to be the symptomatic aftermath of an abortive flirtation. Her hysterical character neurosis had been carefully defended by a rigid façade embodying prim, puritainical representations of herself.

  During the first six months of therapy she very rapidly developed an intense erotic transference. However, Mary found that the analysis of her transference could be defended by writing voluminous love poems, to be demurely presented to me instead of presenting herself. An alternative defense was to mail love poems, which of course precluded analysis altogether, since the patient was not present in person.

The first poem presented here is an example of presentation of self via the symbolization of poetry that is reflected in the form of the poem. Note the simple style, the adulation of the therapist, and the lack of reflection on the self. In terms of form, the poem is typical of adolescent love poems. Thus it reflects her regression at that point in therapy, her experience of herself only in terms of the fantasized love object:

> Snow is beautiful;
> —so are you.
>
> Snow is dazzling;
> —so are you.
>
> Snow is gentle;
> —so are you.
>
> Snow is challenging;
> —so are you.
>
> Snow melts;
> —so do you.
>
> Snow is exhilarating;
> —so are you.
>
> Snow is brilliant;
> —so are you.
>
> Snow is frustrating;
> —so are you.
>
> Snow is laughter and tragedy;
> —so are you.
>
> Snow is a gift, and real;
> —so are you.

In contrast, some six months later Mary had accomplished in therapy a considerable amount of work. Her hysterical neurosis was now clearly presented and reflected upon, and the transference relationship had taken on a more collaborative working tone:

RECIPE

Take one large Oedipal complex
Mix with incestuous fixation
Add generous amounts superego
Blend one chopped narcissus
Stir in gelatine (after first 20 years)

(BATTER WILL BE STIFF)

Press into well-defined mold and
simmer 34 years.

When warning bell rings, stand clear
of container before lifting lid.

(some dish.... you name it)

To summarize these illustrations, each of the poems presented vary in style and content. The symbolic assemblage of each poem represents the personality and conflict of each patient. In the cases of Samuel and Mary, poems at different stages of therapy reflect shifts in the psychodynamic configuration of the patient. Samuel remained severely schizoid, and his poetic symbolization of himself reflected that, whereas Mary demonstrated a shift in her personality style as growth occurred in therapy.

The symbolic representation of the patient in his poetry read in both the form and content allows both basic character elements and shifting psychodynamic conflicts to be seen via the poetic production. The classic dictum of psychotherapy has been that dreams are the royal road to the unconscious. In terms of discussion here, we may observe that dreams are a highly symbolic means of self-representation. Similarly, the patient's poetry is a symbolic means of representing himself. The utilization of his poetic productions, like the utilization of dreams, may provide for patient and therapist another royal road to the unconscious.

Poetry as Catalyst and Defense

Major attention here has been given to the comprehension of the patient via the symbolizing process of poetry, the communicational process in psychotherapy. However, I should like to mention the interactional aspects of using poetry in psychotherapy.

In connection with the poetic examples given previously, I alluded to the fact that how the patients presented and used their poetry varied with the psychodynamic interactions of the therapy. Thus, as with any data in psychotherapy, we must inquire not only into the data itself but also into the contextual behavior of that data.

Samuel's fear and anxiety over his internal impulses—and his schizoid aloofness—made the development of a working psychotherapeutic relationship difficult. The dynamic use of poetry afforded him a means of contact and self-disclosure that he could not allow himself to express directly. The use of poetry in this case provided enough distance from both himself and the therapist to allow him to become involved in the analytic process of psychotherapy.

In the case of Roger, his intellectualized defenses enabled him successfully to defend against either presentation or analysis of his inner self. His bursting out in free-form verse took his ego defenses by surprise. He had revealed himself in spite of himself. Once he had committed himself on paper, however, he found that he no longer needed to defend so strongly. Thus the *communication* in his poetic outburst became the occasion to successfully engage him in the *analytic* task work of psychotherapy.

In the case of Mary, poetry was used as a means of defense. The writing of love poems became a channel to justify her transferred feelings. She presented her poems rather than herself. The demand that I accept this love poetry instead of herself was a means of precluding analysis of the self she was presenting. As analysis proceeded in therapy, the style of poetry changes, reflecting the change in the therapeutic work stance vis-à-vis the therapist and herself, as well as her own experience and view of herself.

The subject of written communication in psychotherapy has received some attention in the literature recently. Most of the discussion has vocused on the dynamics of the patient and his use of written communication.[10,11,15,16,28] However, the therapist may also use written communication either as a catalyst or as a medium for his own countertransference. An excellent example is given by Meyer Cahn[5] in an article in which he recounts how he used his own poetry in therapy to service his own countertransference needs. To avoid involvement with his patients he wrote poems about and to them. But doing so he did not engage himself with them.

Summary

This chapter is concerned with the use of poetry written by patients during psychotherapy. We have said that poetry is a particularly appropriate and powerful vehicle for providing insight, for both the patient and the therapist, into the complexity of the patient. Because symbolization is the communicational vehicle for organizing, synthesizing, and representing the self, the poem as a symbolic vehicle is a potent mode of psychotherapeutic communication. The use of poetry is most appropriate to the first process of psychotherapy, namely associational communication, in which the aim of communication is to share ideas and experiences so that understanding of the person occurs. The poetic symbolization of self can then be used in the second process of psychotherapy—observing and interpreting the presentation of self.

The examples of poetry written by patients indicate how poems represent character style, current psychodynamics conflict, and the interpersonal dynamics between therapist and patient. The examples show how poetic symbolization, like dreams, is an avenue to the unconscious.

The writing of poetry and the use of poetry in psychotherapy may facilitate psychotherapy or may be used defensively by the patient in the service of transference or by the therapist in the service of countertransference.

In sum, the use of a patient's poetry can be an integral part of psychotherapy. However, the therapist must approach this symbolic representation of self in terms of the symbolizing process and not reduce the poetic communication to sign exchange. Further, the therapist must place the use of poetry in the interactional perspective in such a way that it serves as a catalyst and not a defense mechanism.

REFERENCES

1. S. Arieti, *The Intrapsychic Self: Feeling, Cognition, and Creativity in Health and Mental Illness* (New York, Basic Books, 1967).
2. E. G. Beier, *The Silent Language of Psychotherapy: Social Reinforcement of Unconscious Processes* (Chicago, Aldine, 1966).
3. L. Bernstein, and B. C. Burris, eds., *The Contribution of the Social Sciences to Psychotherapy* (Springfield, Ill., Charles C. Thomas, 1967).
4. B. J. Biddle, and E. J. Thomas, *Role Theory: Concepts and Research* (New York, J. Wiley, 1966).
5. M. M. Cahn, "Poetic Dimensions of Encounter," in A. Burson, ed., *Encounter: The Theory and Practice of Encounter Groups* (San Francisco, Jessey-Bass, 1969).
6. J. Ciardi, "Of Poetry and Sloganeering," *Saturday Review* (January 6, 1968) p. 14.
7. S. S. Feldman, *Mannerisms of Speech and Gestures in Everyday Life* (New York, International Universities Press, 1959).
8. K. Goffman, *Interaction Ritual: Essays on Face-to-Face Behavior* (Garden City, Anchor, 1967) pp. 138–139.
9. L. A. Gottschalk, and A. H. Auerbach, eds., *Methods of Research in Psychotherapy* (New York, Appleton-Century-Crofts, 1966).
10. C. E. Kew, and C. J. Kew, "Writing as an Aid in Pastoral Counseling and Psychotherapy," *Past. Psychol.*, XIV (1963) 37.
11. A. A. Kramish, "Former Patient Report on Letter Reading Technique," *G. P.* XI (1963) 320.
12. R. M. Krauss, "Language as a Symbolic Process in Communication," *Amer. Scientist* LVI (1968) 265.
13. J. Laffal, *Pathological and Normal Language* (New York, Atherton, 1965).
14. M. T. McGuire and S. Lorch, "Natural Language Conversation Modes," *J. Nerv. Ment. Dis.* CXLVI (1968) 239.
15. E. M. Pattison, "The Patient After Psychotherapy," In press.
16. L. Pearson, *The Use of Written Communications in Psychotherapy* (Springfield, Ill., Charles C Thomas, 1965).
17. D. Rapaport, *Organization and Pathology of Thought* (New York, Columbia University, 1951).
18. T. Reik, *Listening with the Third Ear* (New York, Grove Press, 1948).
19. A. E. Scheflon, "Quasi-Courtship Behavior in Psychotherapy," *Psychiatry*, XXVIII (1965) 245.
20. D. Shapiro, *Neurotic Styles* (New York, Basic Books, 1965).
21. D. W. Shavo, *The Language of the Transference* (Boston, Little, Brown, 1968).
22. A. A. Stone and S. S. Stone, *The Abnormal Personality Through Literature* (Englewood Cliffs, N. J., Prentice-Hall, 1965).
23. T. Thass-Thienemann, *The Subconscious Language* (New York, Washington Square Press, 1967).
24. C. B. Truax, and R. R. Carkhuff, *Toward Effective Counseling and Psychotherapy: Training and Practice* (Chicago, Aldine, 1967).
25. R. W. Waggoner, and D. J. Carek, eds., *Communication in Clinical Practice* (Boston, Little, Brown, 1964).
26. P. Watzlawick, J. H. Beavin, and D. D. Jackson, *Pragmatics of Human Commu-*

nication: A Study of International Patterns, Pathologies, and Paradoxes (New York, W. W. Norton, 1967).

27. H. Werner, and B. Kaplan, *Symbol Formation: An Organismic-Developmental Approach to Language and the Expression of Thought.* (New York, J. Wiley, 1963).

28. H. A. Wilmer, "The Envelope and the Psychiatrist: A Study of Patients' Envelopes," *Amer. J. Psychiat.*, CXXIII (1967) 792.

29. B. Wolstein, *Theory of Psychoanalytic Therapy* (New York, Grune & Stratton, 1967).

PART III
WHERE

IN PRISON

Poetry in a Cage: Therapy in a Correctional Setting

BILL J. BARKLEY, Ph.D.

Poetry therapy is not only possible, but a most important adjunct to the other psychiatric treatments offered in a correctional setting. Strange as it may seem, it is not only welcomed but sought out as a means of otherwise impossible communication. Within the bounds of the correctional setting we find a great deal of hidden creativity. Supposedly impossible, frowned upon, unverbalized feelings are discovered. The need to express the soul is another often-suppressed wish of the resident of a correctional institution. In attempting to express himself poetically, many times he will be hesitant for fear of making mistakes in spelling, punctuation, or even poetic style. These are unimportant. The important fact is that the individual speaks, expresses, goes on record, and communicates his innermost feeling and hopes through the medium of poetry.

No matter how sick, hardened, and institutionalized an individual is there resides a heart, and that heart needs to be heard. Many times the heart cries out in all too many camouflaged ways, and it is our job as therapists to listen and watch intently for those cries, listen to them, and aid in their expression. Therapy begins only when the faintest signs of communication start to come through, and we must constantly be on the alert for them or a resistance to them. Communication, whether verbal or non-verbal, is implicit in the therapeutic process, and often the non-verbal can become verbal through the use of poetry, written by both the patient and the therapist.

In a correctional setting the writing of poetry, the "dissecting" of it, the content, and above all, the creativity, are not too different from the equivalents in the "free world." The writing is a need. The "dissecting" is of the self. (One of the early trained Gestaltists, I prefer to have my people associate to each part of the poem as a part of themselves, thus the term "dissecting" is preferred to the term "analysis".) The content is a feeling. The feelings deal with love, fear, pathos, hate, compassion, sex, confusion, frustration, longing, loneliness, friendship, transference and very seldom with violence, corruption, and anti-establishmentarianism. Creativity is the big hidden "I." Often the style is weird, but so is "free" poetry in many instances.

I use poetry therapy in the correctional setting the same way that I used it in private practice. Many times, I first attempt to break through a seeming impasse by writing a poem I consider applicable to the individual involved. Then I request that the subject express in poetry what he cannot or will not do otherwise. Finally, both of us "dissect" the poem in terms of what it means to us. Using it in this way, poetry opens many new vistas that are otherwise closed, or far too long undisclosed; thus the total process involved is shortened.

Since writing or using poetry is a creative process, we must first unlock basic creativity. In my estimation, that can be done only by acquainting the individual with the great need for awareness, because without awareness there is no creativity. The development of awareness can only be accomplished by learning to "not only look, but see"; "not only listen, but hear"; "not only touch, but feel"—until all the senses are keenly attuned and can be thoroughly felt and absorbed by the human being. By this means creativity begins to bud and grow. Soon we have poetry, and it is through the use of this poetry in the therapeutic process that we can then proceed to real communication; by contact and involvement and the epitome of interpersonal relationships.

All of the poetry introduced, "dissected," explained, or discussed in this article was written voluntarily (with the express permission in writing for the author of this chapter to use in any way that he saw fit). All persons contributing have been either overtly or acutely psychotic in the past or have deep-seated psychosexual conflicts and/or overt emotional problems.

The first poem to be introduced and discussed is one of hundreds done by one of the most friendly and fascinating residents of the colony. He has been suffering from chronic hebephrenic schizophrenia for years, and he has been considered psychiatrically untreatable. He could be called the "unofficial welcomer" to the correctional setting because he politely welcomes all visitors when introduced, thanks them for coming, blesses them for their interest and, within an hour, will show up with a "thank you" poem written expressly for them. Then he disappears. His poems are always most touchingly sentimental and usually well written. To those who ignore this creativity in him he is a pest, and pest he can be when not appreciated. His poetry, however, has reached me; and I hope that through his poetry, I, too, can reach him and find what lies beneath his inner conflicts. I consider him a challenge, and hope that poetry therapy just might be the answer. Here is one of his typical welcoming poems.

A SMALL TOKEN OF OUR APPRECIATION

The presence of you here, means very much
It's plain for us to see,
The words of wisdom spoken by you,
Will help my men be free
From inter-war, that destroys the soul
    Throughout eternity.

These men here, are not as cruel as they might seem to be.
I started to leave here some time ago
But, the problems of these men, as I talked to them
Seem to grow and over-flow.
So that's why I decided to stay and help them
In every way I know.

So, fare-well, fare-well, fare-well-my-friends.
We wish that you could stay.
God bless you both, for a safe return.
Please, come back again some day.

Even though he presented it in person to friends of mine, it is intersting to note that he wrote it as though I were writing it. I think it is of ever greater significance that, for the first and only time in well over year, he made reference to the possibility of the therapist leaving. Here, again, the unspoken, the uncommunicated, comes through in the form of poetry.

In spite of his long-standing emotional confusion, the following poem reflects his insight, striving, and appreciation for what has to be recognized and acted upon in order to once again establish a meaningful rhythm in our society.

POETRY THERAPEUTICS—ART OF SCIENCE

Po-e-try is a Thera-peu-tic Art, and it—
Is plain for every one to see
It's a Universal Language
To help both you and me.

If we study it very closely
And try real hard to see,
It carries a message very clear
To help us to be free
    From turmoil, sickness, and bitter strife
    The victims, you and me.

If we can grasp the meaning—
Of this wisdom, my friend you see
We'll walk this land, hand in hand
and then we shall be free
From self-destruction that destroys the soul
Of folks like you and me.

There'll be no need for weapons of war
For there'll be a millennium then
Then we'll build here on earth a Kingdom
And as for time, there shall be no end.

Good po-e-try can be put to music
Very easy to understand.
That's why its the Universal language
Chosen and written by wise men—
With our God, all in its plan.
For every woman, man and child
To walk this Holy Land
With love and respect for every one
For that's God's special plan.

If we will rhyme to-gether like po-e-try
Life to us, it would be music
From——, to my therapist
With deep appreciation for your kindness.

In the foregoing stanzas he illustrates his deep appreciation for the value of poetry therapy. I would say that he has grasped it quicker than the average layman, let alone many professionals.

Humor quite often will come through, but not as frequently as loneliness, pathos, the need for love, appreciation, and many other deeper feelings. The following brief example of humor was written by a huge, powerful individual who all too often gives many the impression that his brain does not match his size. His poem, *Mr. Fish* is followed by another, *As I Look in the Sky*, which amazed not only many of the residents but the therapist himself.

MR. FISH

One night while I was asleep,
    A big fish walked up to my bed and said,
"Would you care to go for a swim, my dear old Friend?"

I said to Mr. Fish:
    "No thank you, I think"
And every day since,
    Mr. Psychopath Therapist
Has been fishing for poor Mr. fish.

His *Sky* poem, showing his true self, which he very seldom lets anyone see, but which he lives alone with constantly, also expresses insight and appreciation for therapy. This poem starts out with his daydream that he is in the Army in Vietnam, and reflects the fact that he is trying to find himself again.

As I look in the sky
I awake from my dream
    And out of my mind,
    It's hard to admit,
    That I am a fake.
That the only war I have
    Is the one in my head.

As I look in the sky
I realize that I'm sick
    And for one reason or other
Have been stricken for nineteen years.

As I look in the sky
I can't help wonder why?
    I have been in this nightmare so long
    But with the help of my therapist

I may come out—right not wrong.
As I look in the sky, as I look in the sky.

Many of us who do both group and individual therapy often wonder what goes on in the mind of the bright uncommunicative participant-observer in the group. Without coercion or prodding, I finally became enlightened when one of my most intelligent residents turned in several poems permeated with pathos, unresolved grief, and a preoccupation with death. The following is typical of his unresolved conflicts and how his silence in the group helped him to uncover some of his inner turmoil.

SOLDIER IN THE SNOW

In a land where none can find him
In a hole so deep into the ground
There sits a poor young soldier and
He doesn't make a sound.

You can hear the far-off cannons
And the screams of those who die
And the whine of flying bullets
And it makes you want to cry.

And you see the smoke of bombing
And you see the flames of Hell
And you feel the heat of battle
And it makes you feel unwell.

But he sits there in his foxhole
And he doesn't feel the wind blow
For he died about two days ago
Our lonely little soldier in the snow.

We always have had to, and always will have to, face the matter of "transference" and what to do about it. While some patients can only express transference in a non-verbal manner, and others not at all, I have found that for many the medium of poetry has been a clear, helpful, softening path for them. An example of the depth of transference is shown in the following.

A TRUE REALITY

Man what a guy, this "Barkley of mine"!
A father, a friend, to all who are blind.
Yes, blind in the ways of problems and such,
And a healer to all, with his magic touch.

Oh Damn! All the others who don't give a hand,
To so many in need, they just can't understand!
Yes, this Dr. I call Barkley, (Dad to us all),
Is a healer and protector, always there when we fall.

So God, help him, and keep him,
Safe in your care
For many still need him,
And so many more care.

It is of interest to note that this was written while the resident was in group therapy only; however, he had formerly been in both group and intensive individual therapy with the therapist for two years. He was acutely psychotic and had been chronically psychotic for many years, and had shown marked masochistic and suicidal withdrawal. He asked for therapy and became completely dependent upon the therapist, and it was most difficult to break through the strong transference. The long "weaning" process was accomplished, and now he not only helps others, as the poem indicates, but maintains a strong sensible depth of feeling for the therapist and is willing to share him with others. The resident has been in full remission now for over a year and has not needed medication. He has reestablished meaningful contact with his family, with almost daily letters and weekly visits. He has also graduated from high school. He has minimum custody status. When paroled, he plans to go on to college to become a psychiatric nurse.

The "weaning" process mentioned above can be a most difficult situation to work through, particularly with psychotics. As far as I am concerned, it has to be a casual, open, and honest happening, not abrupt, not coldly calculated, but almost as though it is being handled with a sixth sense. A resident's poem exemplifies it better than I can describe it.

MY WEANING

If it were planned or not
you weaned me well.
I will not again depend
on you, and this I saw
from confidence within myself
not bitterness toward you.

You could not do it better—
this realization had to come,
and glad I am to find it
finished and complete,
a part of me.

To you it seemed to be
important that I see you
real, with faults and foibles, feet of clay
perhaps?

At any rate, this view
of you I see with eyes not looking
for ideals but
just humanity.

You weaned me well
Indeed.

Just recently I tried an interesting experiment using poetry therapy on a young man during his fifth session of individual therapy. I had observed him and worked with him in a compulsory group. It was obvious that he disliked therapy and did not trust a single person. I told him that he was a challenge to me and that I would like the opportunity of working with him in individual therapy. Three days later, he informed me that he would accept the challenge. Deeply depressed about being separated from his young "female" homosexual partner, he was in the neuro-psychiatric section of the hospital for having cut himself. He did not want to live, and absolutely nobody could take "her" place. During the fourth session of individual therapy, he informed me that he was taking an interest in school and that he could hardly wait from week to week for our sessions, granting that he was feeling just a "little bit" better. On the fifth session, I suggested we write a poem together regarding his feelings, thoughts, and phantasies during the preceeding four weeks. The finished poem is as follows:

TO LIVE

I need to appear self-sufficient.
But underneath that shallow front,
I am constantly reaching out,
For the love I need—MY HUNT.

A meaningful word, an interest shown,
Means more than life to me.
Oh, to be needed, wanted, held,
I'm sure would make me free.

Each time I feel it won't come again,
And yet I know it can.
Oh, when will my impatience die
And leave me completed—MAN?

It is of particular significance that the two lines that I contributed to the poem—the first two lines of the second stanza—are the only lines of the poem with which he could no longer identify. He politely, but vehemently, contested that he wanted to live and that those "other things" were not that important any more. He then went on to report that there were many things that wanted to verbally rush out of him, but that when he opened his mouth nothing happened. Here again is an excellent candidate for poetry therapy.

Another example of pain, fear, and loneliness is exemplified in the following short verse:

A MAN CAN'T STAND ALONE

I know the pain and fear of loneliness,
It is like living in the dark.
    Like trying to find a door out,
    Or trying to get some sunshine in
To light up your house or heart.

Being in prison—it may seem strange,
    Is not so bad at all.
    Not near so bad,
As the loneliness I felt for years,
When out working and supposedly "Free."

This short poem brought to light things he had never dared share with others. In his late twenties he was still a lonely, scared, little boy who was always a loner. He was not allowed to date at the age of seventeen for fear he might become like his father, who has spent most of his life in prison. He never had a girl friend and was always worried about what his mother would think. As he put it, "I only enjoyed working, but then was envious of the happy carefree people around me, and I hated to see weekends come." He finally stole a car and went "joy riding."

Proof that there can be shining lights behind the walls and that, essentially, it all rests within the eyes of the beholder is well put in the following selection.

COMPASSION

Prosperity cannot be fenced in for me and mine.
Whatever lies across that fence is my concern;
Every man in need or in trouble is my brother.

This resident lives like this from day to day, and his sunshine and compassion spreads. He was never a patient of mine, but I know his therapist is excellent, and it shows. He has been institutionalized for a long time, but it doesn't show because he lives for his fellow man. He has learned to express joy, enthusiasm, earthiness, to cry when he feels sad—in other words, he lives, he does not merely exist.

Another area of concern—causing frustration, trouble, and even death—that has plagued our correctional settings from the very beginning is constantly presenting itself to the correctional therapist and is typified in the following:

PRISON LOVE

Have I found that one at last?
    To help me forget my bitter past?
How can I really be sure,
    His intentions are true and pure?

He's the nicest person I have met,
    But is it possible for me to forget,
That certain someone, that special place,
    A personality and a handsome face?

It's the little things he does for me,
    That makes me wonder of the possibility,
Of a very happy association;
    Regardless of our poor location.

But what would happen if we meet,
    A few short years from now upon the street?
Would he really remember my name,
    Or avoid me with head turned in shame?

Those are the things I have to know,
    Before I let my emotions show.
Now I don't want to be a fool,
    So I guess I'll have to play it cool.

Many would be surprised at the number of men in correctional settings who are completely ignorant of the facts of sex, and the many hundreds who not only feel guilty, but carry with them many outdated ideas concerning masturbation. The frustration of having to resort to this form of release is explained in the poem dealing with the subject.

MASTURBATION

Is it self-love?
Or purely a substitute for other love, in desperation?
And what is best?
To deny yourself to yourself, pretend
a non-desiring?
Or to let go, unloose desire, and
Let come emotion,
Let come the body-filling, mind-erasing rush
and swell of senses?

All right! Let the rush come, let the wave break,
Let the tide flood, let self love self!
But tide will ebb, too, and then
what?

A physical being unleashed and unbridled,
the flood-tide of senses' enjoyment—
then hush

> with arms empty,
> lips lonely,
> throat aching.
> No ear to say "Dear" to,
> no eyes to watch sleeping,
> no face to relearn in each newness:
> No foot close, no knee touching mine,
> no hand at my chest.
> ———And this?
> This is masturbation.

And then of course, we run into our share of intellectualizing, philosophizing, "hippie" type of poetry, which in many cases is well done and can contribute to our understanding of the individual.

> WHY
>
> where will it go
> when it's gone
> when it's lost
> when it's wondering
> when it's why—
> for how is it   —thank you my friend—
>
> that it is
> what it seems
> what it is
> when it's not.
>
> while resting, the whole of it seems so far and distant
> from my touch of poor piled flesh.
> to concentrate is why when it seems not.
> for to rest.... in the motion of thought
> would be but a small awakening
> to a vast why.
>   —thank you my friend—

Disguised hostility, hatred, loneliness, and youthful frustration is brought out in the following by a young man who lost his father in a war. This individual is alienated from the rest of the family, yet he has both intellect and high aspirations for himself.

THE ANSWER IS THE END

Meaningless rhetoric meant to astound
Platitudes, nothingness, they are just sounds.
Talk of love, grief and strife—does anyone know
the meaning of life?
Man, oh man. What is he? Do you see the ant
D.D.T.ing the flea?

A baby cries, an old man dies.
War is the whore we don't want any more.
The cycle of life again and again,
Failures phantasizing on what might have been.
I love people but cannot see the point of you
or the point of me.

The apex of civilization just around the bend
Is it the beginning of the end?
The fire the next time on all will descend!
That's the meaning of life: To end, to end....

Compassion, empathy, sensitivity, and fear all are expressed in a poem dealing with the gas chamber at San Quentin. The following poem was written many years ago, but it expresses the marked degree of empathy that is supposedly beyond the capacity of the anti-social personality.

RED LIGHT OF DEATH

Behind the high gray walls of Quentin
    Trying to beat the still hot air
I gazed into a Summer sky
    Saw a red light shining there.

Down below walked dear old Padre
    Slowly walking down the hall.
While behind him strolled a convict
    His foot-steps very slow.

The convict's eyes were filled with tears
    So full he could not see
As the dear old Padre sang his song
    Nearer my God to thee.

Not far ahead stood a great steel door
    The color, it was green
The gates of hell stood behind that door
    For a convict, whom we'll call Gene.

They sat him in a big arm chair
    Strapped his arms down nice and tight
Now all he had to do is wait
    As the gas shut out the light.

In my hand I hold a paper
    On front page, you'll find his name
Yes, the Governor sent his pardon
    But the postman never came.

They dug a hole on yonder mountain
    Three foot wide and six feet deep
They carved his name upon an oaken board
    To mark where this convict sleeps.

As I sit here, how I wonder
    How many tears he cried
As he watched the creeping darkness
    Fold around him as he died.

Now who can say I'm sorry
    His innocence plainly seen
Just who now stands in judgment
    Of a convict we'll call Gene.

Now I know what the red light meant
    Against the clear blue sky
I did not know the man who died
    But a tear fell from my eye.

I no longer sit in the big big yard
    Trying to beat the Summer air.
I don't like to gaze into a Summer sky
    And see a red light shining there.

I am sure that the above person is what most people think of when they think of "correctional poetry," but I find this the exception not the rule. Even though many of the residents like this sort of poetry, they do not write it themselves. More often their endeavors deal with themselves and their own problems.

An example of the therapist writing a poem in order to help a resident face the problems that he is not expressing was written for a very young man who was in the process of returning to the "free world" with nobody to return to. He had no previous work experience to count on. He had no early life preparation to live happily and meaningfully in the world that he had left four years previously, let alone the strange one now.

ALONE

Behind the concrete walls
There are big and little bones.
Some wanting to go home,
Others not knowing what or where is home.
Yes, alone, alone, alone!

This stimulated much thought, anxiety (which could be worked with) and, needless to say, effort in preparation on the part of the resident.

In addition to the values of poetry therapy I mentioned in beginning this chapter, I feel that, like bibliotherapy, it gives the resident the opportunity to identify with his own or other characters of phantasy in the poems, and with the problems presented. By this process, he not only comes sooner to understanding himself, but he soon starts relating better and more realistically with his peers.

IN A MENTAL HEALTH CENTER

Poetry Therapy for Psychoneurotics in a Mental Health Center

CHARLES CROOTOF, Ph.D.

A poetry therapy group has been functioning for a year now at the Postgraduate Center for Mental Health in Manhattan. The patients of the group join by first becoming members of our Living Room Club, in the Social Rehabilitation Department under the direction of Dr. Maria Fleischl, psychiatrist. The members of the therapeutic club may avail themselves of one or another kind of adjunctive therapy almost any evening of the week. Dance, art, music, drama, poetry therapy, arts and crafts, and vocational counseling are offered them for a nominal monthly fee. This arrangement creates a supportive atmosphere for the members, many of whom live alone and welcome the companionship of the others. Though most of them are employed, they are troubled by psychoneuroses of varying severity. Some are borderline; some have been previously hospitalized.

Poetry sessions are held once a week for an hour and a half. Attendance ranges from 12 to 20, and during the year 9 or 10 members have attended almost every session. Many of the patients are constantly struggling against the encroachment of feelings of isolation and against slipping into a loss of communication with other people. During a recent session, the intensity of the reaction to the lines

> Today I met a stranger—
> Though for ten years I have lived with him

gave clear indication of the fear of isolation that the patients are struggling with.

Having been the therapist and leader of the poetry group for this year, I have tried to form some answers to the questions: How can poetry contribute to mental health?

The extent to which poetry has provided solace and comfort to humanity through the ages is buried in the history of mankind. We will never know how many hearts and minds have been stirred to feel less alienated and more human by the quiet beauty of the Song of Solomon, by the tragic suffering of a Job or an Oedipus, or by the derring-do of a Beowulf. The imagination of each generation is captured by its own poets. Homer, Chaucer, Shakespeare, Tennyson, Longfellow, and Whitman spoke to their contemporaries in the idioms and the symbols of their day. Where Bob Dylan sings the language of today's youth, their parents were moved by Robert Frost and Carl Sandburg. Just as the classics are best understood through a fresh translation for every succeeding generation, so does each popular poet arouse and intensify the feelings of his contemporaries by means of the current symbols of love and hate, hope and despair.

Once we begin to deal with effecting changes in feelings, we have already moved close to the purposes and intent of psychotherapy. When we consider further that words and language are the means by which those purposes and intentions are to be realized, we have already enumerated two basic ingredients of both poetry and psychotherapy—feelings and language.

It is not at all surprising that in his day the amazing Aristotle had something to say of poetry therapy. Writing in reference to a particular species of poetry—tragedy—he observed in the *Poetics* that the passions pity and terror could be corrected and refined. *Katharsis* is the word he used. Butcher states that Aristotle's use of the word implies the "expulsion of a painful and disquieting element"[1]; it is a homeopathic cure in that pity and fear are first aroused by poetic tragedy and then purged together with the latent pity and fear that were brought to the poetic experience.

Poetry of one kind or another has in fact been such an ancient and universal nostrum for ministering to hurt minds and baleful moods—from the earliest incantations of the tribal priests and medicine men to the vast outpourings of Tin Pan Alley and our modern rock and folk minstrels—that we have been even less consciously aware of its restorative powers than of nature's subtle way of healing a cut finger.

One can only speculate how it came to pass that the ancient Greeks conceived Apollo to be the god of both poetry and medicine. Somehow in their ancient wisdom they must have perceived the relationship between poetry and the art of healing. Thousands of years later, in the middle of the twentieth century, Smith and Twyeffort[2] assert that literature may be used as an aid in treating mental illness by helping the patient obtain a better knowledge of himself and his reactions, thereby improving his total life-adjustment. Between Apollo and the *Cyclopedia of Medicine*, we can only guess at the untold number of souls that the bards have comforted and at how much insight and hope they have given to those perplexed in spirit. The long parade of gleemen, scops, minstrels, balladeers, folksingers and sophisticated poets ministered to the despondent and the defeated, comforted the lonely and the lovelorn, and understood the hostile and the hateful. With venom and rancor drawn off, love and hope could move in.

The belief that a therapeutic essence resides in the nature of poetry has, in recent years, stirred some mental health practitioners to seek out and explore more highly conscious and organized uses of poetry in the service of psychotherapy. On the contemporary scene, the first to search actively for the healing principle in poetry was the late Eli Greifer, who, about 35 years ago, began to write therapeutic poems, later published as *Psychic Ills and Poemtherapy* and *Poems for What Ails You*. In 1959, Greifer used poetry therapy at Creedmoor State Hospital, Queens Village, New York, and subsequently formed a poetry therapy group at Cumberland Hospital in Brooklyn, together with Dr. Jack J. Leedy, psychiatrist, Director of the Mental Hygiene Clinic at Cumberland. Greifer used poetry to help patients develop a philosophy of life that would help them adjust to their misfortunes.

> Patients help to select poems, read them aloud individually or in unison, in some cases memorize them; they carry on group discussions of the poet's life and work, are also encouraged to write poems for the group. Combined poetry and music therapies are developed in group singing of psalms, hymns and poems set to music.[3]

Greifer rejected the cynicism and obscurantism of "modernists" like T. S. Eliot and his followers and exhorted his poetry groups to dispel gloom and depression, to seek out joy and happiness through constructive attitudes and approaches. He prescribed poems with "a noble and healthy outlook on life"[4] and advocated memorizing poetry whose themes center on the basic verities found in such poetry as Longfellow's. He himself had written therapeutic poetry that urges his readers and listeners to strive for the satisfaction and serenity to be found in "the balm of accomplishment and glad images from many happily worded, cheerful-toned songs."[5]

Dr. Smiley Blanton has written of the power of poetry to help his patients when they have felt overwhelmed, frustrated, defeated, depressed, angry, anxious or bereaved. He used poetry with individual patients as an ancillary therapy to buoy their flagging spirits through the use of direct encouragement, hopeful examples, and exhortation, and he urged his patients to memorize certain poems to help carry them through times of crisis. He recommended specific poems to counteract certain moods. For example, when you need courage he recommends Henley's "Invictus" or Joaquin Miller's "Columbus"; when you must leave someone dear, Shakespeare's "Parting is such sweet sorrow" or Byron's "When we two parted"; when you're anxious, Eliot's "Love Song of J. Alfred Prufrock."

Leedy[6] believes that the isoprinciple, which Dr. Ira M. Altshuler advocates in music therapy, can be used effectively in poetry therapy as well. The principle of selecting music to correspond with the patient's mood or mental tempo translates, in terms of poetry therapy, into selecting sad and gloomy poems for depressed patients.

Although I agree with Dr. Leedy that "the poem becomes symbolically an understanding someone with whom the patient can share his despair"[7] and that it is helpful if "depressed patients feel that they are not alone in their depression," I feel that the patient cannot be left in a morass of despondency from which the poet gives no indication of his ability to extricate himself. If the patient is to benefit by borrowing from the ego of the poet, he can borrow successfully only if the poet demonstrates that he himself is not emotionally bankrupt. The patient is more likely to respond constructively to a poem in which the poet reveals that he has suffered the same loss, despair, frustration, or loneliness as the patient, *but* in grappling with the problem has somehow managed to surmount the obstacles that seemed to be staring him in the face; somehow the poet has won through— or hopes to. By writing of the fact that he has experienced the same kind of suffering and has lived through the same purgatory that the patient is now experiencing, the poet is now qualified to serve as a counselor and to hook into the patient's private line of communication.

Having established some degree of communication, to what psychic level is the poet, abetted by the therapist, addressing himself? It is to the level of wish-fulfilling thought, extending into the realm of the primary process. It is to the need of the patient to be well, healthy, adequate, strong, accepted, loved. The poetry therapy session has become a crucible in which an elixir of attention, acceptance and affection is brewed. The poem provides the basic ingredients. The patients add many of their own. The therapist becomes associated with the empathic expression in the poem and is perceived to possess the same kind of understanding that is extended to the helpers in Alcoholics Anonymous or in Synanon, by those who have been "there" and returned.

At the Postgraduate Center for Mental Health, the poetry sessions are held in an atmosphere simulating that of a living room. At the beginning of the session, from 8 to 16 or 17 members may be present, and others may drift in later. Sometimes new members wander in uncertainly, but introductions are made usually at the beginning, sometimes at the end, of the session. One mimeographed sheet containing three or four poems is given to each person present. Occasionally, when it is impossible to get the mimeographing done on time, a therapy session may be held successfully by the therapist's reading the poem aloud twice clearly and slowly, supplemented by reading again certain lines of the poem that come under discussion. But the choice of poems under these circumstances becomes more critical; they must not be difficult to understand or else the therapist will find himself having to restate the poem in his own words, and too much of its effect will be lost thereby. Some verses by Robert Service were presented orally on two occasions and were successfully received and discussed, but there is little doubt that it is best to present each group member with a copy of the poems for ready reference as needed.

The poem should be read well, with proper attention given to creation of the appropriate mood. When you finish reading the poem, you are invariably met with an unknowable silence. Of course, you experience your own feelings and reactions, but you can't be sure how the others have responded. A good opening is to ask, "How do you like it?" or "How do you feel about it?" or "How does it make you feel?"—or some such question that gives the members a chance to blow about some of the surface foam that the poem may have churned up. You can almost do a round robin on this question; almost everyone will have some reaction, even if only "It leaves me cold." The technique of singling out someone to respond is to be used sparingly. At times, however, a response may be teased out through the silence by quietly joining glances with someone for whom you suspect the poem may have had some special meaning.

It has seemed rewarding to permit as many as wish, to respond to the initial question. Having expressed whether they like the poem, they have made some kind of emotional deposit and are more likely to involve themselves in protecting their investment. After several sessions, the group catches onto the opening gambit, and subsequently, more often than not, the discussion is launched without the need of putting a question. Questions will be asked immediately about unfamiliar vocabularly, difficult syntax or ambiguities. Unfamiliar words should be quickly and simply explained; it is advisable to give readily understood synonyms as footnotes on the mimeographed sheet of poems. The therapist should bridge any syntactical obscurities by simply providing an easily comprehensible restatement. Our purpose is not to exercise the intellectual faculties or to improve vocabulary, nor are we bent on giving a course on "How to understand poetry." In the initial stage of the session, the therapist should be intent on zeroing in on the emotional theme of the poem. Of course he has a fairly good approximation of what this theme is, at least for himself. How it will unfold for each group member is at this juncture an open question—and must remain so till each one tips his hand.

Frequently the discussion of a poem will veer off in a direction that the therapist did not dream of when he selected the poem. Let it digress; others in the group may follow the vein, because meaningful associations have been aroused. Other patients, sensing the irrelevant digression, may become impatient and attempt to return to the poem's theme. I remark that we are more concerned here with the members' problems than the poem's, and this usually serves to encourage everyone to draw on extra reserves of indulgence to maintain the cohesiveness of the group.

It is the therapist's job to encourage the development of a nonjudgmental atmosphere. Criticism of others may develop in the initial stage because of varying interpretations of what the poem means. The therapist's approach here may be to point out that every reader recreates a poem in the light of his own storehouse of memories and experiences. "What does it mean for you?" and "Why can't it mean something different for him?" are questions that serve to encourage an accepting attitude.

Herein lies a significant difference between the English class and the poetry therapy session: the first objective of the English class is to determine the poem's meaning, of the poetry therapy session to seek the meaning that the poem has for the various members. There may be as many meanings as there are persons, and each meaning is valid in the context of the individual's peculiar experiences.

At times, when a multiplicity of feelings is being grappled with, when members tend to talk at each other instead of with one another and value judgments are expressed that may, unchecked, readily lead into personal attacks, it is apparent that we have moved into a stage where the basic dynamics of group interaction are about to operate. The potential for this development is always present, and the therapist should be prepared with some formulation whether the approach will be group-centered, i.e., functioning essentially as in group therapy; poem-centered, i.e., focusing on the content and meaning of the poem from the poet's point of view; or patient-poem centered, i.e., emphasizing the patient's exploration of his own feelings in the context of his past and current experiences as these feelings and experiences are made conscious by the stimuli of the poem. In the Living Room, the latter method has been fruitful. We do not countenance the use of one member by another as a target for hostile transference, although in other settings this reaction is an admissable development in the therapeutic process.

Whatever the clinical option of the therapist may be, the interaction of the patient, the poem, and the group has drawn the patient into the stream of human thought and feeling. The poem serves as a catalytic agent. Since the poet is the first to reveal the secret world of his own feelings at the begining of the session, the awkward moments of hesitation frequently experienced at the beginning of the traditional group therapy session are readily circumvented. The poet's feelings function as a resonator in the patient's psyche, where corresponding fragments of memory and experience start to vibrate sympathetically, are shaken loose from their submerged moorings, and rise to the surface where they can be looked at in the daylight of reality. What previously seemed guilt-provoking or "sick" to the patient becomes less reprehensible or abnormal through the process of ventilation.

Just how poetry functions in the therapeutic process is a moot question. There are few research data to serve as a basis for a theory; we are at the stage of hypothesis and speculation. Recent research in dreams reported by Diamond[8] points to the therapeutic function that dreaming serves. Could not the effective therapeutic agent in poetry be similar to what exists in the dream process? Is the stuff that dreams are made on the same as that poetry is woven from? The poem and the dream both originate in the unconscious; both are created by "the spontaneous overflow of powerful feelings." Both rely on the "suspension of disbelief." Whether it be the *willing* suspension of disbelief, as in the hearer of the poem, or the *unwilling* suspension, as in the dreamer, in both instances the processes of reality-testing are either completely disregarded or kept waiting in the wings. The hearer and the dreamer, by suspending or short-circuiting reality, are able to make more immediate contact with their id wishes and their basic drives. In the dream, this is accomplished by paying little heed to the bonds of reality—time, space, and causality. In literature, long before our twentieth century surrealists, writers could not be contained by the so-called dramatic unities of time, place, and action. The Elizabethan dramatists gloried in violating them, and the poets, on a magic carpet of language, have been transported on surrealistic trips without benefit of LSD. As Emily Dickinson has put it,

> There is no Frigate like a Book
> To take us Lands away
> Nor any Coursers like a Page
> Of prancing Poetry—

Perhaps the most remarkable similarity between poetry and dreams is in the fusion mechanisms that both employ. The figures of speech of poetic diction—metaphor, metonymy (use of an associated attribute for the thing meant), and synecdoche ("the mention of a part when the whole is to be understood": Fowler's *Modern English Usage*)—and the processes of the dream world—condensation, displacement and symbolization—are so similar in their treatment of time, space, and the things of reality that one is obliged to consider whether they are not basically the same mental operations. In other words, the reality criteria of the secondary process—cause and effect, logic and reason, time and space—are circumvented through the use of poetic diction. The patient enters the world of primary process—of dreams and wishes, urges and drives, hates and loves, turmoil and fulfillment. But it is a *willing* suspension of reality testing. And he can explore this cave as deeply as he wishes; having entered willingly, he can return whenever he wishes. The rungs of reality are always within arm's reach, and he can readily scramble back through one ego-defense or another: "I disagree with the poet's point of view." "What he says doesn't hold water." "This poem has nothing to do with me."

The poem may touch off a series of psychic events that contribute to the patient's feeling of well-being in a way similar to what is experienced after having been involved in a creative act. In the creative process, the magnet of unconscious interest[9] scans the storehouse of memories and their associated affects, attracting the image experiences related to the conscious theme. The organizing ego so molds and shapes these into a communicable form that other egos that perceive reality in a somewhat similar fashion can sense the poet's ideation and affective messages. Thus it is the world of reality that provides the standard datum that serves as the common medium enabling the patient's unconscious to receive stimuli from the poet's unconscious. The poet's affective theme now serves as a magnet that performs a similar function in the patient's unconscious, bestirring early feelings related to the poet's theme. These feelings coalesce and rise to the surface facilitated by the group setting, sometimes taking the form of highly charged verbal productions, sometimes stopping just short at the preverbal level, where meaningful integrations can still be made.

Thus the patient has shared in a process of re-creation. The poet's affect-images have served as condensation nuclei to which the patient's vaporous and troubled feelings were drawn and given a form more acceptable, conscious, and functional. Perception has been expanded, doubt and uncertainty reduced, feelings validated, and guidelines underscored. A feeling of well-being usually pervades the atmosphere at the end of a poetry session because, I believe, each member feels that he has participated in a creative process. For a brief period he feels he has felt a human feeling that was his very own. For a while he was "with it," in and of the world of human feeling. He has established a beachhead on the shore of a troubled sea and now has the hope of being able to fan out in many new directions.

The presentation of didactic poetry that undisguisedly urged a moral course of action on the reader almost invariably raised hostile reactions from a subgroup, which resented either *1.* the assumption of superiority, 2. the arrogance of the poet, or *3*. the perceived attempt to impose a parent-child structure on the poet-reader relationship. The protests against the dictates of the poet-authorities had the quality of pained cries provoked by the poking into old wounds obtained in authority conflicts.

This type of poem served chiefly to arouse abreactions associated with the authority theme and to stimulate attempts to resolve this conflict. Invariably a poem of this type divided the group into two opposing camps, with each member loyally returning to the same standard he had previously defended. Though poems of the didactic type were significantly less successful in eliciting emotions from the deeper psychic levels—except in connection with the authority theme—I would still occasionally include one of them. They, too, seem to serve a therapeutic purpose. Some they seem to inspire; others they provoke; and still others seem to respond in a style resembling identification with the aggressor. All of these reactions are grist for the therapeutic mill. It is my impression that the following types of personalities are more likely to accept the precepts, dicta, and moralizings of didactic poems: *1*. dependent personalities who have not extricated themselves from old symbiotic ties, who form quick transferences to those who assume the mantle of authority, e.g., the unfaltering voice of the poet; *2*. people who think of themselves as highly moral, who harbor a deep conviction that good deeds will eventually be rewarded and evil punished by an Omnipotent One; *3*. immature personalities.

One of the poems that we worked with was by Louis Ginsberg. (I discontinued giving the name of the poet when I discovered that often some of the patients would seize on the poet's relation to the poem in order to resist their personal involvement.) It extols the pleasure derived from self-denial:

HUNGER AND THIRST[10]

Of all the fruits I ever pluck
   To try to feed my fill,
The plum I leave upon the bough
   Remains the sweetest still.

· · · · ·

The sweetest kiss I ever had
Was one I did not take.

· · · · ·

> So, in the feast that I will set,
> Before my life will sink,
> Hunger will be the richest food;
> And thirst, the sweetest drink!

Some of the reactions and interactions may give an idea of the process that takes place during a typical session. One patient remarks that she agreees with the poet that the contemplation of the ideal fantasy yields greater pleasure than the real satisfaction of the appetite. Most of the group, however, chose not to dwell on this theme. They respond more keenly to the undercurrents of self-denial, delay of gratification, and forbidden pleasure. Another one says, "This poem reminds me of nibbling around a prune Danish to delay eating the delectable center." Still another responds, "What happens if you take too long and the center goes rotten before you get there?" The first says: "It's like the pleasure you get in delaying the orgasm. You prolong the sexual act. It could be good, it could be bad, depending on the condition of your heart."

Another says: "In this poem you don't have the orgasm, you're just left at the dock as the ship goes by. You're just waving goodbye, and just standing there."

One of the patients bursts out: "Why, that's pure masochism!" Someone else quietly agrees: "It's like a sweet lie—it's a kind of tale we tell ourselves." Another is not entirely convinced by the attack on the poem. She says: "When I have a place to go to I sometimes linger on the way. Maybe I stretch out the time anticipating the pleasure to have more pleasure."

This last speaker is supported by a young woman who says: "I dread attaining my [Ph.D] degree." She is delaying the completion of her thesis, she says, because she is afraid its completion would leave a void in her life. Someone points out that she probably had plans to do something with her degree. Wouldn't those plans take up the slack?

One member says: "It's a sort of disallowed life. When the children are sent to bed when the grownups are having a party, they sneak down on the stairway and peek through the balustrade and they see the grownups having a party. It has something of that nature, especially when he says, 'Horizons are horizons when we view them from afar.'" At another point she says: "A woman's life consists of waiting. By nature she has to wait nine months for her children to be born; she waits for her children to come home; she waits for the clothes to dry on the line; she does a lot of waiting all the time. Waiting," she concludes, "is starved living."

No rigorous evaluation of the year's work was attempted. Nine or ten members attended almost every week throughout the entire year. Usually, at the end of the session, they would adjourn to a nearby cafeteria to prolong their enjoyment of each other's company and to continue the evening's discussion over a cup of coffee. Genuine expressions of appreciation were frequent for the opportunity to participate in the poetry sessions. One member credited them with overcoming her writing block. She had recommended writing excellent poetry after many years of inactivity. Another discovered a talent for translating poems from the French; her translations served to trigger some of our most fulfilling sessions, although her appreciation of the poetry sessions alone would have been reward enough. Others often brought their original poems, which were always read and discussed, and they were invariably most rewarding. One disturbed young man was "hung up" on an unresolved relationship with his now deceased father. He would occasionally deflect the flow of the discussion by extraneous references to his special problem. The other members, sensing a special difficulty, at times attempted to help him by going along with his digressions; at other times, engrossed in their own themes, they would deal with him more abruptly. One gray-haired lady came religiously to every session, although she responded to only the most easily understood poems. Occasionally I would tell the members of the group that they need not understand everything in the poem, and I would try always to anticipate difficult lines that could be readily clarified.

One member, a 38-year-old bachelor who rarely missed a meeting, felt that the poetry session was "the high spot of the week," which, to him, was a series of days of otherwise unremitting dullness. Another member, a shy, sensitive, quiet young woman, wrote at the end of the year to say that she felt much better and that the poetry sessions had "helped me the most."

Whatever the therapeutic principle may be in the use of poetry in a group setting—the facilitation of catharsis, the sharing of common experiences in an accepting atmosphere, or the feeling of having participated in an act of re-creation with contributions from one's own "storehouse of memories and experience"—the comments and reactions of the patients and my observations point to the conclusion that the method helps to lift the cover to a deep well of feelings, which can then be discussed, dealt with, and integrated; that the patients can unburden themselves of these feelings in an accepting, nonjudgmental atmosphere; that they can express sad and joyous feelings without retribution; that, at a certain time each week, they can share, if they wish, some hitherto unexpressed feeling or look together through a new window.

REFERENCES

1. Butcher, S. H., *Aristotle's Theory of Poetry and Fine Art*, (New York, Dover, 1951) p. 255.
2. Smith, L.H. and Twyeffort, L.H., "Psychoneuroses: Their origin and treatment," in Piersol, G. M., and Bortz, E. L., eds.: *The Cyclopedia of Medicine, Surgery and Specialties*, XII (Philadelphia, Davis, 1945).
3. "Poetry and Medicine," in MD: Med Newsmagazine *8*:144 (#7, July) 1964.
4. Greifer, E., "Principles of Poetry Therapy" (New York, Poetry Therapy Center, 1963) p. 16.
5. *Ibid.*, p. 17.
6. Leedy, J. J. "Poetry Therapy, A New Ancillary Therapy in Psychiatry" (New York, Poetry Therapy Center, 1966) p. 7.
7. ———, Unpublished paper, 1966, p. 1.
8. Diamond, Edwin, *The Science of Dreams* (New York, Macfadden-Bartell, 1963), pp. 113 ff.
9. Sharpe, E. F., *Dream Analysis* (London, Hogarth Press, 1961) pp. 42ff.
10. Ginsberg, L., in Lieberman, E., ed.: *Poems for Enjoyment* (New York, McGraw-Hill, 1931) p. 101.

IN THE THERAPIST'S OFFICE

Poetry as Therapy—and Therapy as Poetry

MILTON M. BERGER, M.D.

Believing that it is hardly sufficient in itself for the emotionally ill, I do not practice poetry therapy per se. But I have used it for nearly 20 years. For a psychoanalytically oriented psychotherapy to be an artistic as well as a scientific process, it must find its authentic form and texture in a living, creative manner, as therapist and patient(s) relate and communicate. Practicing a psychotherapy in which a continuous diagnostic assessment is integrated with an ongoing working-through of obstructive psychopathologic forces, I have found that poetry brought creatively into the therapeutic situation benefits patients.

Experience has taught me that poetry, created or used during the psychotherapeutic encounter, can often help a patient to reach levels of emotional insight more adequately than conventional dialogue. It enriches the encounter by allowing the patient to identify with other human beings, who have experienced similar conflicts, anxieties, and feelings, and who have been able to state, for all humanity, a universal theme or dilemma.

Therapy is a process akin to life for exposing, exploring, experiencing, mixing, uniting, or integrating the

conscious and the unconscious
concrete and the abstract
feeling and the thought
specific and the general
past and the present
individual and the universal
earthbound and the space-probing

personal and the impersonal
everyday and the unusual
rational and the irrational,
and
what is not yet considered rational
or irrational, although it is
perceivable, being, becoming.

All of these processes are also components of the poetic process. The naked and refined imagery, symbols, rhythm, rhyme and flow in poetry may be therapeutic in life* or in psychotherapy, when the poetic statement clarifies for emotional and/or intellectual understanding and integration a universal experience in a manner comprehensible to the patient-person in one or several levels of his being.

As an aspect of the total psychotherapeutic spectrum, poetry may hope to create order where chaos existed, whether the chaos is in the patient himself or in his relationship with others, including the therapist.

> *If I am not for myself, who is for me?*
> *And being only for my own self, what am I?*
> *And if not now, when?*
> —THE TALMUD

These questions, attributed to Rabbi Hillel,[1] I often share in therapy—with a new patient, perhaps, to say who I am, that is, to give my attitudes, beliefs, values. I imply, and often state openly, that my patient has the choice to remain and work in psychotherapy with one who tries to live by and with such values, or to leave and find another therapist with different values. Patients frequently ask: "How will I know? How can I learn when you should be for yourself and when for others? I am confused." They are asking for a pat answer to obtain structure from me, the authority figure, concerning what is one of the most difficult dilemmas in the existence of every man—that is, each and every man with sensitivity and feeling for others and not for just himself. All this in a world in which John Donne, the Dean of St. Paul's, has admonished us:

> Any man's death diminishes me, because I am involved in mankind, and therefore never send to know for whom the bell tolls; it tolls for thee.[2]

Classically, psychotherapy was considered the "talking cure." Spoken words bring to the listener not only the impact of the meaning of and "free associations" to the words themselves, but also the impact of sound, pitch, rhythm, timbre, accent, aliveness or deadness, feelingness or flatness, and other qualities that affect the listener and the relationship between the speaker and the listener. To bring to the psychotherapeutic encounter symbolic communications other than

---

*"Fortunately, psychoanalysis is not the only way to resolve inner conflicts. Life itself remains a very effective therapy." Karen Horney: *Our Inner Conflicts*, New York: Norton, 1945.

those inherent in the traditional talking cure serves, then, to enhance the probability of a successful outcome in psychotherapy. Such augmentation can occur:

a. through the patient's writing and reciting his own poetry, or poems written by others, or poetry that has stirred him emotionally or intellectually;

b. through the therapist's sharing a poetic line or couplet that comes to him during a psychotherapeutic session with a patient or group, or by the therapist's acknowledging his appreciation of a poetic utterance by the patient or himself;

c. by bringing into the individual or group seession a passage of a poet's writings. A poem that is appropriate and in context to the process and content of the psychotherapeutic hour can be shared. If the therapist is able to trust his patient with himself, he can even use his own poetry.

Another possibility, which I stumbled on recently in working with a 72-year-old presenile patient who had not prepared himself for his declining years, was to write poetry during our session. I encouraged him to write a poem to his wife for their 50th wedding anniversary while I wrote one to my wife, not for our 50th wedding anniversary. He required stimulation, guidance and support en route, as well as repeated assurance that his creative production was in fact worth receiving as an expression of sentiment from him.

Poetry as Therapy

A capacity for appropriateness in timing is a *sine qua non* for successful living and for successful psychotherapy. Timing for some persons is more natural, easy and accurate than it is for others; and often based on intuitive awareness and integration of "what? and how? here and now," is going on intrapsychically and interpersonally and how this relates to past events and people.

During the course of individual or group psychotherapy, situations arise between my patients and me, or in the lives of one or more patients, that suddenly bring to mind the statement of Ecclesiastes. And then I recommend to my patient that he look up Ecclesiastes on his own, or go to my bookshelf for the Bible:

> For everything there is a season, and a time for
> every matter under heaven:
> a time to be born, and a time to die;

> a time to plant, and a time to pluck up what is planted;
> a time to kill, and a time to heal;
> a time to break down, and a time to build up;
> a time to weep, and a time to laugh;
> a time to mourn, and a time to dance;
> a time to cast away stones, and a time to gather stones together;
> a time to embrace, and a time to refrain from embracing;
> a time to seek, and a time to lose;
> a time to keep, and a time to cast away;
> a time to rend, and a time to sew;
> a time to keep silence, and a time to speak;
> a time to love, and a time to hate;
> a time for war, and a time for peace.

Kahlil Gibran's lines regarding time are helpful for those who overemphasize either the past or the future.

> Yet the timeless in you is aware of life's timelessness,
> And knows that yesterday is but today's memory
> and tomorrow is today's dream.
>
> But if in your thoughts you must measure time into seasons, let each season encircle all the other seasons,
> And let today embrace the past with remembrance
> and the future with longing.[3]

For patients who are unable to sense that a present opportunity is perhaps crucial in their lives, and that this exact moment is one in which they may be the right person in the right place to risk constructively moving their own and others' growing edge forward, I turn to Shakespeare's lines from *Julius Caesar* (IV, 3):

> There is a tide in the affairs of men,
> Which, taken at the flood, leads on to fortune;
> Omitted, all the voyage of their life
> Is bound in shallows and in miseries.

In working with individuals—married couples particularly—and families, I often turn to my bookshelves for T. S. Eliot's *The Cocktail Party*.[4] Having just experienced a moment in which a patient, a couple, or a family have been expressing their frustrations due to the non-fulfillment of the neurotic claims that they make on others and on life, i.e., expecting what they have a right only to hope for, I read them the following passage, its essence spoken in the play by Sir Harcourt-Reilly, the "priest psychiatrist":

> *Celia:*   But what, or whom I loved,
> Or what in me was loving, I do not know,
> And if that is all meaningless, I want to be cured
> Of a craving for something I cannot find
> And of the shame of never finding it.
> Can you cure me?
> *Reilly:*   The condition is curable.
> But the form of treatment must be your own choice:
> I cannot choose for you. If that is what you wish,
> I can reconcile you to the human condition,
> The condition to which some who have gone as far as you
> Have succeeded in returning. They may remember
> The vision they have had, but they cease to regret it,
> Maintain themselves by the common routine,
> Learn to avoid excessive expectation,
> Become tolerant of themselves and others,
> Giving and taking, in the usual actions
> What there is to give and take. They do not repine;
> Are contented with the morning that separates
> And with the evening that brings together
> For casual talk before the fire
> Two people who know they do not understand each other,
> Breeding children whom they do not understand
> And who will never understand them.
> *Celia:*   Is that the best life?
> *Reilly:* It is a good life. Though you will not know how good
> Till you come to the end. But you will want nothing else,
> And the other life will be only like a book
> You have read once, and lost. In a world of lunacy,
> Violence, stupidity, greed... it is a good life.

Though this passage may initially be experienced as cynical, resigned or hopeless, repeated experiencing of its meaning may lead one to appreciate its reality-oriented validity. Mature family life requires us to appreciate that perfect fulfillment of our wishes and wants by others is not the common experience of earth-bound creatures.

A colleague[5] informs me that he often shares Dostoevski's phrase, "Hell is the condition of those who cannot love,"[6] and often brings into therapy sessions Hamlet's soliloquy, "To be or not to be...." Sometimes he uses that alone; at others he finds it is appropriate to continue with more: "Whether it is nobler in the mind to suffer/The slings and arrows of outrageous fortune,/Or to take arms against a sea of troubles,/And by opposing end them (III, 1)."

And he confronts his alcoholic patients with their need to blur out reality rather than to face it by quoting Housman,[7]

> "Terence, this is stupid stuff:
> Look into the pewter pot
> To see the world as the world's not."

In family group therapy, when parental overprotectiveness and domination are a key theme, I sometimes turn to Gibran's *The Prophet*[8] and read his "Children," simple to comprehend even by patients without a college education or special capacities for abstract thinking:

> Your children are not your children.
> They are the sons and daughters of Life's longing
> for itself.
> They come through you but not from you,
> And though they are with you yet they belong
> not to you.
>
> You may give them your love but not your
> thoughts,
> For they have their own thoughts,
> You may house their bodies but not their souls,
> For their souls dwell in the house of tomorrow,
> which you cannot visit, not even in your dreams.
> You may strive to be like them, but seek not to
> make them like you.
> For life goes not backward nor tarries with
> yesterday.

In psychotherapeutic sessions with couples or groups of couples, I often refer to Gibran "On Marriage"[9]:

> But let there be spaces in your togetherness,
> And let the winds of the heavens dance between
> you.
>
> Love one another, but make not a bond of love:
> Let it rather be a moving sea between the shores of
> your souls.

Fill each other's cup but drink not from one cup.
Give one another of your bread but eat not from
   the same loaf.
Sing and dance together and be joyous, but let each
   one of you be alone,
Even as the strings of a lute are alone though they
   quiver with the same music.

Give your hearts, but not into each other's keeping.
For only the hand of Life can contain your hearts.
And stand together yet not too near together:
For the pillars of the temple stand apart,
And the oak tree and the cypress grow not in each
   other's shadow.

Gibran has an unusual gift for so communicating the paradoxes of life that clarity arises from confusion, separateness and togetherness can abide in the same house, and self-interest and others' interest can coexist.

Therapy as Poetry

A number of people, I have found, can't stand happiness. The minute that something wonderful happens in their lives, they neurotically "louse it up." A sensitive, robust, intelligent man in his thirties, whose "bull in a china shop" manner frequently denied to himself and others appreciation of sensitive delightful moments in everyday living, brought this poem into his psychotherapeutic session one day. Experiencing and writing it attested to his constructive growth in psychotherapy.

ON A NOTE OF DELICIOUSNESS

Did you ever shiveringly tingle?
Oh, wonder, wonder and more wonder
Close your eyes and feel the catch in your throat
Let it spread and engulf you
Sighing makes it go away too soon
Sometimes I can't stand the bubbling
I swallow hard and shorten my breath
I change the swirling into gas, into a contracted sob
I can't deeply fool myself for long

> My inside smile cannot be kept a stranger
> My eyes are betrayed by their own gaze
> My memory laughs and coughs up the contagion
> It is useless to restrain my own happiness
> I'll live without the everpresent proof
> Without the confirmation of the mystery
> There is no enchantment in the detective
> I will not kill my own wonder this time

Implicit is his awareness that past destruction of his moments of happiness had often been accomplished through a compulsive over-intellectualization, a scientific, objective need to know "why?" and to have visible proof before acknowledging his simple feelings to himself. This poem reflects his growing capacity and willingness to be open to finding his total authentic self through uncertainty, exploration, self-discovery and acceptance.

Cases

In the middle of an individual psychotherapeutic session, a 44-year-old guilt-ridden, marginally depressed bachelor professor of economics, who is often paralyzed with anxieties and self-flagellation, asked: "What is my need to torture myself and feel so guilty that I am not perfect when I am confronted with evidence of my real or fancied inadequacies?" This man—the son of an ineffectual, middle-class father and a guilt-provoking, dominating, overprotective mother—has been driven with high motivation for achievement in life in order to fulfill his mother in ways that his father did not, in order to receive his mother's pat on the head for being "such a good boy." In answer to his question, I said, "Because of your mother in you." He immediately burst into the familiar song: "My mother and me,/And baby makes three,/In my blue heaven"—and then laughed a gallows laugh.

Another example of therapy as poetry occured when a 19-year-old sensitive, gifted, introspective, brilliant high-school dropout temporarily terminated her therapy to resume her education in her home town, located some distance from New York. She sent a letter to her group, in which she shared her feelings and reflections about its various members. Her words moved us deeply:

> What is it to care
> > And to make that caring into life?
> I have hidden from that part of myself for so long
> > That it hurts to break the bars that hold me.
> I get cut in my own shattering glass.
> > But it is all right if I don't bleed to death.
> Now the most painful thing is that I can't
> > Call up the voice and tone of my own thoughts.
> Only some images slide by,
> > In faint colors and fade in dark ones.
> I would give you these colors
> > If I could catch and hold them.
> But it is not easy to give
> > That kind of love
> That occurs from
> > Only a thing called living.

However, in that and later group meetings, none of her words touched us so much as "Loneliness is just not being friends with oneself."

Another incident of therapy as poetry occurred in a psychotherapy group when a 38-year-old divorced, self-effacing mother of three children, who had been trapped within the immaturity perpetuated in her by her mother, shrieked to her group: "If only my mother would stop looking at me with old eyes." This poetic reference to being looked at or looking at others with *old eyes* was later used frequently by members of her group and myself. It says much that's deeply felt, in few words, literally and figuratively.

While this same patient was functioning as a help-rejecting complainer, she remarked defensively of her "weekend blues": "But I get so very waterlogged on weekends." About two years later, having made a fair amount of progress from passive-dependent defensiveness to a healthier state of satisfying self-assertiveness, she stated in a demanding fashion to her peer group member Sam, "So start unzipping yourself and open up." This remark followed a period in which Sam had been busy talking, in his own help-rejecting fashion, about his difficulties in sharing a dream that he had the night before.

I have emphasized elsewhere[10]:

> The bringing into the group of one's artistic creation, whether a painting or a poem, may be experienced as a gift to the therapist or group or may indicate increasing trust in others; decrease in fear of criticism or needs to be perfect; a desire to bring out what has been taboo as an expression of

increasing feeling or self; or a patient may feel his back against the wall and be driven to force himself at least to open up this way.

During the period between Thanksgiving and Christmas of 1955, a patient, Harold R., a 33-year-old schizoid mathematician, compulsively intellectual and socially inept, brought to his psychotherapy group three poems that he had recently composed, one entitled "I Dance." Through the imagery of his poetry, he was able to communicate what his compulsive intellectualization and defensiveness had blocked. It had a profound effect on the whole group and, more specifically, his peer interrelationships. All of them felt much closer to him, were more understanding, and were able to accept him and know him better after the reading than they ever had during the two years they had been together.

One group member cried—Esther, a 42-year-old Brooklyn housewife, who had belabored the group for some time with problems concerning her passive-aggressive husband and her overprotected, rebellious daughter—and shared with the group her interest in poetry, which went back 25 years, and particularly the effect on her of the poetry of John Keats. She had never been able to share this interest in poetry with any adult she respected. The group became aware of the presence of a compartmentalized, refined sensitivity in her, whereas they had experienced her primarily as egocentric and impervious to the deep inner feelings of her husband and daughter.

Another group member, Joan, brought to tears, said that experiencing Harold's poetry produced in her a "startle reaction" that triggered a new warmth towards him. Another group member, Mollie, stated, "I don't understand poetry, so my mind wandered." After a pause she continued, "I do not feel very much—*just* that I had more of a feeling for Harold." Mollie's difficulties in acknowledging "what is," both in herself and others, led her to belittle and only begrudgingly to express positive feelings. Sam spoke of how pleased he was at how receptive the whole group had been to Harold's first attempt at poetry, and he felt that he could now risk bringing to the group the following week some of his photography. He did so; and with the group's continued encouragement of his developing and heretofore secret new direction for his creativity, he eventually gave up his work as Executive Secretary for a Foundation and developed his photographic skills so that today his work receives acclaim both artistic and financial.

Conclusion

Years ago, while looking in *Bartlett's Quotations* for the particular Shakespearean line, "All the world's a stage...," I mistakenly looked in the index under the phrase, "Life is a stage." I experienced serendipity. Suddenly, in this moment of failure to find the correct line, I had stumbled on the making of a prose-poem of my own. I simply utilized the material in the index, which begins "Life is...," and through some alterations and some additions of my own, created a "poem":

LIFE IS

This is—is what life is—
Life is a battle
    a blunder and a shame
    a bubble
    a copycat
    a dance
    a disease
    a dream in the night
    a flower
    a foreign language
    a good thing
    a highway
    a jest
    a ladder infinite stepped
    a lie
    a loom and a game of pool

—and on for nearly 100 more lines.

I have used this "poem" with patients during individual and group psychotherapeutic encounters to demonstrate an experience of a creative process, and to share this impression of what *life is*—which is *all and everything*.

Engle and Carrier[11] claim all and everything as the material of poetry:

> Modern poetry is full of things which many readers never saw in verse before: a brickyard, the evening compared to a patient etherized upon a table, politics, rats on a city dump, the terms of psychology. To the modern poet there is nothing in the world which cannot be put into poetry as long as it

can move the reader. For the purpose of poetry is not to provide a soft bed for the tired reader to rest in when he hasn't the strength to do anything more energetic. The purpose of poetry is to expand and intensify your sense of life by giving you examples of one man's look at the intensities of his own life as the intelligence in his head has ordered them into the shape of the poem.

Poems and poetic expressions, created during psychotherapy or brought in from the territoriality of others, can be valuable therapeutic ancillaries. They can express movement, change and growth in intellectual or emotional illiterates, can allow for the evolution of fantasy and imagery towards expansion of one's growing edge, and can sustain and support an individual moving towards a clearer definition of himself, his potentials, and his road towards self-fulfillment.

REFERENCES

1. Rabbi Hillel, *The Talmud, Ethics of the Fathers*, chap. 1, par. 14.
2. Donne, J., "Meditation XVII," *Devotions Upon Emergent Occasions*, London, 1624.
3. Gibran, K., *The Prophet* (New York, Knopf, 1952) pp. 70–71.
4. Eliot, T. S., *The Cocktail Party*, act 2 (New York, Harcourt, 1950) pp. 139–140.
5. Kronmeyer, Robert, Ed.D., Personal communication.
6. Dostoevski, F. M., *Brothers Karamazov*.
7. *A Shropshire Lad*, 62.
8. Gibran, K., *op. cit.*, pp. 21–22.
9. *Ibid.*, pp. 19–20.
10. Berger, M., "Nonverbal communication in group psychotherapy," *Int J Group Psychother* 8:161–178, 1958.
11. *Reading Modern Poetry* (Glenview, Ill., Scott, Foresman and Company, 1955).

IN THE HOSPITAL

Treatment of a Psychotic Patient by Poetry Therapy

With a Historical Note

ROBERT E. JONES, M.D.

At Pennsylvania Hospital, the nation's first, founded by Benjamin Franklin in 1751, mental patients have long participated in many activities designed to alleviate the pains of mental illness. Franklin himself introduced occupational therapy, and Dr. Benjamin Rush, called the Father of American Psychiatry, introduced music and literature as ancillary treatments for psychiatric patients.

The oldest known poem written by a mental patient in an American hospital is recorded in a leather-bound memorandum book written by Samuel Coates, a Manager of the Pennsylvania Hospital from 1785 to 1825. Mr. Coates always carried this diary with him, in which he noted in ink his reflections upon madness and his deductions drawn from his observations of the interesting patients and incidents that came under his notice in the cells and wards for the insane. The poem was written by Richard N., whose lunacy Coates ascribed to "misfortune and disappointment." Born in England and educated at Oxford, the patient had had a series of five failures in business and farming. Coates wrote:: "To be disappointed Five times was more than he could Well bear; he became low spirited, and to cut the Climax short, he became crazy, & *Now* a poor Lunatick in the Pennsylvania Hospital in Which it is expected he Will End his Days." Soon after admission, he wrote the following touching lines to his wife:

> RICHARD TO FRANCES
>
> Depriv'd of Liberty, and left to prove,
> The bitter want of Frances & her love,
> (That love, which wert thou present to bestow,
> Woo'd sweetly sooth thine hapless Richard's Woe,)
> As burden'd with my Grief, I sat to mourn,

> Thy letter came—Ah why not thy Return?
> Why shou'd the fold, which pleas'd I took, contain,
> The Tale of Absence, which encreas'd my pain,
> While I a double weight of Sorrows bear,
> Sever'd from thee, and kept a Pris'ner here!
> Yet if Through Anguish of a tortur'd mind,
> My thoughts, my Acts were faulty or unkind,
> Though great my errors, great has been my Grief,
> And Richard looks to Frances for Relief.
> Think then in Pity, Love and tender care,
> Upon the sufferings I am led to bear
> And seek to set a wretched husband free,
> Who loses but too much, in losing thee.
> To our Dear Children now let me return,
> To use a Parents labour and Concern,
> Long have I felt both able and inclined,
> To try the powers of Body and of Mind,
> In fit employ to pass thy tedious stay,
> Til hap'ly I may see the favor'd day,
> When I may weep for Joy & own me bles't,
> To hide my Anguish, Frances, on thy Breast.

In 1843, mental patients at Pennsylvania Hospital began publishing a hospital newspaper, *The Illuminator*, which they themselves wrote, edited, and hand-copied. It contained articles about current events, editorials on national policies, jokes and anagrams. Because it was done in beautiful manuscript, its production provided useful labor to a number of patients. A visitor, John M. Galt, superintendent of the asylum at Williamsburg, Virginia, said that its "leading articles would compare favourably with much of the periodical literature of the day."

Pennsylvania Hospital was a model institution, and it had raised the use of milieu therapy to its highest peak of achievement. Under the leadership of one of the great psychiatrists of the 19th century, Dr. Thomas S. Kirkbride, a founder and president of the American Psychiatric Association, it provided milieu therapy in all forms: gardening, riding, work, sewing and occupational therapy, museum, sports, and the like. Dr. Kirkbride even provided a herd of tame deer within the hospital grounds.

Here is another quite early poem written by a mental patient at Pennsylvania Hospital, published in *The Illuminator* in 1843. It describes Dr. Kirkbride's deer park and, like many poems written by patients, has notes of sadness and nostalgia.

> Ye free, ye nimble pretty ones
>   As o'er the mead ye stray,
> Ye mind me of departed joys
>   Forever fled away.
>
> You're happy in your little sphere
>   With pasture rich and green,
> With water from the limpid springs
>   And sunshine o'er the scene.
>
> But we, the tenants of these grounds,
>   The prisoners of these walls
> May view you resting in the shade
>   And sigh as it recalls
>
> Our lost estate, our very love,
>   Our mind's sad overthrow,
> Our friends, our family, our homes,—
>   And sink beneath the blow.

Poetry therapy has been used at Pennsylvania Hospital for nearly two centuries.

THE ROAD NOT TAKEN*

Every choice involves a loss. Whenever we make a decision in life, we must give up something, surrender an alternative. Whenever we decide *for* something, we decide *against* something else. Whenever we select one possibility or pathway, we relinquish another. When we make a decision, in our optimistic aggressive culture, usually we think that we are making a gain, picking the best alternative; and we soon forget the pessimistic aspect of decision-making: the object lost, the alternative not chosen, the road not taken.

    It is my belief that emotionally fragile persons, especially psychotic patients, find that the most distressing and tormenting part of

    *This part of Chapter 1 received the first Kenneth E. Appel Award in Psychiatry, presented by the Philadelphia County Medical Society in May, 1965. Here it has been somewhat edited and enlarged.

making decisions is giving up the alternate choice, longing for the course not chosen, clinging to the object that inevitably must be lost.

A psychiatrist might consider that a patient is experiencing ambivalence when he remains rooted at a crossroads. Or he might believe that the patient is experiencing anxiety when he holds fast to a person or way of life that obviously is not so healthful a choice as some other person or way might be. And undoubtedly, he would be right. But nonpsychiatric language often conveys an idea in better words. One of the best expressions of the human decision-making predicament is Robert Frost's poem

THE ROAD NOT TAKEN*

Two roads diverged in a yellow wood,
And sorry I could not travel both
And be one traveler, long I stood
And looked down one as far as I could
To where it bent in the undergrowth;

Then took the other; as just as fair,
And having perhaps the better claim,
Because it was grassy and wanted wear;
Though as for that the passing there
Had worn them really about the same,

And both that morning equally lay
In leaves no step had trodden black.
Oh, I kept the first for another day!
Yet knowing how way leads on to way,
I doubted if I should ever come back.

I shall be telling this with a sigh
Somewhere ages and ages hence:
Two roads diverged in a wood, and I—
I took the one less traveled by,
And that has made all the difference.

The purpose of this chapter is to relate how this poem helped a psychotic patient. The story will be told not as a case history but as a narrative, in the way it became known to me.

*Complete Poems of Robert Frost, New York: Holt, 1949, with permission.

The Encounter

I first met Mrs. H in the Occupational Therapy shop of The Institute of the Pennsylvania Hospital. A small woman with graying blond hair and an intense stare, she approached me quite unexpectedly and asked, quickly, furtively, "Are you Dr. Jones?"

"Yes," I said, hesitant about getting involved with a patient I did not know.

"May I speak with you in private?"

"This time," I replied, "is set aside for working. Although I'd like to be able to talk with you, I'd be more interested now to see what you're doing in the shop."

Mrs. H looked around suspiciously and led me to a loom, where she was weaving a set of place mats. I admired her handiwork and asked how long she had been weaving the mats. But she didn't wish to talk about her work; she asked again if she could talk with me privately. I explained that it was not possible then for me to interview her, but that I was sure her own resident would be glad to discuss her problems with her. At this second rebuff, following her two requests, Mrs. H lowered her head onto the loom and cried.

The Assignment

Several weeks later, Mrs. H's resident went on vacation, and Mrs. H was assigned to my care for one month. My interest in her had already been awakened, because in our one brief encounter I had been impressed with her intensity and sensitivity. Reading her case record, I learned that she was a lawyer by profession and the mother of two children. This was her fourth hospitalization for a paranoid schizophrenic reaction. After her three previous hospital visits, she had returned to her husband and family in a Southern city.

My eagerness to work with Mrs. H led me to present her case to my preceptor and to tell him that I had a plan of therapy in mind. After interviewing her, my preceptor instructed me to obtain the permission of Mrs. H's private therapist before undertaking my program. The private psychiatrist granted permission for me to change the type of tranquilizing medication that Mrs. H was receiving, then said: "Doctor Jones, we haven't been able to do anything for or with Mrs. H for several months. You may try anything you like with her."

Formulation of the Case

I began my association with Mrs. H with a series of three visits to her ward, during which I attempted to establish some kind of rapport with her. On these visits, she was restless, hallucinating, angry. She believed that there was a plot against her in the hospital and that her two children were being held as patients on another ward. She thought that our conversation was being recorded. She demanded her own discharge, but could not state her future plans. Her expression was rigid, flattened, her conversation blocked. But she clenched and unclenched her fists, and behind her immobile face I thought I detected a well of emotion. However, our meetings were fruitless. The nurses complained that Mrs. H was untidy and careless about her dress and would not eat properly. Mrs. H continued her endless demands to leave the hospital. I wondered whether I could be of any value to her.

Through these visits, however, and a daily reading of her chart, I became impressed with two factors: her strong wish, which had reached delusional proportions, to be with her children, and her heightened distress whenever we discussed her husband. With these impressions, I formulated the theory that Mrs. H was in the throes of attempting to decide whether or not to leave her husband, and that under the stress of making the decision, her ego forces had been fractured and her psychosis had developed. Her psychosis, I reasoned, was a reaction to her anxiety about so momentous a decision. I speculated further that Mrs. H was ambivalent about giving up her husband, with whom she had so many arguments, who put her under so much pressure, who placed his own mother ahead of her. She wanted to choose freedom, to return to her law practice, to give more time to mothering her children instead of bickering with her husband; but she had not been able to reconcile herself to the loss of her husband, to surrendering the father of her children, the builder of their home. She was on the horns of a dilemma, and she was paralyzed into inaction by her psychosis.

The Therapy

Her therapy should take the form of learning how to make decisions. I felt I had to teach her the wisdom of Frost's poem. I designed a simple project: making a small blue daisy by gluing ceramic tiles onto a rectangular piece of wood. Carrying the colored tiles, the glue, and the small board, I went to Mrs. H's room and locked us in. Very firmly I told her about our project. I would put glue on the backs of the tiles and direct her where to place them. I made all the decisions: the background was to be white, the leaves green, and the petals blue. However, Mrs. H would have a single decision to make: to decide whether the center of the daisy would be a white tile or a yellow. Mrs. H sighed deeply a few times as we went to work. She did not speak, but eyed me suspiciously.

When we were all finished, Mrs. H selected a white tile and placed it in the center of the daisy. I complimented her on her choice. A few minutes later, however, she removed it and placed a yellow one in the center. Her perplexity mounted and she began to frown. Then I told her that I noticed that she was having trouble making a decision and sticking to it. "It makes me wonder," I said, "if you are having the same trouble trying to decide whether to stay with your husband." I told her that it didn't matter which tile she chose, that this was a minor decision—either tile would be suitable—but that I was going to remain with her until she decided. If she chose the white one, she would have to give up the yellow one, and vice versa. I would see her through this first small decision.

Mrs. H became markedly distressed: she cried; she threw tiles on the floor; she tried to escape from the room or to lie on her bed. She tried to fit both tiles into the space; she tried to throw away both tiles. Always I insisted that she return to the task. I repeated that I knew she was probably trying to make major decisions in her life; she must learn first about making unimportant ones. I pointed out that if she chose one, she would have to give up the alternative. Two hours later, Mrs. H made the final decision. At the end of the time, when she had finally placed a white tile in the center of the daisy, she collapsed onto her bed exhausted. I told her that I would return on the following day with another decision-making task.

On the following day, I brought two birthday cards, which said

"Happy Birthday, Son." I knew that she missed her children and would want to send a birthday card to her adolescent boy. The cards were very similar; her job was to choose between them. The decision was agonizing and time-consuming, and again, after two hours, the patient was exhausted. But at the end of the time, she had written "Love, Mummy" on one of the cards. This was the first message that she had written to her family in four months.

On the third day, I brought two gifts for her son, and demanded that she choose between them. When she was able to choose, after an hour of deciding and revising, I congratulated her heartily on her growing ability to make a choice. I repeatedly pointed out that whenever she chose one thing, she had to surrender the other.

On the fourth day, we began another tile project, more complicated than the first, in which she was permitted to choose all the colors of a multicolored bird. With more conviction at each choice, she began to fill in the design. Also, we began to converse about other things. She told me that she had been unable to eat for several weeks because she could not select foods from the menu, as she had delusioned ideas that the various foods had special meanings for her—for example, that spinach was a message from her son that she could not decipher. She confessed that she had believed for several months that microphones were concealed in the air vents. On that day, when she began to tell me her unrealistic, paranoid fears, I presented her with my volume of Frost's poems. I asked her whether she were really trying to decide to leave her husband, to choose a more independent course in life. She became silent, but nodded her head in assent. I read to her "The Road Not Taken," and left the volume with her.

On the fifth day, I handed her a book about birds, thinking that she could refer to it in selecting colors for her tile project. But she hurled it across the room. Then she explained that her husband was a bird watcher, that the book reminded her of him, and that she was angry at him. She confessed that she had indeed been considering a divorce, and that it was during the process of weighing the decision in her mind that she had become ill.

When, on the sixth day, we walked outside the hospital, she was jubilant. She explained that for months she could not go outdoors, because if she saw a bird or an airplane, she thought it meant that she had to run in that direction in order to get home to her children. This explained why, to the distress of the nurses, she had tried to climb over the hospital wall so many times. On our walk, she made no effort to escape. She was happy, smiling, appropriate in her affect, rational in conversation, and without delusions. She explained that she had approached me on that first day in OT because she had the delusional belief that a Dr. Jones in her native city had sent me to rescue her.

It was exactly one week after she began making decisions again that Mrs. H joined a group of patients on an excursion to the city art museum, the only patient from the disturbed ward who was permitted to go. Thereafter, she was quickly transferred to an open ward, granted grounds and town privileges. All medication was diminished, then stopped. She began to make a dress in Occupational Therapy. In a series of considered interviews, she decided to divorce her husband. She remained free of psychotic symptoms.

Often in our discussions, we mentioned Frost's poem. It became a text. Mrs. H memorized it. When I presented her to my preceptor again, she recited it for him and stated that she believed that she had recovered from her illness because of it. We both agreed that her therapy had consisted of learning how to make decisions, of reconciling herself to the loss involved in every choice, of studying both pathways as well as she could—then choosing one of them.

Six Years Later

Mrs. H returned home to the same family situation that had precipitated her psychosis. She did not feel a need to consult a psychiatrist on a regular basis, but made a plan to return in six months and again in a year to see her Philadelphia psychiatrist for two or three visits. Now, six years later, Mrs. H is still with her family and still free of psychotic symptoms.

Her final decision was a surprise. When she left the hospital, her plan was obtain a divorce, but she chose, instead, to remain with her husband.

It was the *awareness* that she could make a choice that enabled her to remain with her husband and keep her family intact, trying to improve some aspects of their relationship, accepting other aspects. She had used her hospitalization to look down one path as far as she could—then chose the other.

Poetry Therapy with Hospitalized Schizophrenics

KENNETH F. EDGAR, Ph.D., RICHARD HAZLEY, M.A. and HERBERT I. LEVIT, Ed.D.

It is the purpose of this chapter to demonstrate the effectiveness of poetry in therapy with chronic schizophrenic patients at Dixmont State Hospital, Pittsburgh, employing matched groups, one receiving poetry therapy and the other conventional hospital treatment.[1,3,4]

Procedure

Seven patients were selected for their interest in participating, ability to relate verbally, and average or higher intelligence. A control group of five patients was matched with the experimental group in age, education, marital status and hospital diagnosis (Table 1). Therapists Edgar and Hazley visited Dixmont every Thursday for eight months. The seven patients sat at a large round table with the two therapists in a room designated for poetry therapy. Poems were chosen according to Leedy's isoprinciple—i.e., poems that symbolically represented feelings that the patients were unable to deal with successfully[4]—and were used as levers to involve the patients in discussing their feelings.

Evaluation. Pretest batteries were administered to both groups: the Rorschach, WAIS, HTP, Bender, and a psychiatric interview. Although the same battery was intended for the post test, its administration was impossible: all except one patient in the experimental group were either discharged or going home on visits by the end of the experiment.

TABLE 1. *Experimental and Control Groups*

PATIENT	AGE	STATUS	EDUCATION	DIAGNOSIS*	ADMISSION	HOSPITAL-IZATION
				Experimental Group		
Mrs. S	28	Mar	HS Grad	Par Schz	1st	7 yr
Mr. J	33	Sep	HS Grad	Schz (U) Pas-Ag	1st	4½ yr
Miss H	30	Sng	HS Grad	Par Schz	1st	1 yr
Miss C	51	Sng	HS Grad	Par Schz	3rd	8½ yr
Mr. P	29	Sng	HS Grad	Cat Schz	1st	9½ yr
Mr. R	29	Sng	Col 2 yr	Chr U Schz	3rd	4 yr
Mr. M	31	Sng	HS Grad	Cat Schz	1st	7½ yr
				Control Group		
Mr. A	30	Mar	Col 3 yr	Par Schz	1st	6 yr
Mr. C	36	Mar	HS Grad	Par Schz	1st	7 yr
Mr. L	21	Sng	8th Grd	Ac S Schz	1st	4 yr
Mr. E	24	Sng	HS Grad	Sxl dev Chr	1st	4 yr
Mr. S	40	Sng	Col 2 yr	Heb Schz	2nd	8 yr

*Ac, acute. Ag, aggressive. Cat, catatonic. Chr, chronic. Heb, hebephrenic. Par, paranoid. Pas, passive. Schz, schizophrenic. Sxl dev, sexual deviant. U, undifferentiated.

Results

The average patient was 31 years old, single, and a high school graduate, with hospital residence of just over six years. They came from within 50 miles of the hospital, usually from small industrial towns, and had received medications, EST, traditional group and individual therapy. All had at some time hallucinated and/or been delusional, and several had been aggressive. Table 1 indicates the chronicity of their illnesses.

In their usual attitudes, all of these patients were relatively unresponsive to the hospital programs; they showed little or no enthusiasm from day to day. At the conclusion of eight months of therapy that included poetry therapy, hospital personnel noted a decided change. Of the original group of seven, three had been discharged and four were making visits home. Of the control group, one had been discharged; the four others were not permitted home visits, nor were their attitudes more enthusiastic toward hospital routine, Occupational Therapy, Recreation, and the like.

HYPOTHESES

From observing the effect of poetry therapy on the experimental group, one may state certain hypotheses. Poetry is a means to and a vehicle for therapy. It can help to create a mood in which emotions can be shared and responded to by the group, and so can stimulate interpersonal relationships. The participants' writing poems may be viewed as both sublimation and, more important, a means of symbolic externalization closely associated with dreams.[2] Such projected externalizations may circumvent repressive barriers and break through resistances in the group, since the poem appears to be objective. With its apparent objectivity, it can be dissected and used for the acquisition of insight more readily than personal symptoms or behavior. Patients can feel free to be more spontaneous and even critical, and thus there is more verbal and emotional responsiveness with subsequently less repression. Several patients who had previously both avoided and denied their own problems, and certainly could not verbalize them, were able to react to poems by such comments as "That's just how I feel!" This not only was cathartic but also permitted a sharing of common fears that were secret, personal, and festering until this point. With such objective externalization, they found that others shared their torment, and this brought about a common bond. Further, with the vehicle of poetry, interpretations could be made more easily and quickly and with more safety to the individuals and the group, yet with therapeutic results. Clearly, with a minimum of threat, poetry can put a wedge into the pathology and defenses of the psychotic and provide for relatively unthreatening interpersonal relationships, a structured therapy setting without rigidity, and a means of understanding without pressure.

Discussion

1. SIGNIFICANCE OF THE POEM

While the members of this particular group had been chosen from the hospital population because of their ability to relate verbally and their average or higher intelligence, they had had no exposure, with one exception, to poetry beyond the public school level. It was necessary, therefore, to avoid "difficult" poetry with extensive literary allusions, where the effect of the poem might be lost between the reading and the explanation, or where the interest of the patient might be deadened by the presence of material that he could not grasp. The therapist, then, must take into consideration the structure of his group and its literary level in his choice of poetry, otherwise the efficiency of the tool will be reduced or even destroyed.

As the therapy progressed, the significance of choosing the "correct" poems for each occasion became manifest. Several examples may suffice. After several meetings it appeared to the therapists that certain secondary gains provided by hospital life were perhaps affecting the patients' desire to get well. Within the confines of the hospital, the patient was freed from the ordinary exigencies of life. One patient, asked to describe his day, provided the therapist with a picture of total freedom from responsibility.

> I get up in the morning, shave and dress. If I feel like working I go down to my job. If I don't I go back to bed. After lunch I have a Coke, go down to the barbershop, then go back to my room and lie down and listen to the radio.

What was apparent in this account was that the patient enjoyed his routine enough for that enjoyment to operate as a significant deterrent to his wish to get well. The therapists therefore decided to use a poem that expressed the patient's dependence on these secondary gains, "A Prison Gets to Be a Friend" by Emily Dickinson. The discussion following the poem was lively and provocative and seemed to provide the patient and others with some insight into how, at least to some extent, their confinement was a means of avoiding the normal pressures of life. The poem also served as a valuable referent when this particular symptom manifested itself, as it did from time to time.

Another patient, *R*, had been completely dominated by his father, an officer in the US Army, whose practice it had been to have *R* stand at attention after meals and narrate completely the events of the day. If *R* hesitated in his account, his father would strike him sharply on his forehead with the heel of the hand, and call him "Stupid." He used the same "technique" when he attempted to "help" *R* with his lessons. He demonstrated no affection for the boy, his most common interaction being that buffet against the forehead. *R* had been in three mental hospitals, a patient at Dixmont for four years, and had attempted suicide three times. All of his behavior indicated a massive repressed hostility against his father, which R refused to admit. In conversation he praised him, insisted that he had been a good father though a "perfectionist," and refused to admit of even normal failings that a son would attribute to a father. To attempt to demonstrate to the patient the difference between his conception and reality, a poem, in this case again by Emily Dickinson, was chosen. The poem describes a bird struck by a stone thrown by a boy, and concludes:

> Magnanimous as Bird
> By Boy descried—
> Singing unto the Stone
> Of which it died—

Once again the poem, which seemed to fit exactly the needs of the patient, appeared to provide a valuable insight that began the erosion of the false image of the father that was obstructing R's progress. Shortly after that, R wrote a poem of his own, the last line of which is "Illness is the fuehrer." Through simple word association he equated "Fuehrer" with "father," and then, when asked to provide a grammatical analysis of the sentence, said, "Fuehrer is the predicate nominative which means the same thing as the subject, so I guess I am saying that illness is my father." This was the first occasion in which he had been willing to admit such a possibility; it demonstrates not only the effect that a poem may have but the importance of the patient's own writing in demonstrating that effect. One thing further should be noted. In post interviews, patients commented that "it made them feel good" when a poem was brought in especially for one of them.

2. TRANSFERENCE: TWO THERAPISTS

The presence of two therapists rather than one appeared important in the experiment. The manifestations of transfer indicated that patients tended to identify differently with each of the therapists. In the case of a woman patient S, one of the therapists came to be a father figure ("I feel that I can tell you my troubles"), the other assumed the role of her lover and possible husband ("I'd like to take him home with me. We would pack up my clothes, buy a ring, and go somewhere"). With *S*, whose record showed domination by the father and latent or perhaps overt incest, it was felt by the therapists that this dichotomy of lover-father was beneficial. *S* came to regard one of the therapists as a boyfriend, the other as a father figure. It should be noted that in practice one of the therapists tended to involve himself with the patients, sharing his own feelings and anxieties, and the other did not. Thus the differences in transfer made by the patients correspond to the roles played by the therapists, and, in the situation of this experiment, it was felt that the differences made by the members worked to their benefit. It should also be mentioned that those sessions that were conducted by only one therapist were judged significantly less successful. Not only was the group feeling impaired, as though one parent figure were missing, but the therapy could not be maintained at the same level. The pace of the sessions tended to flag, a situation that did not arise when both therapists were present.

3. IMPORTANCE OF MEMORIZATION

Eli Greifer advocated for some time the importance of memorization—what he has termed a psycho-graft—as an important adjunct to poetry therapy. The experiences at Dixmont indicate that memorization is indeed of value. *H* suffered from auditory hallucinations; particularly when working in the laundry, voices would admonish her, saying that she was a bad girl and should have led a better life. It was suggested to *H* that she memorize the last stanza of Henley's "Invictus" whenever she felt the voices might begin. While the memorization did not entirely banish the hallucinations, *H* reported that she was better able to control them and felt less powerless when they did occur. Post interviews indicated that the patients attributed more to memorization than the therapists had realized. *R* reported in post interviews that he had memorized many of the poems and that he "was having important words pumped into him." *M* reported that "memorization helped him from being depressed." Even with the members of the group who did not show an inclination to memorize, copies of the poem used in each session were nearly always requested and the patients reported that they enjoyed reading them. It is the conclusion of the therapists that memorization should be encouraged and that the poems used should be available. Repeating or reading particular poems appeared to have a beneficial effect on the patients in that they provided occupation for their minds and relief particularly during depressed periods.

4. POEMS AS OBJECTIFICATIONS OF THE ILLNESS

One of the premises underlying this experiment—that poetry could be used as a means through which the patient may objectify his feelings—was utilized in several ways. First, the poem, when correctly chosen, provided an immediate incentive for discussion. Thus the warm-up period, which so frequently takes up a significant part of group therapy sessions, was bypassed. Immediately after the brief salutations, the first poem for the session was distributed, read and discussion begun. Even when it served only as a jumping-off point, the poem was the subject for discussion; there was no need to begin with the customary "Well, what shall we talk about today?" Better results are obtained, it should be said, when the poems are so chosen that they provide a continuity and a progression. Second, the poem provides a means for the patient to begin talking about himself indirectly, that is, via the poem. Through this device, disclosures are made that the patient might be reticent to make in direct discussions. The device also, it was felt, brought about a group cohesiveness more rapidly than conventional group therapy does, and the point at which the patient might reveal himself personally arrived sooner than it does through conventional means.

Most important, the therapists felt that poetry has long been a reservoir for the expression of human feelings. It was hypothesized that in the poetry the patient would find both direct and symbolic expression of his own feelings. It was believed that this discovery would accomplish two things: first, the patient would realize that he was not alone in his particular feelings. Thus, the sense of strangeness and alienation that is so much a contributing factor to mental illness would be alleviated. The alleviation would be furthered by the patient's realization that he was encountering feelings not only that he himself had experienced, but that had also been a part of the lives of men who were recognized and of some eminence. Second, seeing these expressions and talking about his response to them, the patient would be enabled to objectify, via the poem, his own personal feelings. Once that was accomplished, then, through discussion, a catharsis and self-realization would begin that would be less possible so long as the patient's feelings remained internal and were dependent on projection for their expression. In this regard, the therapists soon realized that there was a tendency on the part of some of the patients to intellectualize the poem, to talk about the poet's intention rather than their own feelings, or to make references to world history, cultural epochs, and so forth, thus keeping the poem at arm's length. This, of course, is a defensive maneuver that the therapist should curb. Therapists should make an effort to avoid abstractions and to encourage the patient to talk about the specific relationship between himself and the poem.

5. THE IMPORTANCE OF THE PATIENT'S OWN WRITING

One of the most significant and useful features of poetry therapy is the patient's expression through his own writing. Our general procedure was to discuss a poem and then ask the patients to write a few concluding lines that expressed their own feelings, either in opposition to or in agreement with the poem and the discussion. As in the experiment at Slippery Rock College, the poems were judged not on their literary merits, often few, but as an expression of the patients' parapathy. The discussion of the patient's poem was conducted in somewhat the way that a dream would be analyzed. The significance of these poems has already been mentioned in the case of *R*, who wrote "Illness is the fuehrer." Another significant example is *V*, a woman of 28 who had regressed in voice, mannerisms, and attitude to preadolescence, and who had no realization of where she actually was. She wrote, after a discussion:

> In this interior decoration
> There is some congestion
> That squanders in the mind.

In previous sessions, *V* had demonstrated the ability to tap the unconscious and to write highly symbolic and effective lines. In the context of the discussion, the therapists felt these particular lines to be important. Following *V*'s reading of her "poem," she abruptly looked up and said in a voice that was, for the first time, unchildlike, "Where am I? Is this some kind of a nut house or something?" From that time on she showed a heightened awareness and insight, and progressed from a closed to an open ward to an outpatient basis. It was felt by the therapists that the lines she wrote were critical in her progress and were perhaps the precipitating event that brought about her initial contact with reality.

Summary

Seven patients diagnosed as chronic schizophrenic and with an average hospitalization of six years were treated two hours a week for a period of eight months with a group therapy technique involving the use of symbolism in poetry as a lever to release feelings and, hopefully, to bring about catharsis and insight. Three of the patients were discharged within the eight-month period and the other four began making home visits. Those remaining in the hospital were observed to participate more enthusiastically in hospital routine. Of the five controls, one was discharged, four showed no signs of improvement.

REFERENCES

1. Greifer, Eli, "Poetry therapy," *The Brooklyn Psychologist*, September, 1964.
2. Guthiel, Emil A., *The Handbook of Dream Analysis* (New York, Grove Press, 1951).
3. Hazley, Richard and Edgar, Kenneth, "Validation of poetry therapy as a group therapy technique," in *Poetry Therapy*, Chapter 9.
4. Leedy, J. J., "Poetry and Medicine," *MD* Med Newsmagazine, 1964.

The Double Door

Poetry Therapy for Adolescents

ROBERT E. JONES, M.D.

Normal adolescents have more poetry in their lives than any segment of the population other than English professors. Their exposure to it comes mostly in popular songs—simple direct insights made memorable by simple retainable tunes. Every crop of adolescents supports some idol poet-singer, who addresses himself to their problems.

Consider the current hero, Bob Dylan.[1]

What he is saying is getting an unbelievably intense reaction from a generation thirsting for answers other than those in the college textbooks. Students may very well learn more from Dylan today than from the obsolete educational system, structured by another epoch.... In schools all over the country, students are copying down lyrics of Dylan's songs from records and insisting that the English class study them. A Jesuit high school in Sacramento devoted most of an English class one semester last year to the study of Dylan as poetry, and the University of California, like numerous other colleges and universities, has seen students get together themselves to hold unofficial seminars on his poems.... He has taken poetry out to the streets and put it on the juke boxes and brought it into the lives of everyone.... He has discovered how to speak to youth.

Psychiatrists need to speak to youth, too, and therefore must be able to assess the role of poetry in normal adolescent life as well as to use poetry as a therapeutic technique.

The problems common to all adolescents—identity, security, acceptance—seem to find expression in such metaphor as Dylan's. Adolescents entering mental hospitals bring with them this normal interest in poetic forms. It may even be that nervous adolescents have a more intense interest in poetic forms than their better-adjusted peers. "I am handed sheaves of poetry by our patients," said C. Robert Rubenstein, M.D., research director in the adolescent program at Yale

Psychiatric Institute, "and I try to make use of it whenever possible in therapy."

Theory

What is the theoretical basis for the use of poetry—both reading and writing it—in the treatment of emotionally disturbed adolescents? Searching for therapeutic constructs, we can turn to Freud. In "The Poet and Day-Dreaming,"[2] Freud relates creative writing and the use of fantasy to the imaginative play of childhood: "The writer does the same as the child at play; he creates a world of phantasy which he takes very seriously; that is, he invests it with a great deal of affect, while separating it sharply from reality. Language has preserved this relationship between children's play and poetic creation." The child, in his course toward adulthood, learns to conceal his fantasies as being "childish" and "prohibited," because he learns that as an adult "he is expected not to play any longer or to day-dream, but to be making his way in a real world." But the pleasure of fantasy life persists, even in adulthood, and can be indulged only in certain acceptable ways. Imaginative writing is one of the ways. "Imaginative creation, like day-dreaming, is a continuation of and substitute for the play of childhood," and the artful writer can put us "into a position in which we can enjoy our own day-dreams without reproach or shame."

On the pathway from childhood to adulthood, then, the child learns to convert his wish-fulfilling play into the private exercise of daydreaming, which he can legitimately enjoy as an adult in the form of literature, poetry and song. The period of learning to conceal daydreams and to deal with them in mature ways is, of course, adolescence. For normal adolescents, poetry has a universal appeal because it provides an obviously acceptable means of dealing with fantasy. The disturbed adolescent has an even greater need for techniques to deal with impelling id wishes and fantasies. Freud said: "If phantasies become over-luxuriant and over-powerful, the necessary conditions for an outbreak of neurosis or psychosis are constituted; phantasies are also the first preliminary stage in the mind of the symptoms of illness of which our patients complain."

Poetry can serve as a two-way door, opening toward the world of fanciful childhood play or toward the reality-oriented fantasy-concealed world of adulthood. As a therapeutic tool with adolescents, therefore, poetry has two potentials: to uncover and reveal the wishful dreams of childhood, and to convert these dreams into socially acceptable yet pleasurable adult forms.

That poetry provides a pleasurable means of dealing with fantasy is important. Many childhood experiences are painful and traumatic, and the means of uncovering and dealing with them must be kindly and pleasant. "The art of the writer," said Freud, "lies in the fact that he can soften, change, and disguise the character of the day-dream by offering it in a pleasurable form.... Many emotions which are essentially painful may become a source of enjoyment to the spectators and hearers of a poet's work." The act of writing or reading a poem, then, can provide a way of translating a distressing experience into a pleasurable form.

Not only does poetry offer a means of communicating with childhood fantasy life, it also offers a means of communicating with the emotions attached to particular events. "Poet and novelist," said John Dewey,[3] "have an immense advantage over even an expert psychologist in dealing with an emotion. For the former build up a concrete situation and permit *it* to evoke emotional response. Instead of a description of an emotion in intellectual and symbolic terms, the artist 'does the deed that breeds' the emotion."

Practice

That poetry can work in both directions, that it is a double door, allows it to be used in a variety of ways in the therapeutic setting. At the Institute of the Pennsylvania Hospital, the use of poetry therapy with adolescents takes four forms, in all of which participation is voluntary.

Poetry seminars are conducted two mornings a week for an hour and a half, by Mr. David Fetterman, an English instructor at Temple University. Procedure at the seminars, quite informal, varies from session to session. Usually Mr. Fetterman reads contemporary poems, of his own choosing, and invites comment and discussion from the patients and nurses present. Sometimes he selects prose pieces with marked emotional impact, such as an indictment of Eichmann, or an essay on psychedelic drugs by Ginsburg. Patients may read their own selections or original verse. On occasion they have studied the compositions of guitarist Bob Dylan and heard songs written by their fellows.

Mr. Fetterman sees his role as a poetry therapist as that of activating and guiding the group. He does not offer meanings for poems, but will suggest alternate meanings from which patients can select. "I represent someone who has done this before, a person they can trust, so that they can feel free to associate to the poems." Mr. Fetterman has his own ideas about the value of poetry to the patients. "A poem is a *commune*—a place where things can participate. More than anything else, a poem is the most immediate form of relations between things, an agent for making reality concrete, a model for relationships. A poem is not hopelessly abstract; it clarifies the act of knowing the things that the mind deals with." Most important, he believes, is that the poem provides a way of "dealing with something on satisfactory terms." Mr. Fetterman quotes William Carlos Williams: "A poem is a vision of the facts," he says; "adolescents have to deal with the facts to form convictions about things." For adolescents, he sees a poem as "an adventure with an idea. Kids fantasize, and the fantasies can take over. They can see the reasoning of the poem and see how unreal their own fantasies are. Furthermore, they can identify with a poem. They can say, 'I correspond with this poet.' For them, it's a personification, a step toward a sense of dignity."

The emotional value of poetry has importance for Mr. Fetterman's philosophy also, as a group and as an individual experience. "Poems give a dignified release of emotions, and also a direction, a form." Thus, the poetry seminars are a group experience in the form of a discussion, usually—but not always—using the poetry of professional poets. It permits the exchange of associations to the poetry among the patients. The group is able to correct and modify the interpretations of its individual members.

Adolescent patients are invited to participate with adults in publishing *Insight*, a monthly news and literary hospital magazine, called *The Illuminator* in the 1840's and the *Tatler* in the 1950's. At twice-weekly staff meetings, patients read articles and poems that they have written, criticize one another's efforts, and select the best for publication. The character of these meetings changes with the patient population, at times being very businesslike, at other times resembling the poetry seminar, with emotional sharing. The editorial staff is at times very tolerant of "crazy" poetry, selecting poems that have emotional impact without necessarily having logical meaning.

Being advisor to such a publication can provide a stimulating experience for a volunteer. Over the past seven years at the Institute, several gifted people have held the post. A young poet who donated his services found the job stimulating to his own creative work. The post was filled for another year by a housewife and mother, who had retired from a magazine editorial job to raise her family. When the patients learned that she would have to give up her position as advisor to the publication, they decided to sell the magazine at 15¢ a copy in order to pay for a baby-sitter, so that the young mother could continue to volunteer her services to the hospital! Both volunteers made ample use of professional poetry in group discussions. Resident physicians are required to attend *Insight* meetings for one month in order to acquaint them with the use of creative literary work in a mental hospital. Occasionally, a resident will thereby become interested in this therapy and choose to sponsor the activity himself. When a volunteer or resident has not been available, the post has been occupied by a social worker or a music therapist, but any interested person, such as an occupational therapist or nurse, would qualify if available. As with poetry seminars, the character of the meeting is determined by the personality of the advisor and by the patients present. Of course, the patients elect their own editor and production staff. At *Insight* meetings, adolescents have an opportunity to work with adults and to share with them the experience of writing poetry, thus verifying poetry's reality-testing function.

The Institute's school unit, with its literature and creative writing courses, offers a third exposure to poetry in the therapeutic setting. The approach of the teachers is usually oriented much less toward uncovering pathologic fantasy-life and more toward structure, comprehensible meaning and good writing. Miss Julia Johnson, a teacher of disturbed adolescents at the Yale Psychiatric Institute, points out the difference in approach of the teacher from that of the psychiatrist. With his interest in the unconscious, "a psychiatrist can reinforce their writing bad poetry. By encouraging too many autistic associations, the doctor encourages bad writing rather than good." Thus, the teacher is interested, more than the doctor, in the patient's ability to organize his thoughts and feelings and to give logic and meaning to his work. The teacher, she says, "can confront the student with his craziness, with his statements that don't make sense."

Another aspect of writing poetry is the achievement of the patient. Generally, achievement is praised. For the patient, this may pose a dilemma, because he may assume that the teacher or therapist feels as his parents felt and communicated, "If you achieve, you are competing with me, and I do not want that." The use of an abstract poem may permit the patient to "find numerous ways to get away from it. If concrete, the poem can be a direct stimulus," Miss Johnson says. It is always important for the teacher to work closely with the therapist and to be as familiar as possible with the patient's history and pathology. Miss Johnson gives examples of a patient's blocking on the meaning of a poem because of family pathology. In general, the teacher is a more reality-oriented, ego-supportive user of poetry in the mental hospital.

The use of poetry by individual therapists varies from doctor to doctor. In general, the psychiatrist is interested in a patient's productions as expressions of unconscious conflicts and feelings, although this generalization should not be applied universally, because the therapist's problem is not only to analyze the patient's inner struggles but to develop in the patient the capacity for creative synthesis. The business of making the unconscious conscious is only part of treatment; maturation into an integrated person is the aim, especially with adolescents.

This synthetic process and the importance of metaphor in it are the subjects of a paper by John C. Sonne, M.D.:[4] "Has the effect of our scientific study of schizophrenia been to diversify our materials and forms rather than to create an organic synthesis? Do we not need poetry in the psychotherapy of schizophrenia, in addition to our newfound knowledge about the unconscious and communication?" In one example of the treatment of a schizophrenic family, Dr. Sonne capitalized on the father's use of the "illusion" of love. "In treating families such as this, or in treating their offspring, one must bear in mind that, at times, rather than being analytic, one must be poetic, for the poetry is the reality." The metaphor has a healing power, because it can translate a pathologic unconscious idea into healthy meaning.

The metaphor contains surprise, similarity and contrast, relationship, and power. An apt metaphor can link unconscious, conscious, and interpsychic levels and more, and can be as powerful in health as a dream, a delusion, or a symptom can be in sickness. One might speculate that not until we say something metaphorical do we have a human relationship. Metaphors are the reservoirs of relationships and the instruments for relating. In psychotherapy, the psychotherapist endeavors to establish a poetic and permanent organic unity with the psyche of his patient, and shares with his patient in participating in the experience of composing metaphors. 'You'll live in my mind forever' is a poetic or metaphorical statement, which is meaningless if taken literally, yet to live in each other's minds is a requirement of psychic life, if we are not to live alone.

To Sonne, the metaphor is important for its quality to synthesize and unify a relationship. He quotes Aileen Ward on Keats[5]:

This taking part in the existence—or, as he later called it, the identity—of other beings was one of Keats's most important insights as a poet. What he called "essential Beauty" was a sudden realization of the innermost character of a person or thing, won by imaginative identification with it; and through this insight a new universe was revealed to him. So he could become one with the intense absorption of the sparrow picking for its food in the dirt, or with the loneliness of the oyster asleep in its shell at the bottom of the sea; he could even feel his way, as he once said, into a billiard ball delighted with its own smooth motion and perfect roundness. What he described to Bailey was, of course, a quality which he had often achieved in his poetry without being quite aware of it, when his focus shifted from his own response to an object to the imagined inner life of the object itself: the sensations not only of the astronomer discovering a new planet, but of the star itself gazing down on the earth, or of the lazy power of a breaking wave and the delight of the rock weed swirled about in its foam.

Sonne's statements about the unifying qualify of metaphor confirm the usefulness of poetry as a maturing influence. The individual therapist has a choice of using it as an uncovering or as a unifying technique.

Poetry provides a two-way treatment for adolescents, who find themselves, naturally and by virtue of their illness, at a period in life when the fantasies of childhood need to be mastered. In an adolescent treatment center, poetry can be utilized both to explore fantasy life and to master it: by group-sharing experience; by reading, writing, publishing, and studying it; and by using it in individual psychotherapy. Because of the nature of adolescence, poetry's use with adolescents seems particularly apt.

REFERENCES

1. Gleason, R. J., "The children's crusade," *Ramparts*, March 1966, pp. 29–34.
2. Freud, Sigmund, "The poet and day-dreaming," *Collected Papers*, vol. 4, (London, Hogarth Press, 1953) pp. 173–183.
3. Dewey, John: *Art as Experience* (New York, Capricorn Books, 1958) p. 67.
4. Sonne, J. C.: "Metaphors and relationships," *Family Process* 3:425–427, September, 1964.
5. Ward, Aileen: *John Keats* (New York, Viking, 1963) pp. 137–138.

The Use of Poetry in a Private Mental Hospital

AARON KRAMER, Ph.D.

It has been my good fortune to participate in a long-range therapy program, which, because of its novelty and success, may interest others. In the summer of 1956, I was invited to give a poetry recital at Hillside Hospital, in Glen Oaks, New York. The Group Activities Department admitted some trepidation, since no such evening had ever been attempted there, or (so far as we know) in any other US mental institution. Nevertheless, the staff approached the event as a possibly entertaining experiment, and publicized it widely.

It was explained that Hillside, along with only one or two other US hospitals in this field, operates on a more or less voluntary basis for both admittance and release. Most of the patients, I was told, are above average in intelligence. Their generally relaxed and normal appearance before strangers might fool me into forgetting how deeply disturbed they actually are, and might lead me to introduce material or make statements of a nature violently discomforting and painful to some of them. I was warned in particular not to read long or "heavy" selections, and to shy away from the theme of death. It was pointed out that several months earlier a pianist had destroyed the effect of her musicianship by playing several elegiac numbers, which disquieted and depressed a large section of her audience. As a result, some patients had requested that she not be invited to perform there again.

The publicity bore surprising fruit. I was told to be ready for as many as 50 people—some of whom were expressing, in advance, a great enthusiasm for poetry; others who were frankly curious about seeing a "live poet"; still others who hoped to have a good laugh at his expense. I was reassured that enough matrons would be on hand to cope with any disturbance that might arise—of which there had usually been one or two. A hundred patients showed up. This represented half the entire hospital population. Of the 100, about 75 were between the ages of 16 and 25. I operated on the premise, right or wrong, that most of my audience were unfriendly to poetry: they had come because they preferred "an evening out" to remaining alone in their wards. My aim was, therefore, to surprise and convert them.

I planned to spotlight the widespread disregard and contempt for such "luxury" items as poetry in a crassly materialistic society, aided and abetted by the generally poor teaching of literature in our public schools. I hoped to prove, as dramatically as possible and with ample illustration, that at many times and in many places poetry has not been a luxury but has played most useful and dynamic roles. To lessen their feeling of difference between me, as a two-hour entertainer, and them, as year-long prisoners, I dispensed with both microphone and stage, stood in their midst, and addressed them very plainly in terms of my own creative problems, experience and credo. In general, I followed the admonition of the staff, choosing mostly short, lighthearted poems, and avoiding all morbid themes.

However, while discussing the special role of poetry in evoking the proud past of subject peoples and inspiring them to rebellion, I decided on the spur of the moment to exploit the attentive silence by reading a very long excerpt—with its share of gloom—from Poland's nineteenth century epic, *Pan Tadeusz*, explaining first the historical background and various obscure allusions. Midway through I heard, for the first time, conversation in the back of the auditorium, and looked up in dismay, thinking my choice had been a blunder. The conversation, however, involved three matrons; with a rather electrifying unanimity, the audience turned 'round to "shush" their police! This ten-minute selection won more applause than anything else.

An animated discussion followed, in which perhaps a dozen persons participated, centering chiefly on the Polish excerpt and on remembrances of poetry as "an instrument of torture" in the lower grades. Two young men rose to admit that they'd come with the expectation of mocking poetry, but now—for the first time in their lives—felt that poetry might have value for them. Others asked for advice on follow-up reading.

Afterwards, the hospital informed me that doctors had noted a marked "uplift" in the mood of numerous patients, and asked me to visit regularly, not as a guest artist, but as a workshop leader for those who now wanted to specialize in reading and writing poetry. At the next appearance, however, there were about 50 people, although another activity was offered at the same time. Because like numbers attended each time, the hospital finally decided not to offer any other activity on the nights of my appearance, and to publicize these poetry readings as a regularly monthly feature. The average attendance has been 100. On every occasion, more than two thirds have been 25 or younger.

I've kept no journal of these evenings, and have discarded my preparatory notes. To think or write of my activities and experiences at Hillside Hospital in terms of therapy might have had a harmful effect on my behavior toward the patients: I've always avoided considering them anything other than my peers—at the least—both in intellectual capacity and social potential, and I believe their awareness of this is an important factor in the continuing welcome they extend. For the purposes of this report, however, I will set down the aspects— favorable and unfavorable—of my two-year program at Hillside, and certain incidents that needed no journal to be remembered.

Among the problems to be dealt with, I would list the following:

1. Shifts in audience: no steady attendance, as in a classroom, but always many new faces present and old faces gone; the need is, therefore, to maintain a certain continuity, while avoiding repetition and staleness.

2. Shock treatment: the staff has, perhaps mistakenly, allowed certain patients to attend only a few hours after they've received shock treatment. In many cases, particularly among the more mature people, there is no visible effect except a loss of memory (one lady, who'd come to hear me four times, addressed me as Mr. Copeland the fifth time, then apologized and explained that she was under shock treatment). Among the very young, though, particularly girls, the effect is heartbreakingly clear—one youngster of about 16, in mannish garb, could not restrain herself from moving around and giggling at several references to sex; the other patients strained nobly to disregard her, but the giggling was contagious.

3. Moments of upheaval: besides shock, patients occasionally attend while under great emotional stress, and endanger the mood of the evening. An incident of this kind took place recently, involving two 17-year-old girls who've developed a strong attachment. Both are poets, the feminine partner displaying a rich lyric gift. The month before, both had approached me with poems in tribute to Anne Frank, and I had read the poems at the outset of the evening, announcing their authorship. This time, a few minutes before the program was to begin, I heard a commotion in the hallway. The mannish partner, eyes bloodshot and eyelids swollen with weeping, was arguing violently with other girls. She finally came in, walking past me without sign of recognition, and seated herself at the piano, where she leaned forward and played violent combinations of notes with her left hand, again and again. I strolled over to say hello. Before hearing me, she blurted: "I'll stop playing if you're ready to begin." I asked the fate of the Anne Frank poems, and she responded: "Hers was accepted, mine was rejected." I asked whether she'd written anything new. She told me she'd finished a long series of "wonderful" dialogues—and rapidly indicated the content of each, becoming so absorbed that soon she stopped her nerve-wracking shrieks from the piano. She hoped I'd read some of them.

Then she whispered that her girl friend had escaped from the hospital an hour ago, with the words: "I must go to the sea—if I live, I'll see you again." None of the attendants knew about the escape, and she begged me to say nothing. "That's why I'm acting this way—" she explained, and emphasized that no one besides this girl had ever loved her, and that she feared the possibility of suicide. By this time she was all talked out and rather calm. Another patient gently asked for the use of the piano, and I walked this girl to her seat. She kept thanking me for having listened to her, and having shown an interest in her poems. I urged her to concentrate on the Shakespeare reading, which was about to begin, "since these people have rehearsed for two weeks and deserve your full attention." One of the girls in the cast also seemed most upset; guessing the reason, I suggested that she beg her friend not to keep the secret any longer: it was urgent that the search for the escaped girl begin at once. A few minutes later she returned, whispered in my ear that the attendants had been informed, and went onstage to give a fine performance. The other girl sat through the entire evening without any visible sign of disturbance.

4. Educational differential: this is faced by all lecturers, to some extent, but is especially marked at Hillside. The audience ranges from the extreme of lifelong poetry enthusiasts and even specialists to the opposite extreme of those who've never paid attention to a poem before, except perhaps in hostility or bewilderment. It is difficult—well-nigh impossible—to prepare and carry through a program that will satisfy all: to find poems, and to speak in a language, capable of striking home on many levels. The discussion period gives those more advanced an opportunity to introduce more subtle nuances and more advanced concepts, and to draw the kind of answers from me that will satisfy their intellectual needs; in this "give and take" form, the material is livelier, and those less advanced listen with a good deal of interest.

Sometimes an individual either is or fancies himself to be beyond the lecturer in knowledge of his field. One such case was a Greek boy of about 18, very well-read, and himself a prolific poet. When he failed to attend it, it was interpreted, by me and others (perhaps incorrectly), as a criticism of the program. When he did attend, there was no satisfying him; he always requested that I read the longest and most difficult poems imaginable—wonderful choices for a graduate school course, but impossible in terms of the educational differential here. Among his requests were Keats's "Hyperion" and the entire Book of Job. While praising his taste and expressing enthusiasm for his choices, I read only tiny passages from these works. The patients regarded him with awe; had he prevailed, however, he might have crushed both program and their self-esteem. (The hospital, incidentally, instructed me in strong terms not to cater to this boy's requests.)

5. *Sensitivity to sex and death*: some patients are particularly touchy on one or both of these subjects, tabooed in childhood and thrust suddenly upon them during adolescence. While not ignoring death, one may advisably shy away from too violent and vivid descriptions. As for sex, my method thus far has been to deal with it whenever appropriate. Though occasionally someone squirms, or giggles uncomfortably, or even stalks out, muttering "This is too much for me!" the general effect is so wholesome, in terms of audience gratitude for being handled without kid gloves, that a few minor disturbances may be overlooked.

6. *Exhibitionism*: this constantly looms as a frightening possibility. Very few of the adolescents indulge in this activity—on the contrary, their problem is usually a self-imposed silence and self-abnegation. Several adults are more likely to demand attention. However, there have been a number of such cases—mostly before the program begins, or at the very outset. I've tried at least to neutralize those who make a threateningly noisy entrance: teasing, singing, or complaining—by engaging them in brief conversation beforehand, and focusing my

eyes on them in a kindly way from the beginning of the evening. These "bursting" individuals will usually make more than their share of comments during the discussion period; I try to praise their comments and questions whenever merited, and to treat them respectfully. This seems to give them the attention they really crave, and afterwards they are often among the most stalwart listeners. Twice, at the close of rough evenings, it was heartening to have groups of patients come and apologize for the exhibitionist, explaining that he "didn't know any better" and assuring me that my visit had been greatly appreciated.

7. *Presence of attendants*: this, I think, may have a harmful effect on the patient's ability to concentrate and to enjoy the event; it reminds him of his true status, continually. Being commanded to leave at 9 PM sharp, and sometimes bodily removed while in the midst of a thought, has a most demoralizing and embarrassing effect, dampening the mood of the whole evening. Very few of the attendants, however, perform this function harshly.

8. *Choice of words*: while not seeming careful, one must take great care with one's vocabulary at all times. Patients mentally ill are most keenly alert to hidden or double meanings—even to smiles and gestures. They observe at least as thoroughly as they are observed, and draw subjective conclusions, often unfounded, which cause them to feel "insulted and injured." Words pertaining to mental or emotional disturbance should, if possible, be avoided. In preparing for a reading from *Hamlet*, I carefully circled four or five references to "madness" that were to be omitted. This particular event drew the largest audience ever; I saw at once that a number of patients had supplied themselves with copies of the play, in order to follow my performance, and realized that others in the audience, considering their backgrounds and the nature of their illness, might know the play better than I. Deciding that it would be worse to omit the circled lines than to read them, I went ahead without any deletions. The response was unusually good; a first-rate discussion ensued, centering on the question of Hamlet's "madness." Most gratifying was that none of the comments had subjective overtones, so far as I could observe.

9. *Lecturer's status*: there is always an undercurrent of awareness that the guest is about to leave for home and work "out there"—while the audience is about to march back to their wards "in here." At first,

this separation was more intense, since the hospital, for good reasons, refused to allow any personal conversation after the program. Several times, more recently, there have been opportunities to converse, personally, with those patients who seek me out (usually to obtain my opinion of their poetry).

Following the success of *Hamlet*, I prepared a reading of some Falstaff scenes, from *Henry IV* Parts I and II, and suggested that patients volunteer to take on some of the other roles, so that I could concentrate on the character of Falstaff. An SOS phone call came from the hospital a week before the scheduled performance. The volunteers were resentful: there wasn't enough for the girls to do, and some of the fellows hankered after the colorful role of Falstaff. We worked it out by giving Falstaff to one of the boys, and by choosing another scene in which the girls played an important part. Everything went off smoothly. Giving the spotlight to seven patients meant a great deal, not only in terms of their own healing, but as a flesh-and-blood symbol to the onlookers of their own possible flowering. Two of the girls have begun writing "floods" of poetry, and one of the boys is working on a drama "in Shakespeare's style." All seven actors have established a team-relationship, with one another and with me.

10. Self-centeredness: this ranges from the egocentric variety, which resents my holding the spotlight and actively attempts to usurp it (as in exhibitionism), to the daydreaming variety, which resists my efforts to intrude and make contact and which maintains an even pitch of soul-crushed silence despite all the enthusiasm and debate raging around it. Not being members of a school class, they cannot be confronted or tested, and it is impossible for the lecturer to gauge the extent—if any—of his influence. Yet they return, month after month, applaud limply with the rest, and sometimes a few in this category unexpectedly join the "thank you" line shaking hands with me at the close of the program.

Along with the problems, however, are several factors that have contributed to the success of poetry therapy at Hillside Hospital.

1. A creative figure: the fact that the lecturer is a published poet fills many of the patients with genuine awe and interest. A very large number of these people have hoped, at one time or another, to play a creative role in the art world—as painters, writers, musicians; one suspects that, in some cases, lack of creative success has been a factor in their emotional deterioration; but they are excited by the presence of a poet, and ask no end of questions about the practical problems faced in a creative career.

2. *A semi-classroom atmosphere*: these youngsters, many of whom probably enjoyed their only brief success and sense of safety within the classroom, perhaps feel a nostalgic stimulus and security in the mood of lecture-discussion. At the same time, there is no danger of examination or forced recitation, and the down-to-earth, nonesoteric treatment of literature is an intriguing change from their classroom experience, leading them to reassess earlier attitudes.

3. *Variety of format*: the nature of the evening is not consistent. There have been many surprises that tend to keep and develop interest: national programs: Negro, Jewish, modern Greek, American; media programs: dramatic monologues, ballads, lyrics; theme programs: satire, humor, social protest, love, anonymous poets of the world. Occasionally there is a complete break in the pattern: an evening of poetry recordings, or performances of scenes from Shakespeare, or an all-request program, or a program of my own favorite poems (with explanations why they are my favorites).

At one time, a small group of poetry-lovers became so fervent that they decided to form a Poetry Committee to help me prepare new programs, take care of the publicity, and meet afterward for an evaluation of the evening. Although the initiation of this group was considered a very wholesome development, unfortunately so much dissension arose among the members over what should take place the following month that the committee soon disintegrated. With closer supervision, it might have enlarged and thrived, with interim activities between my appearances.

4. *Freedom of discussion*: generally the most vital part of the evening, usually lasting half an hour, is the discussion period. Even those too timid or benumbed to participate seem animated when their more vocal wardmates take the floor. The questions and comments often show originality of thinking as well as erudition. Having nothing to lose, they are all remarkably candid, and accept equal candor from me. Some who participate preface their remarks with a statement that they've "never spoken up before."

5. *Voluntary basis*: that there is no compulsion or pressure about either entering or remaining contributes to the mood of relaxation. Naturally, the patients will give more wholehearted and friendly at-

tention to a speaker whom they have *chosen* to hear. It would be even more effective, I imagine, if attendance were not taken—though taking it is probably a necessity. Once, at the last moment, the supervisor in charge became ill and asked whether I would mind being at the helm alone, without her introductory remarks or her authoritative presence at the front of the room. Except for a little difficulty in bringing order at the beginning, the evening worked out exactly as well as if she had been there.

    6. *Original work*: a highlight of several evenings has been the reading of poems written by patients. This deserves to be a therapy activity in itself—and a creative writing workshop should eventually be initiated. A sizable number of Hillside people, mostly teenagers, are making poetry their means of self-expression. Few, however, have been courageous enough to let me read their self-revelations before 100 acquaintances—fewer still would face the audience and read the poems themselves. But those few constitute a real triumph. From time to time, the most extreme cases of apparent introversion will amaze their fellows by rising and reading. Even when the poems are too cryptic for general communication, or when the embarrassed poets mumble their lines almost inaudibly, the listeners are consistently polite and warm in their show of approval. That one of them *has* managed to verbalize his or her feelings in an artistic way, and is participating in a respectable poetry recital, has inspiring significance for the others.

    At one such event, in response to an invitation for original verse, a fellow came forward and read several satirical rhymes which, while slightly bawdy, displayed real wit and deftness of style. The audience loved it, particularly as a "breather" after an hour of serious material. The supervisor, however, did not laugh—and privately expressed the suspicion that this patient was guilty of a consciously insulting intrusion, intended to poke fun at my program. The next month, along with others, our humorist brought a sheaf of additional verse. Unfortunately, the supervisor adamantly refused to call on him, though he kept waving his hand. The audience became restive; a cry arose: "Let him read!" At my urgent request she finally, rather ungraciously, gave him the floor, limiting him to a couple of minutes. Again, his verses were really clever and not without ironic content; I praised and thanked him when he was done. The audience laughed and applauded heartily, yet it was apparent that a certain bitterness had been engendered as a result of this strategic blunder. Possibly the supervisor, a veteran on the staff, was basing her attitude on some prior experience; certain patients have a history of public destructiveness. Her effort to control this young man, however, turned many patients against her as the symbol of authority.

A similar situation was narrowly averted several months later. One of the middle-aged patients marched in belligerently, carrying a volume of Nick Kenny "poems" with a dozen threatening pagemarks. He announced that he hadn't ever come to these programs before, and didn't know what I was doing there, or what right I had to decide what poems should be read. Opening the book, he said he'd found some beautiful verses, which he intended to share with the audience. I invited him to read his four favorite poems. Many patients had to turn their faces away so that he would not see how close to laughter they were because of the sentimental and banal lines. However, all applauded politely when he'd concluded, and I thanked him. We utilized the unexpected entry of Kennyism by developing a good discussion on the difference between rhyme and poetry. He then boisterously complimented my reading style, and nearly shook my arm out of its socket.

7. *The nature of poetry*: this, more than any other factor, has been decisive in the success of the program. Were the lecturer weaker, the frequency and attendance might diminish; were the lecturer stronger, more success might be attained. Of one thing I am certain: a considerable nucleus of interest, even enthusiasm, existed from the outset, and is permanently dependable. For reasons that professional psychologists could surely state with more confidence and clarity, a large number of mentally disturbed people at Hillside Hospital have made reading poetry a favorite pastime from the days of early adolescence—and, of this number, possibly half had attempted versification as a means of personal expression and emotional release. Even if no new adherents had been won during my two-year campaign, this nucleus of old-time poetry addicts would have welcomed the program, and it would have been worthwhile as a timely stimulus both for reading and writing poems.

Even more than music, poetry has been an instrument by which especially sensitive individuals, in all lands and ages, record their emotional upheavals and imaginative wanderings. Poetry is the most concentrated and vivid language of both pulmonary and nervous systems; poetry is a challenging outcry from those who refuse to conform and who are in eternal revolt against the status quo; poetry seeks for meanings under meanings; poetry insists on finding a way of saying what is forbidden or impossible; poetry resounds through a silent world, sings arias in a theatre of stammering conversation. These are not scientific or scholarly definitions, but the sum of them may indicate why adolescents who are out of tune with their daily lives, and who are moving with frightful speed toward mental and emotional disturbance, may attempt to take refuge in poetry: a language closer to them than the language of mothers, newspapers, or doctors.

Besides, there is a widespread old portrait of The Poet as a figure aloof and misunderstood, yet ultimately victorious over his time. Intellectually keen adolescents, rejected by society and in turn rejecting society, find in this legend of The Poet a convenient and romantic pattern to emulate. To qualify the "success" of Hillside's poetry program, it must be pointed out that the question has been raised whether it might be better for the disturbed adolescent to begin speaking and thinking socially, rather than jotting down his egocentric thoughts for his own satisfaction. However, I have stressed the role of poetry as a communicative and deeply social art—and, even in those cases where the patient is too timid to make his rhymes public, the consensus of opinion seems to be that by putting his most urgent thoughts down on paper he has taken a long step forward toward self-clarification and eventual health.

It would be presumptuous of me to make definitive statements based on my particular observations and experiences. Hillside Hospital, to begin with, is a most unusual place; what succeeds there might fail elsewhere. Then, too, its intellectual level is proably beyond that in most mental hospitals. That most of the patients come from Jewish middle-class homes should also not be discounted. Finally, I've had little direct contact with the medical staff, which is in a far better position to gauge the effects of my poetry program. Nevertheless, the fact that poetry has had, and continues to have, considerable therapeutic success at Hillside should mean something to those who are looking for every possible instrument of therapy.

IN THE APARTMENTS OF HOME-BOUND PUPILS

Poetry Therapy with Disturbed Adolescents

Bright Arrows on a Dark River

MORRIS ROBERT MORRISON, Ph.D.

> *Because the literary experience tends to involve both intellectual and emotional facets of the personality in a manner that parallels life itself, the insights attained through literature may be assimilated to the matrix of attitudes and ideas which constitutes character and governs behavior.*
> —Dr. Louise Rosenblatt[1]

The effectiveness of poetry therapy is rooted in the power that all literature possesses to assist the individual in his search for self-understanding and emotional liberation. Poetry is especially useful because of its unique qualities: A poem can initiate an intellectual and emotional experience with exceptional immediacy. It is the poet's special gift to involve one with his first lines.

The reader may enter as a guest into the private world of the poet, yet he soon recognizes familiar landmarks. He quickly finds that he is no outsider. Though the poet speaks for himself, the reader discovers his own psyche, his own thoughts and feelings, being expressed. He is not so alone as he had imagined himself. He finds his identity disclosed in the world of a fellow human being. The very pulse of poetry and the pattern of its rhythms appeal to something basic and atavistic in our nature. Poetry, drama, and religion have all evolved from a common ritual whose purpose it was to annul the participant's consciousness of separate personality, exalting him to union with his group and its God.

The secrets of the dance have been traced to our physiology; dance rhythms correspond to those latent in the human system and are capable of evoking them. This, too, is a faculty of poetry. T. S. Eliot has said: "The human soul, in intense emotion, strives to express itself in verse. It is not for me but for neurologists to discover why this is so." The appeal of poetry is to the mind on both its conscious and unconscious levels. Poetry releases one from the world of the particular into the healing ambience of the universal. To one suffering from a sense of alienation, the awareness that another's steps have preceded him on the same lonesome road is comforting for its reassurance. Poets expressing their deepest fears, insecurities, and anxieties give voice to what we feel deepest within ourselves. This helps us find our way back to the mainstream of society.

For the practice of poetry therapy, no special equipment is necessary. All one needs is a room with a fair amount of privacy. Everything else is left to the resources of the imagination. In New York City, recently, "An Evening with Frost" enjoyed a highly successful run. It was presented on a bare stage (no backdrop) with a minimum of props (a table, two chairs, and a lectern), yet all New England came alive to the audience. One saw pastures and woods, farm houses and their interiors, and a west-running brook flowing before one's eyes. It is this very reliance on the role of imagination and the implicit participation that it elicits that account for so much of the therapeutic value of poetry.

Lorene

The first view I had of Lorene was of a girl of sixteen, carelessly dressed and smelling of alcohol, who kept her head averted so that her hair spilled about her face, masking most of it. What she couldn't hide of her skin showed itself covered with eczema. Because of this skin ailment, I was assigned to instruct her at home, a place she never left; she neither paid nor received visits. Her mother, employed as a domestic, was gone most of the day. Her sole companion, her grandmother, 75, appeared just as withdrawn as my pupil.

Though in the early part of the term she had come to accept my presence as her teacher, she made no attempt to improve her appearance. Although she gave up resorting to liquor, she still seemed to wish only to hide behind her hair, behind a book, or, as quickly as possible after I left, in any one of the rooms of the railroad flat in Bedford Stuyvesant. One could only guess at the extent of the agony experienced by this adolescent girl. Along with the emotional debasement caused by her disfigurement, there was the accompanying physical pain of her constantly itching skin. During our lessons she would claw savagely at her face. Still, she would not go when the clinic referred her to a hospital where a series of tests might suggest a cure.

It was Lorene's ambition to graduate from high school with a commercial diploma and to secure employment some day as an office secretary. Her typing was neat and careful. She was orderly in her bookkeeping, and she applied herself diligently to her lessons in stenography. Her reaction to literature, however, while dutiful, was uninspired.

In the course of our work in English we came upon a poem by Emily Dickinson*:

> I'm Nobody! Who are you?
> Are you—Nobody—too?

I studied Lorene's face. For the first time she was not pretending interest. She brightened at:

> Then there's a pair of us!
> Dont tell! they'd banish us—you know!
>
> How dreary—to be—Somebody!
> How public—like a Frog—
>
> To tell your name—the livelong June—
> To an admiring Bog!

Something remarkable followed. Lorene asked me for information. She wanted to learn something of the poet's life. I told her the story of Emily Dickinson—of her idiosyncracies, her isolation, her unhappiness, of the posthumous discovery of her poems and her brilliant position today in world literature. She was fascinated. She seemed to have found a rapport with Miss Dickinson.

Not all of Emily Dickinson's poems were so easy to understand as the first we studied, but Lorene's enthusiasm for the poet, whose life story she reread several times, helped her, with my assistance, to overcome the special difficulties in the writing. This eagerness to learn about poetry and poets' lives was carried through to an interest in Edna St. Vincent Millay and others.

*The Poems of Emily Dickinson, ed. Thomas H. Johnson, Cambridge (Mass.), The Belknap Press of Harvard University Press, 1958. Pages 206–207. With permission.

One day when I came to see her, she had brushed her hair away from her face and had bound it together with a ribbon. Apparently she no longer needed to hide from anyone. She began to go to church. During the summer, treatment at the hospital improved the condition of her skin. That fall she returned to regular classes at her high school. I heard from her later: she was doing nicely both socially and scholastically. When I saw her recently, the eczema had disappeared.

It is clear that Lorene's problem was emotional as well as medical. The lines of communication between her and the outside world needed mending before anything could be done for her at the hospital. The line, "I'm nobody," must have moved her strongly, reflecting as it probably did her own opinion of herself. Additional defenses fell with the question, "Are you nobody, too?" Lorene was also undoubtedly gratified to be included in the admonition "Don't tell—They'd banish us you know." Emily Dickinson had reached her, and Lorene in turn reached toward the poet. In Emily Dickinson she could identify with someone as lonely and as "odd" as herself. This was apparent in her eagerness to memorize as many of Dickinson's poems as possible. Pretty clearly she sought to incorporate some part of the poet into her being. After this discovery of kinship with a celebrated writer, she could accept her own self. When Lorene brushed the hair away from her face and permitted the world to look at her, she had traveled an incalculable distance.

Barbara

I was on my way to John Jay High School when an attractive girl suddenly opened the door of a parked car and rushed towards me, greeting me warmly. She had heart-warming news. She was doing well at school and had recently won a scholarship to art school. It was Barbara, radiating vitality and charm. In appearance and manner, she was incredibly transformed from the hostile withdrawn fifteen-year-old, dressed in sloppy jeans, who had been one of my homebound pupils.

When I first visited her at her home, two years prior to this encounter, I found her drawn into her chair as into a corner. She seemed prepared to defend herself against any intruder and from the beginning was not only openly hostile to her mother but critical of everything and everyone in her environment. When I attempted to interest her in the term's work, she yawned in my face. She soon let me know that she had little use for me or my teaching and couldn't wait for me to leave. Her attitude seemed to scream out, "Leave me alone!"

From her school records, I learned that Barbara had been an excellent student in English. During one of our lessons, I asked her what writers she liked best. In her estimation, none of those she had studied in school were any good. Her current idols were Jack Kerouac and Allen Ginsberg. When I said that I greatly admired Ginsberg's *Kaddish*, she seemed surprised that a square like me could see anything worthwhile in the beat writers. For my master's thesis, I had made an extensive study of the Symbolist poets, Rimbaud and Mallarmé, predecessors of today's *avant garde*. When Barbara heard this she seemed slightly impressed. When I compared Rimbaud to Ginsberg, she listened. I suggested to her, later, that in place of the conventional home work she write a poem. She could select any subject and write in any way she chose. At the following session, when I inquired about the assignment, she said she hadn't done it. Later she did bring out, almost reluctantly, six lines she had written. I praised them highly, though I took exception to the phrasing of one of them. Subsequently she wrote another poem and, as the term progressed, went on to produce an impressive series of highly creditable writings.

The following poem reveals Barbara's talent and illustrates the beginning of a new insight into herself.

> Perhaps if I tried to communicate
> To someone I don't know
> Who wouldn't care
> And wouldn't think of me
> And would carry nothing of me away—
> Or to something not committed to listen
> Some object, some state of being
> That couldn't feel...
>
> I've only negative expressions
> Emptiness
> You would be listening to the sound of no sound
>
> In "you" or "I" there is nothing real
> What is there in front of my eyes
> Besides objects?

She continued to write poems of unexpected merit into which she poured her tortured feelings. "What is Next?" is worthy of inclusion in any anthology.

What is next?
This is the time I pose the question
When there is no wash hanging out in the black night on the line
When little drops of water are falling from the faucet
And the poison food isn't doing much good killing that hungry fat mouse
I look around the room
    And say out loud
Because there isn't anybody around to hear me
    What is next?
All my fingernails are in my stomach
And I want something more than this can of Hawaiian Punch
    Which is too cold and is
    Hurting the back of my front teeth
How would it be if I just went out the door and tried to be friends
    With the few people on the street
Ignoring the quietness of the night
And yell to them
    What is next?
And then run in and slam the door and stand on the kitchen chair
    And raise my arms and feel how the heat is rising
Uncertain, with no answer,
Ashamed, for the embarrassment
So now my teeth are brushed and the involuntary muscles are putting
    Me under the kitchen table
Humming and singing quietly to myself
As the sun comes and night begins again—comes rolling out from in back
    Of my tongue   What is next?

Shortly after the composition of this poem, we passed a significant little milestone. At the conclusion of a lesson, I said as usual before leaving, "Good-bye, Barbara. Have a good day." For the first time she responded, "You too, Mr. Morrison." She began to take more care of her appearance and pursued her studies with greater interest. She seemed particularly intrigued with solving problems in geometry, and responded with a kind of hunger to its coherence and structure. Her homework assignments, from this point on, were done conscientiously.

Old friendships that had been cut off were renewed. She talked about these friends with me. Much of the original tension in our relationship disappeared. There was no doubt that by this time Barbara had reestablished real communication with the world and that there were other things in front of her eyes "besides objects." She did well that June in her Regents examinations and, on the recommendation of the psychotherapist who had worked with her during this period, returned to John Jay High School in September.

Setting into order words that dramatized her cowering posture and her dissatisfaction with the outside world helped her to see herself more clearly in her relationship with that world. She learned to externalize her emotions and become more objective about them. Questioning her ability to communicate helped her to realize that she wanted to communicate. Seeing herself huddled under the table helped her to understand that her real wish was to be out in the open. Even though these poems may prove to be forerunners of distinguished work to come, what is most meaningful at this point is that their creation assisted importantly in redirecting Barbara to a rewarding rapport with life.

Francisco

It was in the orthopedic ward at King's Hospital that Francisco, a sixteen-year-old boy of Puerto Rican origin, first came to my attention. The following poem, done as a class assignment, was written with his left hand, because his right was badly mangled, and it tells of the events that led to his hospitalization.

Bad dreams
What do they mean?
That's what I'm going to explain
There were two dreams
Similar to my accident.

In the first
I charged at some one
Or at myself
I was trying to kill some one
Or some thing
But in that some one
I saw myself.

That was my first nightmare
With the feeling of fear and death
Right upon me.

I remember seeing myself
Going around in a continuous circle
And in that circle there were two
    people
One of them was me.
And the other seemed to be me,
    also.
That's what I could not believe.

I awoke in my bed
Half-scared to death
Then my mother came into my
  room
And asked in Spanish,
"Que te pasa?"

And I said,
"Nada pasa, Mamma."
Then she said,
"O. K. Good night," and left.

I was afraid to go back to sleep
So prayed till morning came.
I began to believe the nightmare
  wasn't coming back
But it did come back in the same
  way
In a second dream
So right there, I knew
Those two dreams meant
  something.
I knew the fear would be back
But I did not know when it would
  be coming back.

It did come back
On September 23
I did everything normally.
I ate
And went to school.
But as evening came
I started getting nervous
And cold.
Then something hit me
It spoke to me
"Get a knife!"
And I went straight out
To find my destiny.

I got my knife.
As I walked, feeling jittery and
  strange
I got more nervous

Then, I thought
I should get high
To do what I must do.
I bought booze and was high.

I caught guts
And went to face it out
The face in the dream—my friend
I was scared
But I showed heart
Only too much

With my blade
I charged at him
To cut him open.
But with a wire
He had the best of me.
Did he disgrace me, Man.
I knew it
As soon as the aerial slashed my
  face.

It was anger and fear
That hit me that night.
Anger began piling up on me
As I kept fighting.
He was my friend
But I knew right there
That I must fight with him
When I stabbed him
I knew it was going to be the
  beginning
Of a long nightmare.
As soon as the aerial touched my
  face
The pain was like in a dream
But this was for real.
I couldn't believe it was right there.
It was like the nightmare falling
  upon me
I acted like an animal.
I wanted to kill my friend.
I charged, but as I charged him
He slashed me.

I fell to my knees
He kept on slashing
I was in great pain
Then another friend
Saw what was happening.
He picked up a garbage can
And chased him off
I got up from the ground and
    touched my face.
I felt the cut and blood
It was unbelievable.

I ran to South 9th street to the
    Center
Because I did not know
Where else to go.

All my friends saw my face, and
    asked,
"What happened?"
I started going crazy.
I kicked and hit at everyone in sight
My friends held me so that I could
    cool down.
One of the counselors took me to
    the basement
To wash the blood off.

When I took the water in my hands
I began to think
How I had disgraced myself.
I couldn't show myself to my
    parents.
Then my madness got to me.
I didn't care
About myself or the world
    anymore.
I turned around.
The first thing I saw
Was a window.
I hit at it.

As my hand pushed through the
    glass

I felt funny and tired.
I did not know what was happening
I cursed like any thing.

Even God!
When I stopped cursing
I looked down and saw my hand
    hanging.
I panicked like a woman

And bled like a dog.
Just then the counselor came in
And grabbed my hand
I yelled
I felt so weak
Like when a bunch of guys are on
    top of you
And when they finish
You try to get up

I begged the counselor
"Kill me, please.
Please kill me.
I don't want to face life anymore."
He put my hand in the sink
And kept it here.
I thought he put water on it
But it was the blood that was
    pouring out
Then he told me to cool it
Or I'd bleed to death.
I played it smart and cooled down.

He yelled for help
Someone came down.

It was another counselor
He pulled off my shirt
And tied it to my triceps
To stop the blood
Then the Priest came
And confessed me.
I was afraid to die
So prayed to Him up there.

After a while the cops came
That's when I stopped praying.
They asked me what happened to my hand

So I told them
Then they asked about my face.
I said I fell down.
They didn't believe me.
They called me a liar.
The ambulance came
And took me to Greenpoint Hospital.
That's when I finally felt bad

When all these people saw me
I knew what those people thought about me.
They said in their minds
"Look at that hoodlum
With the scar on his face."
I could tell by their eyes.
When they took me to Emergency

I heard one of the doctors say
"This boy needs surgery."
Man,
I never thought I'd be operated on.
I once saw a picture
But me? That's something new.
When they had me in O.R. they said to me
"Sorry, son, but that hand has got to come off."

I couldn't talk so I began to cry.
Then the doctor told my mother
What was going to happen.
My mother said, "No"
She asked to transfer me to another hospital
They took me to Kings County Hospital.
There they saved me and my hand.

Here I am in the hospital
Still waiting.
The doctors told me I am very lucky
I didn't lose hand or life.
They are trying to fix my hand
But they told me
That my hand won't be like it used to be
But God! I hope I have learned my lesson

The night of September 23, 1965
I almost knew what death meant.
I was a fool

But I am glad I haven't come to my end.

Thank God.
I've ruined my hand for life.
Please God, give me the power to get used to it
I only pray for that!

In our city slum areas, as the young come into conflict with the cultural patterns of their elders, scorning them for their inadequacies and shrugging off their authority, a new family comes into being. This is The Street, which tramples on gentleness and sensitivity. Here the boys develop loyalties to the street gang and to its leader—frequently a psychopathic adolescent lionized for his ruthlessness. The "turf" is the testing ground of their manhood. For the boys virility is symbolized in the switchblade. In a hail of broken bottles, bricks, stones and other missiles, they battle a foe from another block, and in this "rumble" establish their masculine role.

They adopt a smooth vocabulary: "man," "cool," "turf," living up to the gang ideal. Under cover of bravado they conceal from each other their secret fears, their anxieties and insecurities. It is cool to be conspicuously dressed in tight pants with slash pockets and to wear boots with Cuban heels or sharply pointed shoes. Their girl friends help to romanticize this way of life.

With a kind of swagger, Francisco carried this street style into the hospital ward. He affected a Van Dyke beard. He addressed me as "Teach," and asked me to call him by his gang name, "Frenchy." Exceedingly cavalier about his lessons, he proved clever at devising excuses for failing to perform his scheduled assignments. I permitted him to "outsmart" me and, since he enjoyed telling me about his gang activities, these stories became the focal point for some of our lessons. As his stories of certain skirmishes reminded me of the legends of the *Iliad*, I took the occasion to retell several adventures from this epic poem. He was fascinated. This was my cue to borrow a copy of Homer's poetry from the library and lend it to him.

The hospital nurses told me that he stayed awake all night reading. They couldn't imagine his being interested in anything but comic books. Francisco, however, was insatiable in his eagerness to know all the stories in the *Iliad* and to memorize the names of the heroes. Achilles, Hector, Diomed rolled off his lips as though he had been raised on them. I had him retell their adventures in writing. He caught the rhythms and language of the text so amazingly well that I could scarcely believe he had not plagiarized. I checked; he had not copied. The astonishing thing was that only a short time before this he seemed unable to spell the simplest words and appeared to know nothing of the structure of a sentence. Yet, describing the death of Patroclus, he wrote: "Achilles heard and saw the Trojans coming upon the Greek camp and Hector slaying many Greeks but only the mighty Diomed still showed courage." I could not praise him sufficiently, and he accepted my commendations as though they were food and drink. Recognizing his hunger for praise, I found many opportunities to tell him how well I thought of him. Since he had spoken of his accident, I asked him to write about it. He did. I was moved by the emotional pitch of his writing. Francisco was proud to hear me refer to his talent. Shortly afterwards, he shaved his beard, surrendered his swagger, and began to comport himself with dignity about the ward. He spoke to me about his future, of his new faith in education, and of his desire to marry and become a family man. After he left the hospital, I received word from the psychiatric social worker assigned to his school that she was impressed with Francisco's changed attitude. A plan for vocational rehabilitation was being prepared with his full cooperation.

It would appear that somewhere in the Homeric skirmishes he had dropped the false values of the gang along with his haunted sense of fear and anger. He was able to accept his true role, that of Francisco, a young man with a future. Gone was "Frenchy," cocky but scared; gone also the theatrical routine that led nowhere.

Katina

Her hometown newspaper predicted a glorious career for Katina as, full of romantic hopes and dreams, she prepared to embark from Greece to study in the United States. Her married sister, now a resident in obstetrics at a Brooklyn hospital, had preceded her. They shared an apartment and Katina was about to enter the second half of her senior year at Prospect Heights High School when she developed glomerulonephritis, necessitating home instruction after five weeks of hospitalization.

Lethargic and depressed, she emanated defeat and hopelessness. She had experienced a crushing sense of failure at school. Eager for popularity among her classmates, she felt that they, and some teachers as well, had ridiculed her because of her awkwardness in English. She felt that both academically and socially her adjustment had been disappointing. New acute physical pain brought on by a renal infection added to her despondency.

Aloof at first, she later asked me to address her as Tina. Her notebooks were replete with doodles. When subsequently she permitted me to examine them, I found among the drawings an impressive representation of Christ, portraying His agony as He dragged the cross to Calvary. The exhausted look in Katina's eyes showed that she knew only too well the crushing weight that she dramatized with this great realism. Her other drawings were of coffins and their tenants, of weeping figures and skeletons—all indications of her preoccupation with death and loss. Obviously, Tina possessed extraordinary sensitivity and the talent to express her emotions in artistic terms. I was not surprised to discover later that she could respond to the poetry of Keats and Shelley with an instinctive appreciation of their intent. Having noted her absorption in Keats's "Ode to a Nightingale," I related the mood of the poem to the poet's state of mind and asked her to describe her own emotions in verse form for the next assignment. Her deepseated unhappiness was visible at once in her first poem.

AUTUMN

My dreams
Yellow leaves, lifeless, dead.
My life
Skies gray, dark, filled with rain.
My hope
Pale, cowardly, scared.

The autobiographical reference is too explicit to be missed. I was understandably lavish in my praise and encouragement of her talent. A succession of gifted verses followed this first effort, all alike, sad and heartbreaking.

CONTRAST

Creation adorns the earth with flowers.
I feel the beating of swallows' wings.
The white mountain gets younger.
But dawn has not arrived in my heart.
Only affliction nests there.

WINTER

In my heart
Where cold winter reigns
Are the icicle tears
Of two nightingales
Who died, singing together
Of their golden love.

Shortly afterwards, writing of fate as a woman, she referred to the sterility of her life:

MY DESTINY

She reminded me that eyes were made for tears
She instructed me to respect darkness
My destiny stands over me like a strange lover.

Here she projects the terror that haunted her previous doodling.

Give me your little hand,
The only treasure of my life.
And don't leave me alone.
And don't withdraw from my side.
Now that there appears at the turn of the street
The elevation on which they have set up my cross.

Disillusion is brilliantly described in

EXPERIENCE

Remember
The bright sunsets in the bamboo of your youth
When you sang
Against the shouting of the wind?
Then you were a hollow reed
Easily broken.
Now that you've become a tree
Filled with substance,
You understand so well
The beauty of the sunset
But you don't sing anymore.

The first school day after Easter, I arrived at Tina's apartment for the morning lesson. There was no response to my ring. I was about to leave when Tina's sister opened the door. She had been sleeping and had no idea where my pupil might be. We were both beginning to feel alarmed when I heard some one running up the stairs. It was Tina, out of breath, her face radiant, her eyes sparkling. She had left the house at six o'clock that morning to observe the sunrise in a nearby park. Then to commemorate the event, she had composed a poem, which she gladly showed me. It provided unmistakable evidence of her return to psychic health.

DAWN

The sun has arrived in the sky
Saying "Goodby" to the dark daughter of time.
Life begins with the kiss of the sun.
The sun is a young boy looking at me, lustful,
With his large beautiful eyes.
I am so pretty when his rays caress
These velvet petals of mine that
Barely touch my delicate green trunk.
Everything is so peaceful, so still,
That I can almost hear the heartbeat of this radiant blond boy.
It is a pity that I cannot sing the beauty of the dawn,
But God made me a flower,
Reflecting the miracle of this lovely morning.

The imagery of her later poetry continued to bear the imprint of that radiant morning.

LOVE

Your embraces were created to hold me
And my dreams.
Your eyes to incise my figure,
To let me exist.
Your hands to take the colors
Of my sorrow,
And hang smiles everywhere.

In June, after graduation, she was to return to her family in Greece for a visit. Before she boarded the plane, she confided to me, "I'm happy. I'm so happy." So by unburdening herself of an obsessive despair through the medium of words, she had successfully reintegrated a personality previously damaged by maladjustment at school and the deleterious effects of a protracted illness. I believe that she has also produced some truly memorable verse. The metaphors of Tina's tribute to poetry reveal the therapeutic magic it has held for her.

TO POETRY

You shine on my bitter days
Like a sky full of stars
Like the sun that breaks his arrows

On a dark river,
My beloved poetry
Folds my soul into blue elements
So that I can be water,
Tempest, or flame.

REFERENCES

1. Rosenblatt, Louise, *Literature as Exploration* (New York, D. Appleton-Century, 1938).
2. Drew, Elizabeth, *Discovering Poetry* (New York, Norton, 1933).

IN PUBLIC SCHOOLS

Self-Discovery for Teacher and Youngster through Poetry

ART BERGER, Ph.D.

The behavior that gets labeled "disturbed" is, as R. D. Laing says, a strategy that a person invents in order to live in an unlivable situation. And children are presented with a situation that is hardly livable at an early age. Their elders impose upon them thorough and rapid brainwashing techniques, so that by the time they are fifteen, they are, like their elders, "half crazed...more or less adjusted to a mad world."[1] This is the normality for which the present age strives.

Behavior in both home and school becomes a game that is played in compliance to others. What to do, say, or experience is taught, imposed from outside the body and mind. The effect of all this violence done to the growing psyche in the name of love is to seal off any inner life or fill it with terror.

The poet, through the exploration of his own inner space and time, becomes a specialist in those inner experiences called dreams, images, visions, reverie, memory, and hallucination. This is why the poet has always had affinity for both the child and the madman—both victims of the denial and repression of self fostered by family, school, and society.

I have worked as poet-in-residence in both inner city and suburban schools. In this work the poet aims, through inventive techniques, to encourage children to express themselves creatively through poetry and stimulate creativity in teachers and administrators through workshops and seminars. This work has convinced me that the dull prose of programmed learning stands in the way of the child's being free to construct his own being. The tool the child needs is his own free imagination. With this he builds extensions of himself, bridging the gaps from his inner self to outer space. Building bridges comes naturally, since the infant mind has always identified with his environment. In this sense the child has always been aware of the "tissue of living skin" that McLuhan proclaims is the nature of all matter on our world.

Metaphorical thought comes naturally to the child and creates the model for him to grow by. The spontaneous release of this creative energy allows the child's personality to unfold like a rose. Aid from the teacher can come only from the arrangement and manipulation of environmental factors that will foster this growth. He also brings about exposure to sources of inspiration that will nurture the growing soul of the child.

According to Maria Montessori, the first act of the educator should be "to stimulate life—leaving it free to develop, to unfold."[2] Thus the teacher becomes a director of the spontaneous work of the children. Jerome Bruner has said that by the same token, "spontaneity can be expected from the students to the degree that the teacher demonstrates spontaneity."[3]

I have been consciously applying this thinking to my own work as poet-in-the-classroom. I have functioned existentially. I face each day as it comes and try to generate creative energy in the class out of fresh layers of consciousness every time. Anything that I have given too much thought to in advance and structured into a plan had become stale and uninspired by the time I introduced it. My response to the moment and place, drawing reservoirs of inner resources and materials in my large bag to supplement and alter the environment, was what worked best. Working from the top of the head (soul would be more correct) becomes a way of life. Responding to the day—it could be the sky, weather, the headlines, vibrations from the school, something going on in the class as I entered—gave me the cue as to what my "thing" was to be. Building a supply of resources, both material and spiritual, all the time, made this process possible.

The lesson plan is a "middle-man" that filters out the freshness of discovery and dehydrates the living presence of the teacher. Building bridges from the inner world outward and encouraging the child to express what is in his mind, whether it is peaceful or violent, without censure or direction produces the drama, joy, variation, and unpredictability of the open classroom. Where creativity is nurtured, explosions in poetry and art are produced. Art is doing, and from doing comes learning.

Montessori places the "psychic salvation" of the child above the mere obligation to provide instruction as the goal for which schools should aim. She equates it with "beauty of Nature as an end in itself."[4]

If spiritual forces working and developing within the child are dependent on exposure to external forces, the freedom to develop these physical needs becomes a responsibility of the teacher. To be comfortable, this movement from the inner man outward, from the known to the unknown, from the organic to the inorganic, must be nourished by the imagination.

The fruit of the imagination is linked to observation of the real: "There is a vast gulf between the delirious confusion of thought and the metaphorical eloquence of the imagination."[5] Following this reasoning, the child perfects himself as he originates images that are more perfect. It is necessary to help children find the material required by the imagination from out of their sharpened perception of the environment.

The taking on of characteristics from the environment, the mimicry that in many animals is adaptive, such as the white fur of the polar bear or the leaf shape of butterfly wings is a "psychic phenomenon which occurs in childhood."[6] The child absorbs the life going on about him and becomes one with it. Impressions so profound take place that psychochemical changes occur by which his mind becomes the environment.

Much of the writing I have evoked from children by creating concerns for environment by varied visual material, rock music, and selected poetry, has been metaphorical. This whole exercise of calling on the child's own resources to reach into the mind for something to say nourishes the inner eye and preserves a child's own true personality.

Eliciting free expression through writing or any other medium serves the function of childhood which is to construct models of living which make him free to act in and influence his world. An examination of the children's writing included in this essay is typical of the insights into the problems of the times that the children have. But we have not been listening to the children, and as Montessori states:

> It is man's own fault if the majority of human beings are inferior, for the formation of their characters during the constructive period has been prevented. We have to make an effort to

> recapture the true human level, letting our
> children use their creative powers.

Considering the state of the nation, these lines from Jane Stembridge's poem, *The Children*, makes sense:

> I want a president who's nine years old
> to organize the country from his
> treehouse home

But Montessori's appraisal of the insensitivity of the elders to the real needs of the children still holds true: "... We regard as manifestations of evil instincts the rebellions of the child treated as a beast, his obscure protests and desperations...."[8]

The technological revolution makes imperative a corresponding revolution in the sociology and psychology. The children have an instinct for this, while the adults are blind to the obvious. The whole question of our present and future is wrapped up in the "social question of the child."[9]

The plight of the American middle-class child is presented in these words of Montessori: "Where our lives are oppressed, there can be no health for us, even though we eat of princely banquets or in splendid buildings."[10]

This same thought is poignantly conveyed in the following poem by a sixth grader:

> People walking in the street
> Almost mechanically doing the
> Same things they've been doing
> Year after year, eating the same
> Meat and potatoes stew every
> Wednesday for supper.
> Gertrude and friends, playing
> Their regular mah jong game.
> Always the same doing the
> Same thing day after day,
> Year after year. No change,
> Nothing different, shutting out
> All other people.

But parents want their children to do as they do, and any "diversity is called 'naughtiness' "[11] This naughtiness is, in reality, the struggle to grow, to develop creative energy and form personality. Yet, "we adults stifle these wants."[12] It is only when liberated from such tyranny that their spirits have "sprung up like a jet of water from an internal fount."[13] When this happens powers are released that can take us to a bright new world, led by the child become the New Man.

The children show in their writings that they can dream up visions of the utopias they would like their future to contain. This poem by another sixth-grader is typical of many:

> Soft springwater
> A court of order
> Warm summer days
> Cool fresh air
> Everything natural
> Everyone would share
> Just a penny for an apple
> Love sweet love
> Peace for all
> Throw a party
> Have a ball
> No king
> Just peace and love
> Just like a dove
> Alas, its just a dream,
> A thought
> Something other men have
> Sought.
>
> I guess I'll have to give up
> Like most other men
> But if I have a chance
> I'll start my dream again.
> *Howard grade 6*

The writing that children do opens up windows into their heads. This is an accomplishment that seems to frustrate teachers and counselors. This function is defined in the words of a New Jersey high school student after a particularly revelatory outpouring of spontaneous writing: "Mr. Berger, you must be some kind of shrink."

I really began to realize the nature of what was happening after reading these notes of a teacher/observer at a session in a fifth grade class:

Sound-Metaphor-Image
Eye in Ear

These are the words I carried away from the sessions. The rest is unable to surface as words of criticism or analysis.

The only explanation I can offer is that I was stirred so deeply by each multi-faceted experience that my unconscious is still in a state of turmoil and the experience is not ready to surface and express itself in verbal form.

I do recall the sessions—in terms of color, sound, and mostly feeling. But no analysis comes forth—only poems. Each time I recall the poetry sessions out comes a new poem or part of a poem. I can't offer suggestions from a teacher's point of view until I have ridden the wild horse to where I am going. Then I can look back to describe the journey.

Marjorie N.

To have released a typically structured teacher from her world of sterile curriculum and lesson plan into the milieu of soul and feeling that is crystallizing into her poems, something must have been happening there. A retrospective search of my diaries showed me that what was happening was that the mystique of the poet made possible a rapport that transformed the class into a group encounter. The outpouring of writing contains within it an acting out in writing of all the problems of identity, security, mystery, and wonder that beset kids and are generally out of bounds in the classroom.

The following is a compression of my notes and may give some clues on what the mystique is that brought forth writing that the school psychologists and counselors were to find valuable in dealing with these children.

An aspect of the youth culture that has worked well for me in the classroom and that I want to discuss is the pop music. If one has ears, one knows that the most pervasive aspect of their culture is the sounds and message of soul and rock. These, born out of that most poignant expression of personal and immediate human experience, the blues, are here to stay and cannot be ignored. In fact, their music and lyrics are the literature of a large portion of young people today.

The music has been the most evocative material that I have used.

I have accumulated a treasure of writing bearing its imprint. The building of a nation, social and racial inequality, industrial growth and rural decay, the move to the cities, personal protest, and spiritual solace are all in the blues.

I start by telling how it all began with the *blues* in the deep south with the work song of the field hand wrapped into the lyrics. The heat of the Delta sun and the surge of the Mississippi reached into their souls, throbbing out the beat of the blues. The movement of the cities added the tempo and tension to big beat city blues, and now the young have added the magic of poetry and electronics.

The bluesmen are always at my side in the classroom by way of my portable stereo tape player. John Lee Hooker's *Teaching the Blues* gives the basic beat and discipline, while Lightning Hopkins' *I Heard My Children Crying* really moves the class. Then we talk about the injustice of hungry kids in a world of plenty. B. B. King's *Why I Sing the Blues* brings it all up to date.

In a typical class hour I may use a singer like Otis Redding, who helped convert teen-age America to rhythm and blues, to start the creative energy going. He sings *Satisfaction* and *Shake*, causing vibrations to surge from everyone. I use the line "shake it like a bowl of soup" to show how words can make one see (imagery) and "Sat-is-fak-shun" as the articulating of sound in language that starts fingers snapping.

After reading blues lyrics with the proper beat stresses and intonation, I ask them to write a small blues, three- or four-liner, four beats to the line, with the last line running on to achieve resolution of the question or problem raised in the first line and emphasized in the second. This "blueslet" is to carry a personal message with words that have a jazz sound. I always do whatever I ask of them myself and chalk one up on the board.

> Some people think that school is just a mess
> Some people think that school is all the best
> But I think that together in this class
>   we sure can have some fun.

While their pencils are working, the player keeps spinning out a blues sound to give them a beat to write to. Sometimes I play my harmonica. Some kids may stare empty-eyed at their paper, but as I cruise around I talk with the idle ones in an effort to turn on their imaginations. Sometimes I suggest that they try the title or a line from their favorite song and try to build their own thing on that. One boy answered my query as to what idea he had with "Nothin'." I said, "Okay, let's write a blueslet about "Nothin'." This is what he turned in:

> Oh man I have nothin' to do
> I can't call my baby nor sing the blues
> I have nothin' to do... Nothin'
> Mark

School seems to be one of the most popular themes among these sixth graders for singing the blues.

> The blues is when it rains watch out kid
> Here comes the blues
> The blues is when you have to go to school.
> Con

> Today is a test oh what a mess
> Oh my! I just remembered, two tests
> I got the blues. I got the blues.
> Bonnie

Some of the blueslets are very topical, especially at times when urban problems are in the news.

SUBWAY BLUES

> You make better time if you walk the track
> Man I want my money back
> Watcha think I have a lifetime to lose
> That's why I have those subway blues.
> Valerie

POLLUTION BLUES

> Its funky junk in the air it stunk
> don't go near it or you'll flunk

> I can't help it if junk is in the air and sea
> Cause dontcha blame it on me.
> *Linda*

> In this city of old New York
> I think we all feel like a cork
> Its like a cap on a bottle
> Everyone keeps putting you on.
> *Eric*

Many of the pieces point to personal concerns of family, identity, future.

> I left my job because I had to eat slob
> and I was sad and I had to sit
> in a garbage can and I was a bum
> for seven years and never had a wife to pinch my ears.
> *Neal*

> My father didn't know the meaning of work
> he disrespected mama and treat us like dirt
> So I got into a car and had a wreck
> So all you need is a little respect.
> *Linda*

And some wrote purely in a spirit of having fun with the sound and rhythm of words.

> Its my thang and a rang a dang dang
> Do what you want to because
> Its my thang and a rang a dang dang.
> *Angelo*

Times have not changed since William Shakespeare found the same joy in the sound of words:

> In the springtime, the only pretty ring-time,
> When birds do sing hey ding a ding, ding.

Self-Discovery for Teacher and Youngster through Poetry

Using the present to build bridges to the past works, provided you tell Shakespeare like it is, "with a hey, and a ho, and a hey nonino."*

Rock starts at this elemental level of incantation that conveys mood:

> Sha da da da sha da da da da
> sha da da da sha da da da da
> ... get a job.

and

> Who put the bomp
> In the bomp-pa bomp-pa bomp.
>
> Beep beep mother she cheap
> She walk in the street
> and talk in her sleep
> and she get me a beep
> I weep in my sleep.
> *Cheryl*

• • •

> Man man I lost a man
> His name was Sam Sam Sam
> Bop bop ram Sam man
> I loved that man
> He went bam bam slam.
> *Larry*

> Pata Pata whats the matter
> You got to have soul to go go go
> Nice and fly people always
> get high why why why.
> *Erica*

Erica's verse voices a concern about those who seek escape from boredom in drugs. But poetry shows a way to a new high. In fact, after one stimulating session one boy said, "Mr. Berger, this is better than sniffing glue."

*From *As You Like It* by William Shakespeare

Using words that snap, crackle and pop is fun and generally loosens up the mind. Taking advantage of this, I make the point that to make poems and lyrics have rhythms it is necessary to go by some rules, just as basketball is played by the rules and a pie is baked from a recipe. One could either make one's own rules or use an established form. The classical cinquain is useful. I ask for 22 syllables in a 2-4-6-8-2 pattern using crisp words that convey soul, feeling, and personal concerns. We call these poems jazz cinqs.

> The street
> I love it baby
> cuttin 'tween the zooming cars
> you gotta split when the seconds
> right.   Split man.
> *Alex*

• • •

> The gang
> the gang in the
> street is bad with me we
> hustle we fight we laugh out loud
> the gang.
> *Vincent*

Vincent was writing out of his life, which at that point seemed inevitably running toward the dead end that so many urban poor kids face. Writing out of his own experience became an absorption of his and gave him new direction. When I last saw him before he entered high school he said that his goal now was law enforcement.

> People
> Some people think
> they're hip. Some people
> they cool but me—I know
> I fly.
> *Beryl*

• • •

> Its love
> its love that keeps
> the bells ringing sharp cracks
> the two of us are making time
> its love.
>
> *Julie*

One could pursue this diction and sound into other forms. Applying western idiom and beat to a Japanese form, the haiku, we invent the *rocku*. Verses of this genre generally deal with environment.

> My pretty blue sky
> was nice then the junk came
> and now it is gray.
>
> *Monique*

• • •

> Oil and other junk coming out
> of drains the poor Hudson
> suffering all those pains.
>
> *Lee*

Tracking the rock trail in search of what there is in the sounds the kids are listening to becomes a key to turning on their own writing. I have found that rock—in addition to being history and ballad—is metaphor. Artists like Simon and Garfunkel are masters at it in pieces like *I am a Rock*, with the beautiful line "and a rock feels no pain, an island never cries."* The lyrics of artists like *The Doors, Jimi Hendrix, The Temptations,* and others are loaded with magical metaphors that I use as models. With this influence the children's writing takes on self-searching dimensions like: "I am the wind/because I am as cool as a breeze"; "I am a dot/I stay in one spot"; "I am a sponge/I want to sop everybody up."

> I'm a number
> And when I'm in the deck
> No one knows me yet.
>
> *Adriana*

---

* © 1966 Paul Simon. Used with the permission of the publisher.

I am a tree
and trees can see everywhere
up there its cool and
I find the inside of me
is made right
nothing is wrong
except for the outside
the people who do not dig
love and peace
but they should dig it.
                    Joan

• • •

Me
I was an egg
I became a baby bird
I became a bigger baby bird
I became a bolder bigger baby bird
I became an even bigger bolder but still a baby bird
Maybe I'll be a big bold baby bald Eagle.
                    John

The imagery of rock verbally colors the grey of urban life with "...a rose in Spanish Harlem/its growing in the street/right up through the concrete."* It is emulated in much starker terms by a seventh-grader.

THE STREET

Its big and black
with a white line.
Its very long
and it never stops.
Its good for cars and trucks
and I like it.
                    Allen

---

* © 1960 and © 1961 by Hill and Range Songs, Inc. and Tris Music Co., Inc. Sole selling agent: Hill and Range Songs, Inc. Used by permission.

Self-Discovery for Teacher and Youngster through Poetry

Just as Simon and Garfunkel acknowledge the problem of nature in the city by greeting the lamppost with a big hello and telling it they've come to watch its flowers grow, city kids become skeptical and make statements like this:

> When the moon
> comes through pollution
> a miracle has occurred.
> *Henry*

A song like the Beatles' *Nowhere Man* speaks to the question of identity that most kids are struggling with and can evoke writing like this:

> ABOUT DAVID
>
> David digs this girl
> But don't know how to tell her
> So the man is uptight
> In a world of his own.
> And can't break out of his bag.
> When the words come out
> They sound like his rap is
> But they don't last long
> And he wish his rap was strong
> then he have to be right.
> *David* grade 8

> THE KIND OF PERSON I AM
>
> I was born in the slums and I
> was looking for a ball then
> this guy came and said that I
> was a Chink and that what bit
> me I took him and I knock the
> hell out of him and then let go
> from then on I became a bum and
> I don't care for myself and
> thats the whole truth, but
> I'm changing inside in the outside.
> *Jose* grade 5

The concept of soul, in so much of the music, is very close to identity with the concern for color woven into it, and provides much stimulus for writing.

> The color of a soul
> It's yellow and red and black & white
>   all joined together.
> What do you do with a black man's
> soul in a Baptist body?
> The hair in the braids & the afros too
> Burnt-marshamallow-colored skin
> Black is beautiful too.
>   *Barbara* grade 6

And as alien as the sound of the pop music is to the adult ear, the theme of love is always there, and one is never too young to talk or write about love.

> What is love, is it a sickness or spring fever?
>   Some people do not know what love is.
>   Some will never find out.
> You are hollow without love, you are nothing
>   without love. But some people
>   will never find out.
> Love is a picture on a canvas. Without love
>   your canvas is empty.
>   *Yvonne* grade 6

And the child whose frustration with the emptiness of the learning process as it is, is always with us:

> I CAN'T THINK
>
> I can't think, my head is like a loose TV spring
> that's why I can't think of anything to write.
> It's like I've never learned anything before.
> So I just sit there doin' nothin.
> Ain't nobody around c'n learn from.
> I can't think! Can you?
>   *Laurie* grade 6

The quest for identity comes by painfully in preadolescence. But for black children it is compounded in a world where whiteness is the norm set up for them to emulate. Fortunately their culture resists this, and the poetry and music provides the nurture that is lacking in the curriculum. A child who had been written off as brain damaged and relegated to a CRMD class, came to flower when she discovered Black Power, and has been shaping her identity in writing since.

THE WORD

The word man
the word has power man.
People on the street man,
can't write a thing baby.
Sit up man
do your thing baby.
Black Power is my thing.

Oh baby that not it
You aint doing
what I told you man,
us Black People are proud
of our color.
Baby you white people
are nothing.
Us Black People
are beautiful.
      Do your
           thing.
Sherry grade 6

And from an undersized, undernourished street boy comes this manifestation of strength:

I am 90 pounds of black meat
And these pounds are really sleek
Color me dark because thats what I am
Power and Power is what I am
Brother to Brother is my game
Power Brother Power Brother is my name.
           Mark grade 6

Following the kids into their world, I have found that the street is a garden of poetry where they pass on by word of mouth a rich collection of folk lore that grows and changes with each generation.

This is an area where I can both share and learn from them. There is nothing they like to talk about more than their own thing. And counting out, clapping, rope-jumping chants, graffiti, soundings, rank-outs (Dozens) are their thing. I approached this street culture as a hunt for treasure and came up with rich findings from the sixth-, seventh-, and eighth-graders that I visit regularly. Here is a sampling:

Ballads are plentiful—

> Old Dan Tucker was a mighty man
> he washed his face with a frying pan
> he combed his hair with a wagon wheel
> and died with a toothache in his heel.

The images are seldom abstract and basic sex education takes place.

> Milk is Milk
> Cheese is Cheese
> What is a kiss
> without a squeeze

• • •

> Pork Chops, Pork Chops
> Makes a little gravy
> Your thing, his thing
> Makes a little baby.

Constant exposure to the TV commercials creates a new source of imagery. The following item contributed by a fifth-grader gives insight into how the kids view the world as constructed of commodities. The inversions in it form a keen lampooning of the material hangups of their elders.

> Smoke Coca Cola cigarettes
> Chew Wrigley spearmint beer
> Kennel-ration dogfood makes your wife's complexion clear
> Chocolate covered mothballs, they always satisfy
> Brush your teeth with Lifebuoy soap and watch the suds go by
> Take your next vacation in a brand new Frigidaire
> Learn to play the piano in your winter underwear
> Simonize your baby with a Hershey candy bar

Self-Discovery for Teacher and Youngster through Poetry 245

> Texaco's the beauty cream that's used by every star
> Doctors say that babies should smoke until they're three
> People over 60 use a brand named Liptons tea
> If you want to make this song a better one today
> Buy a record of it and break it right away... Hey!

The topical nature of the poetry of the street is shown by the way this one swept the country via the children's grapevine within a few months of the popularization of the black power slogan. On a trip I made to the West Coast at the time I heard versions of this in Chicago and Watts. This comes from a school in South Jamaica, New York.

> Ungawa black power
> what you gonna do
> box the boogaloo
> what you think is best
> hit 'em in the chest
> I said beep bee, bang bang
> Ungawa black power.

Obscenities become a language of their own, foreign to teachers who reject the culture because the language does not fit into their antiseptic model of the world, thus making of the classroom a truly sterile place. This one, loaded with taboo language, is really a caricature of adult figures, very possibly the teacher.

> Little Orphan Annie with the greasy granny
> Frankenstein with the big behind
> Cleopatra the titty snatcher
> Motherfucker the titty sucker.

Innumerable connotations come from the sensitive oedipal words that can mean anything from hatred to admiration, depending on the situation. On the street, words like this take on meanings and express emotions in a mode that is foreign to middle-class experience. A boy discovers, especially in the environment of a public school, that he cannot express what he feels about anything meaningful—like sex or race or discovery—in the language taught at school. This conflict is especially true for black youths because their lives give the lie to what they are taught in school. This is why the vulgar euphemisms of sex and body functions take on for school youth such ambiguous, underground, yet viable meaning.

This language is used artfully in a schoolyard game more common than basketball called the Dirty Dozens. Its aim is to make the opponent "blow his cool" that is, cry, yell or fight, by making funny, insulting, sexual remarks about his family and his mother in particular. Boys get reputations for being good Dozens players just as they do for being "bad." (On the street, "bad" has good, even heroic connotations.) Often the Dozens rhyme like this one:

> The way he's talking about you is a cryin' shame;
> He say he rather ride your Momma than a choo-choo train!

On New York streets "ranking" is a different name for a less sexual version of the Dozens that has gone beyond the black community. Rankouts transcend mere four-letter words; creativity and imagery are their forte. They are a form of found poetry that pick at the sores of poverty. The insults focus on ragged clothing, cramped and broken down apartments, the scarcity of food. They amount to an urban bestiary, featuring the roach, bug, mouse, and rat.

After generating some strong dialogues among seventh- and eighth-graders, I transformed the verbalization into writing by telling them to "stop running off at the mouth and run it off the ends of their pencils onto paper so that we can publish them and let others know what the young folks are saying."

> If the man in front of me didn't have more plaid
> stamps, I would have got your mother first.
>
> Your mother is like a doorknob
> Everybody gets a turn.
>
> I walked in your house and I saw your father
> directing roach traffic.
>
> I slept in your house last night
> and the roaches pushed me out of bed.
>
> The walls in your house are so close together
> that the mice have to walk single file.
>
> I walked in your front door
> and tripped over the backyard fence.

> Oh man, there's so much dust in your house
> the roaches be playing Lawrence of Arabia.
>
> When I asked your Ma for a glass of water,
> she said, "Wait till the tide comes in."

This bitter humor is an attempt to deal with realities these children see and feel helpless to change. Their inability to understand or solve these problems leads to an obsession with them. Adults misinterpret this attempt of children to explore the reality of the world around them by telling them that they are bad. For instance, after having been shown some of the rankouts written by a boy in her class, one teacher said, "Why encourage that, that is just what we are trying to take them away from. Why don't you have them write an essay on brotherhood."

A child's writing should be considered as an intimate revelation of his feelings and impressions, one to be respected. Therefore teachers must learn to accept the language of the children without imposing arbitrary standards of usage that frustrate the free flow of expression. Early emphasis on 'correct' usage can make the act of writing no more than an anxious, crippling exercise for many children.

No arbitrary limits should be placed on the range of experience and language used in the classroom. If children or teachers feel that words or references or ideas that are important to them must be censored or are "out of bounds" then the classroom itself can become a sterile and irrelevant place.

The poetry explosion that takes place when the child is free to take spontaneously from the external world material in order to compose, is necessary for the health of his inner life. As Sylvia Ashton-Warner, the New Zealand teacher who concentrated on "organic writing," said, "the reaching back into the mind for something to say, nurtures the organic idea and exercises the inner eye;"[14] it is this that can preserve and protect for a little longer his own true personality.

REFERENCES

1. R. D. Laing, *The Politics of Experience* (New York, Pantheon Books, 1967) p. 58.
2. Maria Montessori, *The Montessori Method* (New York, Frederick A. Stokes, 1912) p. 176.
3. Jerome S. Bruner, *The Process of Education* (New York, Vintage Books, 1963) p. 90.

4. Maria Montessori, *Spontaneous Activity in Education* (New York, Schocken Books, 1965) p. 127.
5. *Ibid.*, p. 256.
6. Maria Montessori, *The Absorbent Mind* (New York, Dell, 1967) p. 59.
7. *Ibid.*, p. 214.
8. *Spontaneous Activity in Education*, p. 196.
9. *Ibid.*, p. 17.
10. *Ibid.*, p. 24.
11. *Ibid.*, p. 298.
12. *Ibid.*, p. 323.
13. *Ibid.*, p. 324.
14. Sylvia Ashton-Warner, *Teacher* (New York, Simon & Schuster, 1963) p. 79.

Poetry Therapy in a "600" School and in a Counseling Center

Creative Writing as a Therapeutic Instrument

DOROTHY KOBAK, Ph.D.

Creativity, when appraised as an inborn or natural tendency, can be used therapeutically in the healing of emotional disturbances and disordered attitudes. It builds on the innate facet of every person's inheritance, *Eros*, the will to live. For to create is in some sense to be born again.

Creative writing can be a therapeutic vehicle that offers the client an opportunity to turn his attention inward towards repressed and unconscious material, without having this material modified or camouflaged. Through it, first thoughts are expressed, which in oral expression are often censored, edited, or distorted because of the presence of a listener (therapist). Thus in writing resistance is lessened, and the most flagrant fantasies may be more freely expressed with less danger of conversion from their raw form by the need for approval or fear of disapproval. We have studied the therapeutic efficacy of this process in both a group setting and individual therapy.

The "600" School

We programmed poetry and story writing in the group setting at a "600" school, a specialized educational facility operating within the framework of the New York City Board of Education, for the socially and emotionally maladjusted pupil. Since we were working with many boys whose inner controls were weak or minimal, structured conditions appeared advantageous. Thus, rather than have them write on anything they chose, the therapist encouraged them to amplify their thinking for the broadest possible response offered the topic. The paucity of the boys' inner resources was a determining factor in this. To burden them with choice of subject matter might have reinforced their always painfully present sense of inadequacy. A set topic added security and comfort to the process and gave them a springboard from which to develop their ideas.

The four boys chosen for this pilot group were of the passive-aggressive type, with clinically revealed diversity as well as similarities in their problems. Their conduct changed significantly as familiarity with this new mode of self-expression increased. At the beginning, attention span in writing was short, but there was never any resistance to writing. Both during the writing and discussion sessions, however, great anxiety was manifested by immediate body movements. At times, their scrawls and pencil doodlings over their own writing often rendered it illegible, indicating an unconscious self-deprecating mechanism as well as an attempt at concealment. Gradually, both of these conditions diminished. Initially, writing was sparse, both in quantity and depth, and the group often attempted to escape into generalities.

Written while the group was in session, the following poem illustrates the endeavor of one boy. It served as a springboard for discussion of "sentimental" material hitherto frowned on by the boys as "square."

A FISHERMAN

There once was a fisherman who lived at sea.
He had a boat, it sailed so free.
He knew some sailors big and strong
Who sailed with him the whole day long.

One day they went out for a swim,
And found a rowboat neat and trim.
It was piled with flowers red and white,
Roses, and violets shining as light.

They pushed the boat up to the shore.
They hoped that they could find some more.
But there was no more to be found,
Even though they searched around.

So they went back to their own big boat.
They set the sails and went afloat.

They ate a meal and went to bed,
Thinking of flowers all white and red.

The next was achieved in the manner of a "Round Robin" enterprise; that is, each boy added a sentence until the poem was completed. It afforded a tremendous "togetherness" for the boys, who, mostly self-centered loners, rarely gave of themselves in cooperative ventures. Their sense of satisfaction in building something with others corroborated this method. The end goal was the stressed factor, not the immediate satisfaction of contributing a line. The project was an "instant success," despite the need to contain themselves until the poem was finished. When it was, there was a mirthful boast of mutual congratulation at the success of their common effort. This was particularly gratifying, in that these boys hitherto had always evidenced low frustration tolerance.

THINGS WE LIKE

I like trees because they are green,
I like to eat especially beans.
I like the sky but I don't know why.
My hair is black and I am shy.
I like the sea because it is blue.
I like you because you are true.
I like a boy who has a gun.
But to have a gun would spoil our fun.

The introverted boy offered the lines about the "green trees" and the "blue sea," yet he added the hostile line on the gun. Our obese member contributed the line about "eating beans," but gave the concluding lines about the gun "spoiling the fun": he had sublimated his angers through eating. The rejected boy, who desperately craved a relationship both from peers and therapist, described his shyness and pointed to the therapist when he gave his line, "I like you because you are true."

Although the writing activity was structured, the talking periods following the writing were free and always animated. In reading their material, the boys only rarely seemed embarrassed to reveal their productions or to expand on them. The discussion would often digress far from the original written material, very much in the manner of free association. A small point mentioned by one member would often touch off a tangential train of thought in another and then be further developed by the group.

In one discussion, one boy said, "We get love in this group." Appraising what this meant, one boy thought that he must mean that the therapist "likes him better than his own mother does." Another said that the therapist acts like a nice mother, and this could be what he meant. A third, who had a deep hostility towards his mother, moved on to say he wished mothers could be changed. The discussion wound up with comments concerning the killing of parents, the role of punishment, aspects of life the boys would like to see changed. Much of the undercurrent of the conversation reflected hostility and personal deprivation.

The therapeutic effect of these talk sessions following the writing lay in the fact that one boy's ability to express his feelings overtly often would free another boy to discuss a sensitive area that had previously been too threatening for him to discuss. This form of "derivative insight and spectator therapy" had therefore more than a small element of emotional contagion. It led to a lessening of resistance towards self-revelation and to decreased feelings of isolation.

In terms of their story writing, their fantasy lives were exposed and unrealistic flights into unattainable goals discussed. Writing a "Round Robin" *story*, which again required that each member add a sentence until the story was completed, the boys unleashed hostility to authority and angry expressions of violence. They introduced certain questions of morality, and evidenced a need for sheer revelry in make-believe adventurous escapism. Yet their *poems* showed a melancholy search for beauty, a pathetic loneliness, and sometimes a hopeless depression. In contrast to this, they wrote a *play* in which they experienced a vicarious identification with a hero who was a millionaire tycoon of the toilet paper industry!

By creating something, the boys saw themselves eventually as participants in a socially valuable or "building situation" rather than in the antisocial "breaking down" arena, which had previously characterized their lives. For boys who had rarely experienced recognition or success, acknowledged accomplishment here tasted sweet, and feelings of inferiority diminished.

The peak of emotional impact came when a boy read his "own work" to both therapist and fellow members. He was "on stage" with his own creation, making his contribution to the group process. By tapping his own creative potential, he had opened new avenues of responses, hitherto unused, which, as they became second nature to him, equipped him more fully for even rougher encounters with these emotions in future experiences. If once he had been an isolate, a failure with no sense of belonging, he was now back in communication with his fellow man. By creating—by giving of himself—he was no longer "different" but now was contributing. His own thoughts, from his depths, avenues of estrangement before, now, by writing and expressing, had become *the avenues of permission* to rejoin the society as a person committed to its functions.

The Mid-Way Counseling Center

At the Mid-Way Counseling Center, a religiopsychiatric clinic, poetry therapy was practiced in a joint endeavor with Dr. Joseph H. Gelberman, Director. In individual therapy with adults, writing poetry became an effective tool for uncommunicative and constricted clients impotent to express their feelings. The creative efforts illustrated below had the therapeutic effect of releasing on paper thoughts that clients had difficulties saying—difficulties due to a damaged ability to relate, originating from early insecurities that prohibited trust in people, especially with emotionally charged material. Written between one session and the next, this poem represents a dialogue with self as the "listener" and thereby lessened the resistance to expression of feeling.

> Because you have paved the way,
> I now know the gift of life
> And see light in every day.
> I now have the strength,
> To face each day
> And I know I will prevail.
> I now can hope,
> And I know I will find success.
> I now can share—
> My thoughts, my dreams, and fears.
> I now feel life—
> Its sorrows and its joys.

> I now have patience
> And know, that in time
> I will give, and receive,
> The blessings of Love.

Examination of this poem with the client suggested honest self-appraisal, delineation of problem, ambivalence, despair, but hope for the goals that she herself defined: "And know, that in time/I will give, and receive,/The blessings of Love." We could then establish with the client that when this had occurred, healing had taken place.

The following are excerpts from poems written by a client who "could not feel" and "could not love." Sessions would usually elicit only arid, factual, question-like relating. However, her poems revealed the depth of the transference, the therapist as ego ideal, and a testing-out need for trust.

SESSION WITH GOD

> What a sweet repast
> To sit and behold
> The still, small voice
> Of God speaking through you.

TO YOU WHO ARE

> She is dear to me,
> Dearer with each step up.
> To be as loving as she,
> Could I but become.

FEELINGS PREVAIL

> I want your understanding;
> To be near as I ascend.
> Sharing with you the joys
> As once we shared pain.

Later, when there was much improvement in relating feeling, she wrote the following excerpt seeking the therapist's praise and approval.

> It is Love that shows me how.
> It gave me Soul to speak now.

Please look at me anew,
See how much I grew.

Another client, who sought withdrawal from people for fear of his own impulses and of failure, describes his loneliness and self-imposed exile.

LONELINESS

As an old friend, you walk in,
Ever ready to taunt,
Always accompanied by tears—
Yet you bring me joy.
You are silent, and strong,
I am glad that you are with me.
Yet—I hear a knock at the door
I will open—good-bye—
Good-bye loneliness—don't rush back.

However, the confrontation that followed a discussion on the ambivalence between the enjoyment of the loneliness and the desire to be rid of it prompted the following poem, in which, at last, he asked himself the decisive question and answered the regression that he evidences in the middle of the poem.

WHO AM I

Will someone
Tell me who I am?
I seem quite unable
To find myself.
There is a certain Power
Driving me to uncertainty
And to me that seems like my security.
But then—
That same old voice
Trying, never tiring
But always inquiring
Who I am.

A highly immature client with great dependency-needs could not verbalize, for shame and guilt, her own narcissistic egocentricity. When asked to write a poem about herself, she described what she "saw" and added her own goal—which, ultimately she achieved:

THE FIGHT IS ON

I have taken flight from preoccupation with man
Compassion and sympathy—just two words!
Poverty and pain—just too bad!
I have taken flight.
A deed undone, a smile forgotten.
A thought of hate—who cares!

But a fight goes on in me.
I must stop the flight.
I start within, and work without.
The fight is on!
I shall arrange my Soul
Now I am ready for man.

In summing up the experience of clients who have been involved in creative self-expression, as in writing poems, there appear to be some far-reaching gains in this process in therapy. As the client writes, talks, and reacts to his own written word, the material produced serves as a therapeutic tool, which, when added to the traditional therapeutic process in individual or group therapy, enables the client to accelerate his healing.

To create is to build, little by little, until a completed or whole entity is achieved. This emerges with a new form—a re-creation, a rebirth. Thus creativity is a natural companion to the therapeutic process, which builds step by step, until mental health *wholeness* is attained.

IN A SCHOOL FOR DEAF CHILDREN,
A COMMUNITY GUIDANCE CENTER, AND
A SCHOOL FOR EMOTIONALLY DISTURBED CHILDREN

Opening New Worlds to the Deaf and the Disturbed

LUCIEN BUCK, Ph.D. and AARON KRAMER, Ph.D.

In the spring of 1969 an experimental course, *Poetry and Interpersonal Communication*, was introduced at Dowling College, Suffolk County, New York. It was open to advanced English and psychology majors, the three earned credits applicable toward a degree in either area. Credit for the concept of a college course dealing with poetry as therapy must go to Dr. Jack Leedy, editor of *Poetry Therapy*, for he first planted the idea in Dr. Kramer's mind and persistently returned to it. Such a program, however, requires the theoretical and practical dimensions of a professional psychologist. Dr. Kramer enlisted as co-director Dr. Buck, a man deeply concerned with the nature of communication and eager to test the possibilities of poetry as an approach to emotionally disturbed persons.

Since our goal was not to train therapists, we rejected "Poetry Therapy" as the title. Our stated aims were: (1) to examine the characteristics of a poem with regard to the responses they produce; (2) to analyze the psychological dimensions of interpersonal communication; (3) to use poetry as a means of facilitating communication within a group of hospitalized schizophrenics; (4) to gain insight into the ways by which schizophrenics communicate; (5) to experience an interrelationship with hospitalized mental patients as people.

As an educational experience, the plan of the course was to combine classroom theory (psychological and literary concepts) with the application of poetry to human interaction. This was an attempt to remove ourselves and the students from the aseptic classroom environment, and to emphasize understanding and the use of knowledge rather than rote memory. Finally, this approach attempted to involve students in problems of relevance to contemporary society (i.e., mental illness and language deficiency).

Because our hospital contacts fell though at the last moment, we were obliged to revise our plan in accordance with what was available. There would be three kinds of encounters, each lasting a month: a school for deaf children, a community guidance center for outpatients and their families, and a school for emotionally disturbed children. The hours for visiting did not coincide with the time-slot of the course, so that all kinds of extraordinary adjustments and sacrifices were necessary; it is worth noting that these were achieved without a murmur and with nearly perfect attendance throughout.

Preliminary to these field experiences, the class met as a group three times in order to explore the concept of abnormality, some characteristics of deafness and speech impairment, and interpersonal communication. Readings were recommended as background material in order to supplement these discussions. An understanding of deafness was emphasized because the first field experience was to be at the school for the deaf; other readings were introduced in regard to later field work.

The purpose of these introductory classes was not merely didactic. We intended to use the dynamic processes of the class as a group in order to open up the degree of honesty of communication required for our field activities. We felt that students had to become more aware of their own prejudices and silent assumptions regarding psychological or physical abnormality before they could interact with people having these difficulties. We also felt that we must become sufficiently open with each other so that we could discuss as much of our experience as possible. We would have to discuss failure as well as success, personal biases and prejudices. Finally, we wished students to experience interpersonal interaction as a two-way process, to become aware of themselves as givers and receivers of communication. As participants in a human relationship they would be less likely to think of themselves as trying to "cure" the other person, and would be more likely to focus on the interaction.

A special class period was arranged in order to discuss the poetry which students selected in preparation for our work with deaf children. In order to maintain small-group, face-to-face interaction and individual interaction, we split our over-enrolled class into two groups which would meet separately with two small classes (six and eight students) of deaf children.

Our Tuesday group's first field trip struck us as a disaster. The children, ranging in ages from 10 to 12, seemed stone-deaf and half-mute. We made almost no headway in arousing discussion or getting even simple concrete answers; appalled, our own students contributed very little. Words as common as "admiring" (Emily Dickinson) had to be taught. We made some efforts at group reading, using props, and acting out; but their head-nodding, smiles, and friendly goodbyes did not strike us as proof of communication.

However, it later became evident that these feelings were primarily those of the college group, not the deaf children. The eagerness with which they awaited our second appearance, and the openness of their welcome, dispelled any questions concerning their feelings. They had expressed themselves openly on the first occasion, and had accepted our difficulty in understanding them. The question became one of our ability to respond to children with severe handicaps (in terms of the anxiety developed in ourselves based upon the implied threat to the intactness of our own capacities).

In addition, we were confronted with the very difficult task of accepting these children fully in terms of their severe language difficulties, and attempting to work with them at their level of communication rather than our own (with sufficient patience, concreteness, pictorial representation, etc.). We could no longer pretend that we were there to "cure" the children; we would have to "cure" ourselves first. We would have to learn to listen, to see and to participate. We would also have to learn to express our feelings and ideas to the children nonverbally, since words were frequently of no use in communication. As the children had the task of learning verbal communication, we had to relearn the meaning of expression.

That apparent disaster and our analysis of it turned out to be most valuable. For, encountering the second class, instead of facing their semi-circle with ours (a diverse confrontation, or at least an isolation of the groups), our Wednesday students paired off, sharing desk and poem. We mouthed words more slowly and clearly, gesturing and dramatizing with less fear of appearing grotesque. Our students relaxed and participated; they did not just wait and observe. Although we still functioned as a group, there were occasional consultations on a pair basis.

That the children in this class were two years older (13 to 15) and had studied a few poems already, made a difference; but we credited a superiority in hearing and intelligence as the chief factor in our success. It was a shock to learn that neither their hearing nor their intelligence was at all superior to that of the first class, that what had worked was primarily our own revised approach. While these children were older, with greater language facility, their grasp of language was still severely defective. The major difference was that we participated in a human relationship which placed greater emphasis upon mutual understanding and acceptance. It was the improvement in our hearing and seeing that counted. While this second session was more adequate than the first, the difficulties that occurred demonstrated that it is impossible to prepare students completely in advance; it is necessary for them to participate.

From here on we discarded the group structure except when a general point had to be made. For the next three weeks, in both classes, each deaf child worked with a particular student. They got to know and understand each other very well. We limited the number of poems presented for study, working in greater depth and with specific goals. Our choice of poems became more strategic. We also asked the children to teach us poems of their choice. By the third session they recognized rhyme, internal rhyme, half-rhyme, alliteration, free verse, various stanza forms, and such literary devices as sense-imagery, simile, personification, and hyperbole (not always by the technical terms). While we ended each session drained, the children showed increasing vigor and delight. They loved "making sense" to us and being able to answer our questions. They enjoyed reading the poems aloud with or for us and beautifully echoed our corrections of their mispronunciation.

We also attained a greater sense of understanding the children, and enjoyment of our progress in communication. However, this development was not universal. One student was working with a girl who was not only deaf but showed indications of organic impairment (expressive aphasia). The discrepany between understanding and the ability to express one's knowledge had to be relearned with a child who had more severe limitations than the other deaf children.

Halfway through the third session Dr. Kramer went from pair to pair, suggesting that they try to make a poem of their own. He asked each child to tell him about a sibling, a pet, or anything else of special interest. After drawing out the pertinent characteristics of the subject, he left the child and his partner to shape the material into a poem. By the time he was working with the fifth child, the first brought him her poem, "A Day in May":

> I like to smell the sweet flowers!
> I like the rain falls the heavy showers!
> I like the warm weather!
> I like to wear jacket or the sweater!
> I like to see the blue jays!
> I like to feel the beautiful day!

Joyously she held up her poem and accepted his praise. Within three sessions, aside from having a new set of "big-brother and big-sister" friends with whom she could now comfortably chat, she had learned to listen to the voices of great poets and had gained for herself a new way of speaking—or, better yet—singing!

Before the session ended, she and the others were excitedly crossing the room, sharing their new poems with each other, with us, and with their teacher. Some produced a second poem that day, or the makings of one to be completed next time. We extracted a promise that they would try to write more poems, and their teacher agreed to copy them for the following week's visit so that everyone would have a chance to read them.

That fourth visit was unforgettable. The children stood proudly in line awaiting us, each with a copy of his poems. For half an hour they worked busily in pairs, producing new poems or going over verses chosen from their textbook (which their teacher had not used before our program began). Then we asked them to form a group, explaining that this was our last time and that it would be good to discuss the nature of poetry, since we had been involved with it for a month.

The children suggested definitions and characteristics, some of which had to be qualified: it rhymes, it tells a story, it teaches, etc. Other answers (such as, it sings) could be fully accepted. For each definition we tried to get or give examples from what we'd read. Then each child in turn read aloud one of his own poems. In every case our questions led the group to focus on what a particular poem *did* as a poem: it makes us see more clearly what is there; it makes us see what isn't there (use our imagination); it makes us know how the poet feels; it makes us feel the way the poet feels.

Aside from summing up and leading them to a crystallization of what they had learned, this discussion made them exceedingly proud to provide the central focus and to have their work publicly praised for specific merits. However, it was at least as important that these experiences occurred in relation to a new group of friends who were not a regular part of the school situation. One of the severe deprivations faced by these children is the limited number of friendships they have outside of school. Even their school friends are usually not available outside of the classroom.

Their teachers expressed surprise at the extent of our accomplishment; they remarked that the children had been enriched and inspired, and indicated that they would try to continue our program. The children pledged to buy poetry books, borrow from libraries, and produce more poems.

We too were surprised by the children's ability to write poetry. We had begun this course with considerable humility in regard to what might be achieved. We would have considered the experience a success even were we able to communicate with them only somewhat more effectively. Instead we relearned the idea that performance cannot be confused with ability: children will perform in unimaginative ways if we make clear that this is what we expect, but when given the opportunity and the encouragement, they will use their imagination and creative ability fully.

Of their later poems, mailed to us in the weeks that followed, L's best typifies their naive, exuberant lyricism:

> I saw the red rose.
> I saw the cowboy clothes.
> I saw the freshwater lake.
> I saw vanilla cake.
> I saw the moon.
> Also, the sky blue at noon.

Of the many individual problems that arose during this month, we will mention two. One—psychological—was successfully resolved; the other—ethical—remained unsettled. When E's partner was absent, Dr. Kramer substituted. He soon discovered that she has no hearing and is aphasic beside. Her continual nodding and smiling had indeed meant (as her teacher warned us) nothing. With her he therefore used written dialogue accompanied by gestures and skits.

Building on her own lines ("The dog saw the cat/I love you said the cat") he tried several times to create new verses personifying both animals; but she did not come through with a second line or even the last word of a second line, though the right word seemed inevitable. Nevertheless, she kept roaring with laughter as he finished the couplets himself.

Suddenly she asked for the pencil and began furnishing first lines, some of which showed real imagination and wit, about humanized cat-dog situations. She would then hand the pencil to him, breathlessly wait for him to create the rhyming line, shriek with delight at its humor, and rush off to show her classmates what she and her partner had created. Here are a few examples:

E: The Cat said "I love
K: to wear a white glove.
E: To dress in shoes
K: is what I choose."

E: The Cat washed her hair,
      took pocketbook, dollar,
K: and went to the fair
      in her bright new collar.

E: The Cat and the Dog went to a party;
K: the Dog told a joke and the Cat said: "Smarty!"
E: The Dog and the Cat went to the dance;
K: she wore a pretty
E: dress
K: and he wore
E: coat and pants.

For E, who can't sum up or bring matters to a unified conclusion, but is good at setting up an idea, this turned out to be a priceless adventure with rhyme, rhythm, teamwork, and outlandish situations. The difficulty was less in the child's expressive limitations than in our inability to understand and facilitate her imaginative expression. When an appropriate context was found for the communication of her ideas, she was able to function creatively.

What may be an ethical problem involves one of our most promising and mature children. She submitted to her partner, Joe, three poems signed by herself which were so expert that he had to ask whether this was indeed her own work and not copied from a printed page. She became indignant, and he desperately wished to believe that these fine verses were the product of their partnership. We decided not to challenge her claim further. Joe, however, asking her to discuss them in depth, was gratified by her thorough grasp of their form and content. They had, in a sense, really become "hers."

It is, in fact, still not clear whether this is an ethical difficulty. An understanding of words, particularly abstract words (moral values), requires a level of functioning that is poorly developed in deaf children. As their language functioning is developmentally retarded, they can be expected to show a variety of defects. It is likely that most of these children function, in terms of language, primarily at a concrete level. It is unlikely that many of them have any degree of facility in discriminating between such difficult verbal expressions as "the poem is mine," "I wrote the poem," and "I chose the poem."

As the month's work progressed, it became increasingly clear that our students should have been far more knowledgeable about the nature and creation of poetry before being permitted to enter this situation. A more adequate psychological background would also be desirable. The crucial element is to provide the time necessary for this training.

The following extracts from student reports reflect the kinds of learning which took place during our first month of field work:

LINDA: The program with the deaf children was not only a course experience, but a life experience as well. At the time I felt alienated from people in general and had little or no contact with other people. I had trouble hearing what people were saying, not because of poor hearing or stupidity, but because I was too busy trying to find out what the person *was* instead of what he was saying. And so, having to listen so intently to the deaf children in order to get any sense out of what they were saying was good training for me. I especially enjoyed working with D. Her hand gestures are very relevant to what she is saying and the importance she places upon them is a lesson to me in encountering others. She is more shy about gesture when in a group and so would not demonstrate tip-toeing until Dr. Kramer did it with her.... She pointed out the o's in the second stanza of Frost's "Stopping by Woods" without any suggestion on my part. This was a pleasant surprise....

JOHN: The major obstacle was K's initial shyness. I can readily understand the uneasiness for an adolescent girl to be placed in a novel situation with a strange young man.... We established a meaningful rapport. In the subsequent sessions K's enthusiasm never dwindled. The next week she had a couple of poems to share with me and some questions to ask me concerning them. This was an excellent development because the relationship no longer resembled the teacher-student dichotomy that often occurs, but rather an expression of mutuality in ideas and understanding. We dealt with the formal aspects of poetry such as rhyme, alliteration, repetition, and contrast, and by the end of the sessions she could identify these elements in any poem which contained them. Furthermore, she could employ these tools in her own creative attempts.

ARNIE: I must admit that prior to and at times during the course I had vague notions that I would become a sort of Annie Sullivan trying to get through to an unbudging catatonic schizophrenic.... All too often I gave N answers when I should have let her give them to me. I suggested ideas and rhymes when I should have let her initiate them. I was overanxious; working too fast... I should also point out that the *Poetry Therapy* textbook destroyed some of the realism I had been able to accept and I was the dragon-killer again, floating on case histories of poetry-"cures" and success stories, an unfortunate position to take, as I later found out. (The fault was not with the textbook, but with me for interpreting the articles one-sidedly....)

MIKE: The last lesson I was able to teach J was about meter. I thought it would be difficult, but it wasn't at all. For that class I prepared (Mike's modest way of saying "I wrote"; in fact, his poem is superb, another achievement of the course) a special poem about sailors, that I brought with me. The poem was written with a simple, steady meter, constant rhyme, and a narrative. After reading the poem with her I read it one more time, tapping my hand on her desk on every stressed syllable. I then asked her to do the same, and she did. Next I asked her to do the same with another poem, and she did it well. The next poem we wrote had a strict meter, and it told a story.

BUS RIDE

The bus picks me up.
It takes me to school.
We come to the room.
Miss Liao is there.

>   We learn with her help.
>   And by afternoon
>   The bus picks me up
>   To take me back home.

VIRGINIA: We asked all the girls to take turns reading; we asked for their impressions of various passages, and we gave ours. We tried to use our hands and arms as much as we could in describing what we felt; and at times we acted out certain things (hiding, waking up). The girls seemed to derive enjoyment from the fact that we were willing to prance around and play-act, almost like children.... It was apparent that a great deal of communication and enjoyment had been mutually experienced.... The most important thing that I learned from this session was something Dr. Buck had pointed out to us over and over again: the children are "handicapped children," but they are children first, and that is the most important thing to remember.

The second phase of our semester consisted of three Saturday sessions, two hours each, at a community guidance center. In advance of our first meeting with the outpatients and their families, Dr. Kramer was invited to speak before the staff about our goals. He was then given a somewhat vague orientation about what kinds of people were likely to participate. A student volunteered to visit the center a week ahead, meet some of the outpatients, and report to the class. The student's contact with patients at the center indicated that we would be working with many people who had had sufficient difficulty in their lives to require hospitalization. Many of these individuals would be diagnosed as schizophrenics.

The circular distributed by the center had clearly labeled our work: "THREE MORNINGS OF POETRY: favorite poems will be read and discussed under the direction of special guest poet AARON KRAMER.... Do you have a poem of your own? Bring it if you'd like to share it." This structured our meetings at the center as a voluntary program which was open to all members as well as the parents, mates, and children of patients. This also meant that the number of participants would vary from week to week. Our total class participated in each session. Since we were expecting perhaps 30 people from the center (40 showed up), we did not feel that our numbers would be overwhelming.

There was much in the first session to satisfy the staff, since an exceptionally animated discussion did develop, often to the point of passion, and once to the point of abusive cross-yelling among several members. The crux became a youth-age confrontation, with several middle-aged outpatients and parents of young adult members expressing resentment at the notion that only the young are enthusiastic and visionary. This discussion had arisen from poems that appealed to the imagination and demanded more from the reader than a flat, literal response. The point was that adults tend to adapt to the commonplace reality and learn either not to feel strongly or to conceal strong feelings—a show of so-called sophistication.

The central theme of youth versus age or awareness versus practicality (inhibition) arose from the very nature of the group itself, composed of approximately 55 people (including our class), fairly evenly divided between college-age students and adults of middle age or beyond. This silent assumption focused both the selection of poetry presented and the discussion that followed. The emergence of this theme was facilitated by the flexibility of Dr. Kramer's leadership. (We had intended to let the group develop its own structure and its own leadership. However, some indirect leadership was required. Dr. Kramer began to function in this capacity.)

Because a relaxed atmosphere had been established, the issue of youth versus age, which initially divided the group, was brought out into the open and was sufficiently explored so that some resolution was evident by the end of the session. Though most outpatients were silent, the few who spoke spoke often and with excitement. Our own students were equally caught up in the debate (not realizing, perhaps, the impact of their very physical presence as a large young group bursting with poems and academic phraseology). The dispute was resolved at last: some, at 70, remain young; others are old at 20. After the meeting, interaction continued in smaller groups; some who had seemed uninvolved now spoke up. Both therapists were pleased, because we had demonstrated to them that poetry can serve as the springboard for a genuine expression of personal feeling.

That other forms of communication had also taken place apparently went unnoticed by one therapist; nevertheless, his patients and their families *had* been listening with fascination to poems, to discussions about those poems and the nature of poetry itself. A large number had afterward expressed satisfaction with what they'd heard, and some had promised to bring poems the following week. Several of our students, unobtrusively observant, described the nonverbal signs of communication. "There were many there," Ginny remarked, "who did not say a thing but were very much involved as could be seen from the expressions on their faces."

Dorothea's chronicle is particularly vivid at this point. "One lady near the door became quite anxious. She hadn't been really reacting visibly to what was going on—a few 'I agree's' to the lady next to her. ... When we started this, she seemed to 'lose her cool'—her hands and fingers started twisting and her forehead wrinkled and she crossed and uncrossed her legs until the discussion ended; then she regained her composure. Another woman who never moved except to see who was coming in, got really upset when we were talking about Hopkins and religion. She tried to hide it and by placing her arms at right angles and using the upright arm she effectively prohibited the action of the horizontal arm. Her fingers were white with tension. After the discussion ended, she calmed down and moved to say something to her neighbor. She looked relieved and slightly embarrassed, looking around to see if she was being watched."

The distinction between the expression of personal feeling relevant to the dynamics of the group versus the more general discussion of poetry began to lead to a divergence within the college class regarding the goals of these meetings. Poetry could be selected in order to deal with the emerging group theme of youth versus age, or each individual could be left to choose his selections on the basis of potential interest or general stimulation of group discussion. The first emphasis focuses on the resolution of group tensions in order to facilitate openness of communication (the therapeutic effects); the second choice emphasizes a more didactic exploration of poetry and energetic discussion. These differences sometimes led to opposite impressions within the class as to the success of our sessions. Some students preferred vigorous intellectual discussion regardless of the number of silent outpatients. Others advocated quieter, more evenly paced sessions where all of the outpatients would be clearly involved either verbally or non-verbally.

From our class meeting the consensus arose that too many of us had done the reading and talking, allowing too little time for a point or a poem to sink in so that a response might gestate in sensitive minds. We decided to move more slowly next time and to allow far more room for outpatient participation. In the second and third sessions the percentage of poems offered by "them" and their families increased to half; much of the discussion, too, was carried by non-students. Dr. Kramer felt that his leadership was becoming too dominant, but some leadership was obviously necessary in order to extract the maximum value from a poem or comment, and in order to give shape to what was going on.

"During the second session," Virginia noted, "people were talking and listening. The week before, people were swaying the focus of the discussion into a personal, often irrelevant gripe session. Perhaps for the ends of therapy this is more desirable, but from the point of view of understanding and sharing poetry, a calm, communicative discussion seems more valuable."

The discussion usually focused on the poem itself and seldom drew forth the intense, subjective expression which one staff therapist had hoped for. Thus, when our students asked to continue working with his young adult group for their term projects, he approved on condition that the use of poetry be minimal. The evaluation by Dr. Buck (who had been a participant-observer throughout in order to focus on the style of communication) contrasted sharply. He found that two-thirds of the non-students had spoken up at least once; others had made relevant comments privately, and all had laughed, frowned, or nodded at appropriate moments. He found that all were meaningfully involved and was convinced that even those who said nothing were deriving values from what their family members and others were saying.

The burst of applause that followed the close of the last session seemed to bear this out. Many expressed the hope that we'd be back next year. After hearing a student read *The Love Song of J. Alfred Prufrock* and the discussion that ensued, a father of an emotionally disturbed boy declared: "Poets seem to be centuries ahead of the medical profession in their knowledge of the psyche." An elderly outpatient, who during the second session sighed that there were two poems she'd like to write someday ("What is Man?" and "The Trouble with the World"), and who was urged to try, brought in a first draft the following week. A girl who'd initially been silent felt encouraged enough to bring a poem the next time. This poem was criticized for being too shallow and explicit. Instead of being squelched, she brought in a Byron poem the final time; when asked why she'd chosen it, she explained that she liked its mystery, which makes the reader think.

A "very sick young man" who'd come to the agency three weeks earlier but apparently had not been considered ready to attend our sessions, participated superbly throughout our third morning. The therapist might criticize our use of poetry on the grounds that it relieved the boy of the pressure of facing his personal situation; but the poems to which he responded with great gusto and sensitivity were far from escapist; what moved him most were two large, affirmative but unsentimental excerpts from *The People, Yes*. Afterward he chatted vigorously about problems of scholarly criticism.... When all this was pointed out to our host, he acknowledged that his concept of communication might have been too limited, that apparently even the academic elements of each session had been of value therapeutically and had been received with gratitude.

His interpretation of poetry as communication failed to grasp the complex nature of communication. One of our initial assumptions was that anything that occurs in a group setting may be used for purposes of communication. When people sit together and talk there is a constant meaningful exchange on several levels simultaneously. We indicate how we feel and think toward each other with our words (those we select and those we don't as well as the meaning of the words themselves), but also with our bodies in terms of expressive movements. The type of poetry selected, the discussion of the meaning of that poetry, and the nonverbal responses can have indirect relevance to immediate interaction among the people in the group.

For example, the previously discussed theme of youth versus age reflected the reality of a division within the group. This theme was discussed, not openly and directly in terms of the personal feelings of these young people toward these older people, but in terms of poems that reflected the theme. A group of rather shy, sensitive people were able to deal indirectly (at their own level of preference) with this issue, and were capable of partially resolving it. One indication that the group had moved toward a resolution of its differences was the atmosphere of the second and third sessions. The quieter, more reflective mood allowed more time for individual participation by some of the previously silent members of the group. It communicated a greater degree of tolerance and acceptance of the different participants, and probably increased respect for each other.

Thus, the use of poetry as a means of interpersonal communication is an attempt to provide an indirect way of initiating personal expression while allowing the participant to speak at a level of openness consistent with his own comfort. In addition, poetry provides a creative form of expression that facilitates the communication of feelings and thoughts that the individual cannot deal with in other ways.

Our work at the outpatient guidance center was somewhat frustrating, for all of its positive results. Three sessions are simply not enough to achieve a really lasting effect. At best we captured the attention and awoke the literary tastebuds of a group of emotionally disturbed persons who are trying to leave the hospital world behind and are seeking purpose. Certain poems planted seeds of insight and feeling that may grow wholesomely or helped begin to express feelings that have not previously been communicated. Pleasant relationships were established, but only on a temporary and superficial basis, except for those students who agreed to stay on. With more sessions, deeper explorations might have resulted; further creative efforts would have been stimulated; the sheer pleasure of sitting interwoven—a group of outpatients and a group of college students considering the same verses and comments—would not be diminished by the knowledge that this was one brief segment of one semester. We might also have become more strategic and less haphazard in our choice of poems and have avoided scholarly terminology in our comments.

Part of the group's silence would be impossible even for the most dramatic poetic reading to melt; but in the presence of a dozen radiantly healthy young people tossing off easily poem after obscure poem, an overawed silence was the natural effect. Had we not been so pressed for time, so involved with the severe complications of schedule, we could and would have done what was initially planned and what is absolutely essential. We would have considered possible approaches in advance, carefully, as a group; we would have arrived at specific aims for specific poems; we would afterward have compared our expectations with the results, have learned more about poetry as communication, have learned what to avoid and what to emphasize.

Yet the format had much to recommend it. Opening the floor to "favorite poems" meant being willing to deal with whatever poem anyone might bring, and that kind of relaxed hospitality was well worth the risks; nor could we in good conscience have stopped Joe from reading "Prufrock" (though he was warned of its great length and allusiveness). Had he read it less engrossingly, it might have been a fiasco. However, we should have placed greater emphasis upon helping the students learn to understand the consequences of the poetry that they introduced, by explaining more deeply the relationship of poetry to the nature of interpersonal communication.

The trouble is, several students *did* read poorly; and if they expected listeners not thoroughly attuned to verse to understand and discuss a difficult poem heard just once, even individuals who are not involved in emotional crises, then of course they were naive and this experience should have taught them so. Most of the time Dr. Kramer felt very much like an intellectual juggler working with unrehearsed paraphernalia. For no matter how bad the poems offered by outpatients, he had to extract some discussion value from them and if possible find something kind to say about them; and no matter how obscure or unrelated a poem read by a student, he had to find some relevance, make some efforts at clarification so that a discussion could build around it. Had there been no leadership on an experienced level, the sessions would either have collapsed or have moved in altogether different directions than poetry.

This would not have been the case, however, had the poems been reproduced so that all could follow what was being read and could afterward return to passages they wished to comment on. Nor would there be much danger of anarchy or deadness if our students as a group had considered in advance what they hoped to accomplish in a particular session. But our stated aim at the beginning of the semester was to try out all sorts of things; why then not "Prufrock"? Certainly, much of what the students read *was* pertinent, useful, and well presented—increasingly so. And where questions were raised about the advisability of reading a suicide poem like "Richard Cory," the results proved that a truthful poem which may shock a bit is a better choice than an innocuous piece of garbage unrelated to life. As Ginny put it, with reference to another discussion, "It was our poetry which started the challenge.... and at last everyone had something very important to themselves to say to the group." However, it should be continuously asked whether the particular poem reflects adequately upon the lives of the people who are present.

It seems fitting to end this part of the paper with a picture of the rather remarkable way our Saturday series opened. That morning was momentous for Susan, and her courage made it momentous for the 55 people present. Her fiancé had recently died in an auto crash, and she was determined to withdraw from the human race. She had absented herself from school for weeks; it was at the urgent invitation of Dr. Kramer that she "surfaced" for our first Saturday session. Her narration is as honest, unselfconscious, and casual as was her performance:

> Our first meeting at the out-patient clinic meant more to me than anything this year. This was my first time back from my absence, and I wasn't even supposed to be there. I noticed the tension that was rippling through the room as soon as I sat down. None of the people in class knew exactly how sick these people were going to be, nor what was expected of us, nor what we expected of them. I brought along a book of poetry and, to tell the truth, I wasn't sure whether I was going to present any of it or sit in the back and read it myself. One good thing about the seating *non*-arrangement was that our group could not possibly cluster together in a tight fist because seats were at a premium and we had to grab what we could. We were introduced as students of poetry from Dowling College, and then Dr. Kramer left us with the show, so to speak. I'm sure everyone in our class was as terrified as I, but I couldn't stand the thought of a pregnant silence. I had been doing a paper on William Blake, which I was having a hard time with, mainly because I didn't like so many of the poems in my selection, so I stood up and tried to see if anyone there could change my mind about one of his poems which I especially disliked. I think this must have been a rather good angle to work from because the out-patients could see that I had just as much difficulty with poetry as any of them. Dr. Kramer said, this was "probably the longest discussion ever given to this poem that I've been involved in." I was quite surprised that these people, who professed a lack of sensitivity toward poetry, remained so focused on one "mediocre" poem.

The third phase of our semester's work took place at a school for emotionally disturbed children, with three selected classes of four, five, and six students ranging in ages from approximately seven to thirteen.

At an orientation conference with the three teachers and the director, we were told what their goals and methods are, and what kind of poetry-work interests them: personal expression not for the sake of relieving feelings or expanding fantasies but to establish discipline, logic, reality, and form. We attempted to prepare our students for this field experience by recommending readings related to childhood schizophrenia, autism, and symbiotic relationships, and by an initial discussion of these types of behavior. A major emphasis was placed on the understanding of these children as human beings rather than as some psychiatric type.

Our students wanted to discuss the characteristics of autistic children rather than the behavior of specific individuals. While general descriptive characteristics had some value in orienting students for the situation, such descriptions did not prepare them adequately for the individual uniqueness of each child. However, this orientation was relearned more quickly because of the two previous field experiences.

An additional problem became evident as a consequence of our initial contacts with the staff of the school. It became clear that the goals of poetry and interpersonal communication that we had been emphasizing were inconsistent with those of the school. While we were interested in developing freedom of expression and communication as part of a human process involving warmth and acceptance, the school focused on developing order, control, and rules for behavior. There was some overlap between the two approaches; but our emphasis was placed upon the experiencing and communicating of ideas and feelings which had not hitherto been expressed, whereas the school appeared to be more concerned with control over expression than with its meaning.

The staff warned us against encouraging the children's imagination, but this was one of the goals which we had hoped to achieve. We were aware of the limitations involved in uncontrolled expression of repressed thought, but we wished to encourage creative use of the imagination and stress the positive experience resulting from creative achievement. At the same time, when poetry serves as a vehicle for the imagination, it can help to reveal the inner person.

These differences were explored in our class, and we attempted to relate to the children in ways that were consistent with the school's policy so that they would not be placed in a position of conflict. Many of our students had difficulty working within this context and felt uncomfortable at having to enforce rules and control.

The teacher of the first class we visited had challenged our motives and feared we would use the children as guinea pigs; apparently, other adults had intruded into the classroom with destructive results. He warmed up quickly, however, moving constructively from pair to pair. He seemed relieved to have been placed by us in the key role. M and R worked happily with their partners, but one of the withdrawn boys became restless and didn't get down seriously to creating a poem. As for B, he said very little beside "Yes," and vibrated his hands furiously when pressed to cooperate. However, the face of his girl partner enchanted him: he eyed her for a long time, then touched her face slowly. She felt she'd failed completely and was terrified of her next encounter with this child, but she got him to agree that they would write a poem about food at the next meeting. (His great obesity gave her the idea.)

On our second visit the teacher again supervised helpfully and gave the kind of biographical information about the children we'd hoped for the first time. M was disappointed that his partner (for whom he asked by name) was not back, and he would not settle down unless he could make up a Richard is Sick poem; this was followed by one about his pet. T was still somewhat restless and seemingly uninterested, but he did write (by himself) a nice little Stormy Day poem which he playfully tried to keep us from reading as if inviting us to beg.

B was amazing. From a long session of gazing at his partner's face again, sniffing at her (for perfume, perhaps), and taking her hand, he moved to a good job of reading aloud, barely indicating by a twitch of the lips that her praise pleased him; then she began gathering materials for their food poem. A catalog of dearly loved dishes came pouring out, in a hollow-sounding but strong voice: first desserts, then special holiday foods. She got him thinking about Easter, and a brand-new catalog rolled forth. From Easter Day he moved to "a sunny day." Her approval was quickly followed by "a cloudy day" (this bewildered her, but she wrote it down), then "a cold day, a rainy day, a snowy day, and a church day" (Easter again). She drew a line between the two categories—food and days. He then offered "hot dog," which she listed, in puzzlement, as "hot dog day," but it soon became clear that he was back with his foods, and there now erupted a whole assortment of meats and fish; she could scarcely keep up with him. Toward the end he began calling out types of autos—a third list! Her success overwhelmed her. We had, as his teacher had warned us, totally misjudged this boy's capacities and awareness. Most important, we hadn't expected him to open up so completely to us. The next step, we decided, would be to expand on both his trust and his lists, to find a way of teaching him how a list can become a poem.

During our third meeting the makings of poems were extracted from all four children. M bossily demanded that whatever he dictated be written down exactly, and shot the words out one by one. They didn't entirely make sense to Richard, but he wrote them anyway. The policy of the school, however, would be to reject the words until they became "logical." Meanwhile our elation about B was shattered upon our learning that he'd created lists before and is to be kept from that practice. However, no one at the school indicated that they had tried to help him use his lists creatively. They simply fell back on the necessity of emphasizing structure and rules rather than considering the possible meaning of these lists or their potential use as the basis for a poem.

Having already planned her strategy, Dorothea was permitted to work with B's auto list. She suggested to B a fantasy poem linking the various autos and turning them into a train according to type and color. Asked for an appropriate refrain that would link the "cars" of the auto-train and turn them into a song, B at once offered "Beep! beep!" Although the poem that follows was composed by his partner, B felt involved in its creation, was consulted about every word, provided most of the basic ingredients, and experienced the shaping of something intimately connected with him into a poem:

> All the cars I know
> came to my house one day,
> tied together like a train.
> > Beep, beep, beep
>
> All the green cars came together:
> they were the engine in the front—
> the Cadillac, the stationwagon and the Dodge.
> > Beep, beep, beep
>
> Next in line came the Chevrolet,
> the only yellow car
> in the line.
> > Beep, beep, beep
>
> Now both the blue cars:
> first the Mustang,
> then the Corvair with Mrs. West.
> > Beep, beep beep
>
> And now comes Daddy
> with his car:
> he has an Impala, big and red.
> > Beep, beep, beep

> Last in line were two cars of white,
> a Plymouth and a Volkswagen—
> the caboose at the end.
>   Beep, beep, beep.

Returning to the college, we discussed with the rest of the class the problem of making the children see the difference between a poem and the raw materials they gave us. The fact is, however, that most members of the class—even English majors—were weak in this area and needed much more advance briefing than we had time for.

On our fourth visit, nearly weeping at certain points, M told of his guinea pig's death. When challenged about contradictions in his story, he grinned and burted out "April Fool!" Once the "facts" had been pretty well ascertained, Richard helped M turn the story into a song-text, with rhyme and rhythm, using—almost entirely—the original words. Richard promised to set the verses to music and play it on his guitar next time. This week, for a change, M did not half dig his tooth out with a pick or bite his half thumbnail till it bled. B spoke much more frequently and openly this time, did some writing on the board, and read aloud. T and R managed to stay seated and work for long stretches. The compass T mouthed and fooled with was turned into a poem with Virginia's help; R and his partner made a train poem. We were obviously gaining their trust. They seemed to regret our leaving. Their teacher reminded us of our ealier suggestion that his class visit us for a "grand tour" and picnic.

We arranged for their transportation, and the Director (despite her strong reluctance) allowed the visit. Dr. Kramer's plan had included a discussion of poetry, since this was to be our final session; but several students felt it might be better to omit formal work, and they were right. One hour on campus barely gave us time to play host. The children were generally well-behaved (though T opened a dean's desk-drawer in front of the dean, M pretended electric shock from the President's rug and swiveled in the President's chair, and B had a brief fit on the subject of food). We held the cafeteria in reserve and headed for the river, which they enjoyed fairly quietly, then toured the library and student lounge, went up the winding lobby stairs, examining the tapestry and art-work on the way, touching the statuary gently with our permission, admiring the hanging lamps and wrought-iron window lacings. Their tendency was to plunge ahead; they constantly had to be made to stop and look.

After an orderly lunch, apparently unperturbed by scores of smiling collegians, they came out to the lawn and we all enjoyed Richard's song based on M's guinea pig poem. M rolled over with hysterical delight, even more when our applause brought a repetition of the song. On the way back to the school B was relaxed and friendly; he named his siblings and told us where he lives. T, apparently unresponsive to Dr. Kramer in previous encounters, this time left his seat, climbed over B, and sat on the professor's lap all the way back. He chatted merrily and lucidly to the driver, the girl who'd worked with him and had so often felt altogether frustrated. The children hugged us goodbye.

We thought it an afternoon of total rapport. (Typically, the participating staff failed to transmit any indication of what had been achieved; thus, the school's official comment was that the children had had "too much fun.") To have intruded poetry formally would have been mechanical and unfeeling. The hour itself was poetry. The sun, river, lawn, and trees, the mingling with college students, the swans noticed in ponds on the way back—all this will be part of what they remember about the group that helped them read and make poems. Perhaps they will even turn this swarm of impressions into poetry; at least they promised to try.

Our practical difficulties during this final month were even greater than at the school for deaf children. We now had to split our forces into three groups, roughly equal in size to the three classes we were assigned. Our visits were on three different days, to three different school sites. This made it impossible for both of us to be all meetings; however, some of the problems were shared during our weekly class discussion and at individual conferences.

The almost total difference in philosophy between the school staff and us remained a serious difficulty. We felt that the long list of proscriptions (including a large poster swarming with don'ts) inhibited not only their pupils but our students and ourselves. We felt that needles were being stuck into our "achievement balloons," that we were being repeatedly assured we had accomplished nothing new or important.

In the Friday group Susan worked with P and C. C was "out of it" one day, but she'd succeeded in extracting "five lovely lines" from the usually reserved P. Along came the teacher: "You should work more with C, he's one of our best." Since Susan nevertheless continued working with P (having got nowhere with C), the Director approached and scolded: "P's not the poetic one; C is so sensitive and creative!" She actually took over and primed her favorite (according to Susan) until he responded with an outpouring of "nonpoetry" while P simply went off to play on the jungle gym. This obvious difference in terms of the understanding of poetry was brought to light in a subsequent evaluative meeting with the school staff when some of them admitted that they did not know what poetry was.

The previous week a similar episode had occurred. An uncooperative little girl finally dictated some lines to Mike, which he praised:

> I got liked by a fly
> Somewhere else on my skin.
> I got liked by a moth
> Somewhere else on my skin.
> I got liked by a Katydid
> Somewhere else on my skin.

He was, however, sternly instructed to dissuade the children from using incorrect verbs. Perhaps the school's strategy requires that children learn to use language in the commonplace manner, but from this, poetry does not emerge. This child had used a verb in a new way to create a clearly understandable and enjoyable effect, with "liked" being vividly tactile and reminiscent of "licked." What the school was guilty of here, in the name of discipline, was murder of the creative impulse. All unique or idiosyncratic usage had to be controlled in the name of teaching rules and logic; poetic license was not distinguished from regressed communication.

Despite the unpleasantness of such encounters, however, it was valuable for our students to experience divergent opinions and practices. They are likely to meet plenty of professionals who see only their slant, lack the flexibility to doff the hat to achievements outside their sphere, and try to mold into "usefulness" whatever or whoever comes their way. Our students must learn how to work with them and derive as much as possible from their greater experience and differing approaches.

In general, we felt that working with emotionally disturbed children was the most difficult yet fruitful phase of the semester. The hospitable mood established by the teacher of the Wednesday class made it easier for students like Joe to move from a sense of total failure to gradual accomplishment. During the first session one of Joe's charges, D, taunted the slower one, P, as "crazy," and often left his seat. D's few poetic efforts seemed unsatisfactory; from what Dr. Kramer had told him and from the child's earlier poems, Joe expected a great deal. The second meeting began even worse. P opened more, but D shut up and said he didn't want to participate. Ignoring him, Joe worked steadily with P, and won D's sidelong interest. When D announced that he was not interested in poetry, Joe started the third session with an old poem of D's. He gave no indication of the authorship; he merely taught and praised it. The boy was captured. Later, following the suggestion that Shelley's "The Cloud" might be an exhilarating rhyme experience, Joe read it superbly and galvanized both children. By the end of the month he had been a party to the creation of some imaginative little pieces. Among those composed in partnership by P and D is "Volcano Erupting":

> The big brown mountain
> hot lava, birds fly,
> rabbits run, the bear growls.
> The moon so bright
> in the darkest night.

D wrote a few on his own. One of the most playful is "Rabbit":

> His face was black and white
> His eyes were pink
> Half as mean as a tiger
> and half as mean as a hamster.

Perhaps the chief value of our poetry sessions for these children was the modest but steadily increasing degree of communication. Although a month was, as we had been warned, too little time to achieve more lasting or more comprehensive results, our students were able to observe and record many "glimpses" of the inner child—his fears, questions, and enthusiasms. This was partly the result of the trust they had won, partly because of their youth and unprofessionalism, and largely because the apparent focus on an objective poem gave him the freedom to speak subjectively, through touch, movement, "extraneous" conversation, and the content of the poem being shaped.

These children showed themselves to be ripe for poetry; the rhythms and color-images, the narratives and humorous strokes, the fantastic situations and the moments of recognition offered by poetry appeal to and enliven them. Even when they frown and call a Cummings Halloween poem "scary," they then reread the poem aloud, acting it out with the same gusto they witnessed in our rendition. They seem to have an insatiable appetite for information and literary experiences. The possibilities for creative and human communication seem infinite.

Had each pair worked in a separate cubicle rather than all being cooped together, much more might have been accomplished. Dr. Kramer enjoyed such a moment of illumination with the "terror of the school," a long-hospitalized 13-year-old who had never before allowed himself to join the poetry partnership or even speak in more than a neutral monosyllable. Isolated from his classmates one Wednesday, J appeared accessible for the first time. Softly answering Dr. Kramer's questions about a particular verse, he mentioned trips to the country. Asked what kinds of animals he'd seen there, this well-policed child at once responded: "Free."

Working out-of-doors from time to time can also bring surprising rewards, as John discovered one Friday afternoon:

I feel that I must include D's poems. They are almost entirely his creations.

DAFFODILS

Daffodils bloom in the early sun.
They are pretty and nice.
When I see them I have fun.
They are yellow and white.
And they stay for the summer.
They smell pretty, like perfume.

SANDBUGS

Sandbugs crawl in the sand.
They go faster, faster and faster.
And they curl up like a bouncing ball,
So that no one can hurt them at all.

> Then they uncurl and crawl away
> Into the shade of the grass.
> And the grass is green
> So they can't be seen.
>
> And they crawl under the leaves.

These poems were written while outdoors with a daffodil in hand and a cup of sandbugs, which D decided to release. We also had fun discussing the poem by Lilian Moore, "Hey Bug." D built a finger-hill and a tower for the sandbugs. I really believe that poetry became alive for him; this was my most exciting and rewarding experience during the semester.

By the third meeting, it was clear that our students had established a sense of comradeship. The work went quietly and well in all three classes. The following week the regular Wednesday teacher left his class completely in the hands of our students and disappeared. There wasn't a single discipline problem. All were absorbed in creating or considering poems. Toward the end Dr. Kramer came in. He read aloud the verses each boy had produced, pointed out their virtues, and got the children to define poetry. Afterwards our students brought their month's work to a close:

JOE: When Dr. Kramer left, P asked me if I was leaving as well. I asked him if he wanted me to leave, and he replied, no, he didn't. We talked about certain poems which seemed to elicit little response. I then went back to the more personal talk of before, and this he liked very much. We talked of things that made good subjects for poetry, such as flying like a bird. I had a book of haiku and quickly found a poem about birds, an eagle. I drew a picture of the image in the poem. This he liked, so we did this several more times. P then asked me to draw a picture of the bathtub, the subject of the first poem. This I did; then he wanted me to draw him in the tub. After I did this, he asked me to add to the picture myself in the tub with him. I did this and it brought a laugh from him that was, for me, the finest reward of the entire period of time we spent at the school. This kind of personal interest was sorely needed by P. The poetry was actually the medium through which we were able to establish this relationship, although we went far beyond the poetry in the manner of feelings we penetrated. The session ended all too soon.

* * *

An excerpt from Barbara's report illustrates the mood of that final session. A week before, this short girl with brown hair and wide eyes had allowed F to smell and touch her red carnation.

> This time F told me he wanted to write poems. His first subject was himself:
>
>> I'm short, and have blue eyes and brown hair.
>> I'm thirteen years old.
>> I like baseball, football, knock-hockey, girls and school,
>> and most of all I like vacation.

F was talking about himself quite a bit. He told me he had a sister in a hospital and that he wished he was his mother's son. He also expressed the wish that he could have friends to play with. I listened attentively and I felt badly that he had missed these valuable experiences. Then F told me to write down the title of his next poem.

>> MY FRIEND
>>
>> My friend plays with me.
>> She is my friend,
>> with brown hair and wide eyes.
>> She is short.
>> I like her because she is nice to me.
>> She makes me think of the red flower.

A few weeks later we received a packet of letters from the school. Each child had thanked us for our visits. Not surprisingly, in the case of two classes, this opportunity for a personal gesture had been turned into a writing exercise resulting in a batch of identical form letters. The teacher of the Friday class, on the other hand, had allowed her children free rein, and the results were moving—especially in the case of children who had given the impression that we were not welcome.

> Dear Dr. Buck and Dr. Kramer,
> I liked the poetry people. I liked talking to Linda best. I wish they come back again. P.
>
> Dear Linda and Susan,
> Thank you for visiting. I love to write with you. I like to write with you about tonsils and everything else. C.

Dear Dr. Kramer,
Thank you for coming back. I liked you best. S.

Dear Dr. Buck and Dr. Kramer,
Thank you for visiting our classroom. I liked the semi-circle on Friday. I liked the rhyming games I played with Michael. S.

That these notes were genuine expressions of feeling was borne out at our evaluative session, when the staff informed us that our impact on the children had been considerable, and asked us to return next year.

While the success of this course cannot be easily assessed in terms of purely objective criteria, it was the unanimous opinion of the students and faculty that it was an exceptionally meaningful learning experience for us all. The course began as an experiment. We knew that we did not have all the answers and would have to make mistakes in order to learn. Therefore, we attempted from the beginning to establish an atmosphere which would make this a joint venture to be explored together. Difficulties were anticipated, but we expected to learn from them, and did.

With some change in emphasis, we believe that all the goals of the course were achieved to some degree. The aim of examining the characteristics of a poem and the responses they produce was achieved more adequately in terms of the effects of poetry than an analysis of the nature of poetry. One difficulty was a failure to spend sufficient time exploring poetry. At times, students did not understand sufficiently the nature of what they were trying to teach. On the other hand, there frequently emerged a clear awareness of poetry's effect on the people involved, and the class achieved unanticipated success in the creation of poems (e.g., with the deaf and emotionally disturbed children).

Analysis of the psychological dimensions of interpersonal communication began with the first class meeting and continued throughout the semester. Our final session, an evaluation of the course, was both an indication of how much we had grown in our ability to communicate and an example of growth still in progress. The openness and honesty with which we examined and criticized the course demonstrated our increased communicative freedom. The hesitation, on the part of a few, suggested that more could be achieved.

The last three aims (poetry as a means of communicating with a group of hospitalized schizophrenics, insight into the ways schizophrenics communicate, and the experience of attempting to relate to people hospitalized for emotional difficulties) all had to be revised due to the shift in field work facilities. Not being able to work with hospitalized schizophrenics led us to a much broader program (a school for deaf children, an outpatient clinic, and a school for emotionally disturbed children). The complexity of these field experiences did not allow as much depth of exploration or the time for facilitation of communication that a single situation would have provided. However, the contrast between the communication difficulties of deaf children, emotionally disturbed children, and emotionally disturbed adolescents and adults provided an added dimension that we had not anticipated.

It is also our impression that we were able to make considerable progress in opening up communication between ourselves and the individuals in the field situations, and to relate to these people as people rather than patients defined by diagnostic categories. This progress was not the same for all students in all situations. They found satisfaction or understanding in various parts of the field experience.

The feeling of having been involved in a meaningful relationship was acutely confronted as we faced separation from each of these groups. Each time there was a strong desire to continue with the involvement which had developed. In some cases, the feeling was so intense that students did continue working with individuals beyond the regularly scheduled time.

On the basis of our first semester's work, we prepared a revised course for the following years, which corrected some of our most critical difficulties. The main thrust of our revision was to provide more time to achieve our aims. Credit for the course was increased from three to four, and the number of field work situations was reduced from three to two. The increase in credit has allowed greater class time for an exploration of psychological concepts and poetry, and also the time necessary for a detailed exploration of approaches before and after each field visit. The reduction in the number of institutions used for field work has allowed some variety and contrast in terms of difficulties in communication while allowing a longer involvement and greater depth of exploration in each situation.

Our first field experience continues to be with deaf children, including many of the original group. Increasingly, they have moved toward the creation of poems which reveal their imaginative life and express their most urgent emotions. Each year, after six weekly visits to the school, our students play host to the children, who recite a full program of their latest poetry in the college theatre. Our second field experience is with a sizable group of patients at the rehabilitation center of a state mental hospital. After six weeks of discussion, based largely on poems produced by the hospital and college people, there is a final two-hour session that begins with a poetry discussion and ends with an outdoor picnic. By this time the two groups have become considerably integrated. One year the hospital issued a small collection of the work that had been produced. More recently, in a year when the creative harvest was extraordinary, the college undertook to publish a collection of about a hundred hospital poems, by patients and students, approximately titled *Long Night's Journey Back to Light*.

We have limited the number of students in the course to 12 so that we can maximize individuality of instruction and coordinate our activities more easily with the participating institutions. Our approach to learning has continued to stress a combination of theoretical understanding and practical application. In addition, this has remained an interdisciplinary effort emphasizing student involvement in the direction of the course. Finally, we have held fast to our original focus, working in an area of critical importance and relevance for contemporary society: mental health.

IN A DRUG REHABILITATION CENTER

Poetry: A Therapeutic Tool in the Treatment of Drug Abuse

RUTH LISA SCHECHTER, C.P.T.

... while medicine is an art, art in turn may also serve as medicine ...

—ROBERT VOLMAT[1]

Pretty as the poppy is, the heroin extracted from its flower is creating a frightening plague throughout American society. Accelerating to epidemic proportions, many new drug addicts now seen are 9- and 10-year-old children. Hospitals report rising mortality and overdose statistics.

The experience of Odyssey House, founded in 1966 by its director, Dr. Judianne Densen-Gerber, is that drug abuse indicates symptoms of personality disorganization. The adolescent drug addict has a profound sense of alienation, does not know who he is or where he fits in—an ideal candidate for the current drug subculture thriving in an era of social change that is vast, sweeping and dramatic. Odyssey House was the first rehabilitation agency to establish residential units exclusively for adolescent treatment and, recently, programs for pregnant drug addicts and their babies. At present, this psychiatrically oriented agency has about 15 residential units in New York City, Michigan, Utah and New Hampshire.

As a visiting poet, serving voluntarily at first once a week at the Female A.T.U. (Adolescent Treatment Unit) in the Southeast Bronx, I observed new poems emerging at the center of life, rather than at its periphery. In early May 1971, I was invited to join the staff on a full-time employment basis, in order to expand poetry therapy further. Some emotional breakthroughs had occurred, showing that poetry therapy was a valid therapeutic tool in the treatment of drug abuse. One of the first poems was prophetic, written by a 14-year-old girl, Victoria:

MOVEMENTS
> like a bee gliding
> like a stone rolling
> like a cloud drifting
> I move.

Victoria, who was very non-verbal in group therapy, exited from a second floor window shortly after she wrote this poem. Residents had begun writing "the unspeakable." As the program developed, poetry therapy proved to be a curative bridge, demonstrating that a poem can snap the lights on, offering clues for preventive medicine, hastening self discovery. Response from residents often was, "Yes, now I see."

Scheduled daily for group poetry therapy sessions at each residential unit throughout the city, I met with 10 to 20 residents, ages 14 to 30, of diverse ethnic and economic groups. All were school dropouts whom drug abuse had brought to the edge of suicide. Many had committed criminal offenses to support their drug habits: prostitution, muggings, larceny, etc. Some were referred to the agency from the courts; some entered voluntarily. Many were natives from as far as Alaska and California. When poetry therapy sessions were first announced, disinterest, suspicion and fatigue were evident. Comments ranged from, "Lady, who are you... a teacher, a social worker?" When I replied, "... a poet," some mild curiosity was shown about an actual poet being there. After a few sessions, it was increasingly important that I memorize the colorful and compressed drug-addict's jargon to further communication. My sincerity was constantly tested. Although it was obvious that dormant interest and curiosity could be stimulated in new directions, it was more imperative that trust be deepened and heightened. At first, I offered books of current, relevant poetry and contemporary anthologies, placing them around on tables for visual impact. Eventually, poems by Anne Sexton, Allen Ginsberg, Stanley Kunitz, Langston Hughes, Denise Levertov, Pablo Neruda, and Seferis were welcomed.

By trail and error, I stumbled into an emergency curriculum relative to "live or die." Since survival was the theme, emergency treatment of priorities might work, offering poetry, not as a lulling tranquilizer, but rather as an urgent "telegram" applied much as a respirator or cardiac message—intense, dramatic and immediate. Of necessity then, literary techniques, form, grammar, spelling, rhyming, philosophy or history of literature, were neglected. Although as the program continued, all techniques emerged naturally and spontaneously via exposure. Attention span was extremely brief due to physical weakness and emotional exhaustion. Depression, loneliness, withdrawal, morbid suspicion and disorientation from drug abuse were the pervading symptoms. Applicable was the last line from William Carlos William's introduction to Ginsberg's HOWL, "Hold back the edges of your gowns...Ladies, we are going through hell."[2]

Flexible guidelines encouraging universal major emotions such as love, life, death, birth and loneliness were offered. Immediate writing of hidden feelings and language on a gut level erupted. Self discovery clues were heard in new ways, urging honest, precise and concrete revelations in poems. Imagination stretched toward personal identity and human values. Residents listened attentively to one another's poems, showing concern, offering help and interest. The spirit was: if you can't say it, write it!

Sheera's new poem, Gone, proved to be an exciting breakthrough for her as well as for her peers. Sheera had been expressionless and apathetic for some time, since she had received news of her father's illness. She appeared stunned, in a zombie-like trance, and resisted talking about her father's sudden death from cancer. She was unable to move in any direction, especially since she had constructed fantasies about her father whom she had not seen for many years. She was encouraged to try "writing it out." Shortly thereafter, this 15-year-old girl offered the following poem at a poetry therapy session:

> Betty Lipshitz's
> middle aged son is DEAD.
> I saw him in Hellman's funeral parlor
> a skinny, ghostlike, colorless head
> on interior of white silk that lines
> his bed of walnut wood, that shines
> in his Sleeping Beauty World
> I KISS!
> but DADDY you are still
>   **FOREVER**
>
> So, pops
> where are you at?
> tell me!

where are you really at?
still in your box
down deep in Jersey soil
have you risen?
have you sunk
are you there?
only you know your boundaries
you can't hurt anymore
'cause I'm still HERE

times were bad
but there was good
I still remember
picnics in the park
picking Princess out of whining
puppies at the Bid-a-Wee Home
you telling me...happy birthday
sitting on your knee
summers on beach 67th Street
in our Rockaway home
6:00 a.m. out on the beach
buried in sand
castles you made me from a 39¢ pail
open school week at P.S. 31
hiding the afikoman on passover
giving me a dollar, if I found it
or not, watching wonderama on Sunday morning
holding my hand as we sat
on the cyclone, going faster, faster
at Coney Island, winding it up at Nathan's
tucking me in
saying "good night"

                thank you DADDY

I love you for these times
they're over though

            DAMN IT!

    Lively discussion began about this poem. Sheera shared her feelings with her peers, crying, talking more. Many locked-in feelings, fantasies, and anger about her father were discussed. She began to recover slowly from the shock and trauma of her father's death and cooperated more actively towards getting well in the program.

Constance, a black resident, felt she was ugly. She expressed shame about her blackness and appeared sullen and sad. Soon, she was writing:

> With my skin dark as night
> As I look at myself
> I feel no fright

and later

> running
> when I was running
> what was I running from?
> was it Eva, my mother
> give me some answers
> 'cause I'm not afraid anymore
> no...not anymore

Free association poems resulted in immediate writing from visual objects—photographs, posters, everyday objects—selected at random to heighten observation. We talked about time. Is it on the clock? Is it what you remember? Is it when something happened, painful or joyous? Soon a group of "time poems" like Sharon's poem evolved:

> Time is people
> Time is the leaves on a tree
> Time is food
> Time is clothes
> Time is a book
> Time is smoke rising from my
> cigarette
> BUT DIG!
> Time is everybody, everything
> 'cause you see
> without time
> we're nothing.

Most of the residents who never wrote before were more terrified. Encouraged by their peers to try, since it helped more than mainlining, they began new poems. Eventually, self-pride and widened observation broke into stanzas, finding their own form. Poetry flooded in a surge of personal honesty, original language and relevant imagery. Residents stuffed their pockets with poems, pinned them up on walls;

exchanged new poems as part of everyday living. Some drew cover designs for manuscripts, in creative, spontaneous acts. Poetry therapy was contagious throughout the agency. Residents enjoyed coming forward to read new poems aloud, indicating even in their posture, new feelings of self-worth and enthusiasm about having made a poem. Poems were challenged by peers asking, "what do you mean...are you really saying it...are you telling the truth...why do you use the word 'blue' in all your poems...tell us why?"

The residents wrote many "portrait poems" about one another, exploring further whether they were aware of one another. Those who were most inarticulate began "writing it out"—ventilating frustrations, wishes, anger, anxieties, nightmares and apprehensions, in down-to-earth language relative to repairing troubled psyches and exploring self-identity and value. Limited vocabularies expanded. Since drug addicts superimpose phantasy artificially via drug abuse, residents were encouraged to rechannel energy toward realistic goals via the catalyst of poems that named specifics i.e., time, place, person, season. Typing committees formed to type poems, since they were deemed valuable. Copies of poems were included in residents' charts as part of their medical history and progress.

Occasionally guest writers visited, stimulating new poems. (Interest was shown in my poems, but not until about 6 months later, when I was invited to read some of my work.) Residents exchanged poems with guest writers and actively discussed ideas, feelings and books. Other beneficial extensions of the program were new friendships and social exchange.

Although early poems reflected almost total self-involvement and pity, i.e., "me, mine," after a process of more writing, negative poems moved outwards fostering new attitudes and behavior. Clicking into other dialogues, this delicate poem of hope by George triggered a series of "green" poems:

> Green a tree.
> Green a lizard in the shade.
> Green the sea in a storm, raving.
> Green a banana.
> Green a house in the shade.
> Green the summer or the winter.

Pertinent poetry applied directly offers valid, constructive insights and solutions to human needs, fears and aspirations. It helps to express the feelings at the center of life rather than at its periphery, especially since poetry uses "the word" as truth-seeker.

When drug abuse disorients the psyches of troubled young people, the healing power of poetry illuminates, hand-in-hand with psychotherapeutic modalities; it helps restore, rehabilitate and widen self discovery.

REFERENCES

1. Robert Volmat, in Norma Haimes, "Guide to the Literature of Art Therapy," *American Journal of Art Therapy*, XI (January 1972) 26.

2. William Carlos Williams, in Allen Ginsberg, *HOWL* (Los Angeles, City Lights, 1956).

A LIST OF POEMS

Suitable for Use in Poetry Therapy

One supposes that a therapist who knows the great body of English and American poetry (not to mention one acquainted also with the poetry of other nations), and has lived with it for some years, could find a thousand, possibly even five thousand, poems suitable to his therapeutic needs and purposes. But vast numbers are unnecessary: a practicing therapist might be hard put to use more than fifty or a hundred poems in a year; and excellent large anthologies and smaller paperbacks are available to the searcher in many good bookstores and probably many college classrooms. This list does not intend to be complete in any way. It derives from the suggestions of the Contributors.

ANONYMOUS
    Alysoun
    Sumer is Icumen in
    Western Wind, when wilt thou blow?
BIBLE
    Ecclesiastes
    Psalms
WILLIAM BLAKE
    Cradle Song
    A Little Boy Lost
    A Poison Tree
    The Fly
    The Lamb
    The Little Black Boy
    The Tyger
ROBERT BROWNING
    Epilogue, *Asolando*
    Home-Thoughts, from Abroad
    Meeting at Night
    Prospice
    Rabbi Ben Ezra
    From *Paracelsus*
    Song from *Pippa Passes*

KENNETH BURKE
    Alky, Me Love
ROBERT BURNS
    A Man's a Man for A' That
    My Luve
    The Banks o'Doon
    To a Mouse
THOMAS CAMPION
    There Is a Garden in Her Face
THOMAS CARLYLE
    Today
LEWIS CARROLL
    Beware the Jabberwock
    The Hunting of the Snark
JOHN CLARE
    I Am
    Young Lambs
ARTHUR HUGH CLOUGH
    Say Not the Struggle Naught Availeth
SAMUEL TAYLOR COLERIDGE
    Dejection: An Ode

A List of Poems

Kubla Khan
The Ancient Mariner
Work without Hope
WILLIAM COWPER
Light Shining Out of Darkness
STEPHEN CRANE
The Wayfarer
E. E. CUMMINGS
Buffalo Bill's
dying is fine) but Death
no man, if men are gods
one's not half two
voices to voices, lip to lip
what if a much of a which of a wind
will you teach a/wretch to live
you shall above all things be glad and young
WALTER DE LA MARE
The Listeners
EMILY DICKINSON
A Prison Gets To Be a Friend
A Triumph May Be Several Kinds
Because I could Not Stop For Death
I'm Nobody
I Never Saw a Moor
I Went to Heaven
Magnanimous as Bird
Not With a Club, The Heart is Broken
The Mountains Grow Unnoticed
There Is No Frigate Like a Book
JOHN DONNE
Death, Be Not Proud
Holy Sonnets
Song (Go and catch a falling star)
Song (Sweetest love, I do not go)
The Ecstasy
The Good-Morrow
The Sun Rising
JOHN DRYDEN
To the Memory of Mrs. Killigrew
ALAN DUGAN
Love Song: I and Thou
T. S. ELIOT
Four Quartets
The Cocktail Party
RALPH WALDO EMERSON
Give All To Love
The Problem
ROBERT FROST
Birches
Mending Wall
Stopping by Woods on a Snowy Evening
The Road Not Taken
The Secret Sits
Tree at My Window
Two Tramps in Mud-Time
ISABELLA GARDNER
That Craning of the Neck
KAHLIL GIBRAN
The Prophet
LOUS GINSBERG
Hunger and Thirst
GEORGE GORDON, LORD BYRON
Maid of Athens, Ere We Part
She Walks in Beauty
When We Two Parted
ELI GREIFER
A Poet Wants a Sepulcher in the Form of a Book for His Works
A Song of Emancipatory Renaissance
Creative Smiling
Life Triumphs
THOMAS HARDY
Afterwards
The Darkling Thrush
WILLIAM E. HENLEY
Invictus
GEORGE HERBERT
The Altar
The World
ROBERT HERRICK
Grace for a Child
The Argument of His Book
To Daisies, Not to Shut So Soon
RALPH HODGSON
Time, You Old Gypsy Man
HOMER
The Iliad
The Odyssey
GERARD MANLEY HOPKINS
God's Grandeur
Pied Beauty

A. E. HOUSMAN
  Loveliest of Trees
  When I Was One-and-Twenty
  Terence, this is stupid stuff
BEN JONSON
  Oak and Lily
  To Celia
JOHN KEATS
  Bright Star, Would I were Stedfast
  Ode on a Grecian Urn
  Ode to a Nightingale
  On First Looking into Chapman's Homer
  When I have Fears That I may Cease To Be
EDWARD LEAR
  Nonsense Verse
HENRY WADSWORTH LONGFELLOW
  Hymn To The Night
  The Day Is Done
  The Rainy Day
  The Tide Rises, The Tide Falls
RICHARD LOVELACE
  To Althea, from Prison
ANY LOWELL
  Patterns
GUSTAV MAHLER
  They melt, the shadows of the night
EDWIN MARKHAM
  Outwitted
CHRISTOPHER MARLOWE
  The Passionate Shepherd to His Love
ANDREW MARVELL
  The Garden
  To His Coy Mistress
JOHN MASEFIELD
  Sea-Fever
EDNA ST. VINCENT MILLAY
  Renascence
  The Return
JOHN MILTON
  On His Blindness
MOTHER GOOSE
  Hinx, minx, the old witch winks
ARTHUR O'SHAUGHNESSY
  Ode

PATIENTS' POEMS
  As an old friend, you walk in, p. 255
  As petals open one by one, asserting, p. 26
  Bad dreams/What do they mean? p. 218
  Because you have paved the way, p. 253
  Creation adorns the earth with flowers, p. 224
  Did you ever shiveringly tinkle? p. 169
  Environment, heredity, p. 24
  Give me your little hand, p. 225
  God is Godot, and God is time, p. 27
  Harold—Your heart is as big, p. 98
  How came such poisoned pap from so excellent an udder? p. 93
  How can one bear the awful loneliness, p. 23
  I bounce in late, p. 97
  If the world were my oyster, p. 97
  I have taken flight from preoccupation with man, p. 256
  I like trees because they are green, p. 251
  I never say/What I want to say, p. 99
  In my heart/Where cold winter reigns, p. 224
  In this interior decoration, p. 191
  I sank into a well, p. 23
  It is Love that shows me how, p. 254
  I wanted to ask Nancy, p. 99
  Like the child waiting in the night, p. 90
  Move and change, p. 25
  My dreams/Yellow leaves, lifeless, dead, p. 224
  My universe is small, you see, p. 97
  No man is an island, p. 98
  Of wounded times the grave bird wails, p. 92
  Perhaps if I tried to communicate, p. 216
  Remember/The bright sunsets in the bamboo of your youth, p. 225
  She has new leaves, p. 86

A List of Poems

She reminded me that your eyes were made for tears, p. 225
Short sleek and witty sits this gravid owl, p. 94
...the arching goddess/a silken lure, p. 111
Then sleep, your dark head warm, p. 26
There is a dark place where sometimes, p. 23
There once was a fisherman who lived at sea, p. 250
The sun has arrived in the sky, p. 226
Today I meet a stranger, p. 150
To mine own execution/Be true, p. 91
To walk the virgin snow alone, p. 86
We sat in a room, p. 96
What a sweet repast, p. 254
What is it to care, p. 171
What is next? p. 217
Will someone/Tell me who I am, p. 255
You shine on my bitter days/Like a sky full of stars, p. 226
Your embraces were created to hold me, p. 226

ALEXANDER POPE (*passim*)
JOHN CROWE RANSOM
   Essay on Criticism
   Lady Lost
CHRISTINA ROSSETTI
   A Birthday
   Does the road wind uphill all the way?
CARL SANDBURG
   The People Will Live On
   The People, Yes
WILLIAM SHAKESPEARE
   Plays (*passim*)
   Sonnets
      29. When, in disgrace with Fortune and men's eyes
      30. When to the sessions of sweet silent thought
      33. Full many a glorious morning have I seen
      73. That time of year thou mayst in me behold
      116. Let me not to the marriage of true minds
      130. My mistress' eyes are nothing like the sun
PERCY BYSSHE SHELLEY
   Love's Philosophy
   Ode to the West Wind
   The Cloud
   To a Skylark
CHRISTOPHER SMART
   A Song to David
STEPHEN SPENDER
   I think continually of those
WALLACE STEVENS
   Tomorrow
   Which is Real
ROBERT LOUIS STEVENSON
   Resurgence
   Romance
   The Celestial Surgeon
SIR JOHN SUCKLING
   Why So Pale and Wan
ALGERNON CHARLES SWINBURNE
   In Harbour
   Love at Sea
   The Garden of Proserpine
ALFRED LORD TENNYSON
   Locksley Hall
   Ulysses
DYLAN THOMAS
   Fern Hill
   If I were tickled by the rub of love
FRANCIS THOMPSON
   In No Strange Land
THOMAS TRAHERNE
   Wonder
HENRY VAUGHAN
   The World
EDMUND WALLER
   Go, lovely rose
   On a Girdle
JOHN HALL WHEELOCK
   The Black Panther

WALT WHITMAN
    A Child Went Forth
    I Celebrate Myself
    I Hear America Singing
    Song of Myself
    Song of the Open Road
JOHN GREENLEAF WHITTIER
    My Soul and I
    The Eternal Goodness
    The Light That is Felt
WILLIAM WORDSWORTH
    A slumber did my spirit seal
    Intimations of Immortality
    It is a beauteous evening, calm and free
    My heart leaps up
    She dwelt among the untrodden ways
    The world is too much with us
    Tintern Abbey
WILLIAM BUTLER YEATS
    Dialogue of Self and Soul
    The Lake Isle of Innisfree

INDEX

A

Achievement, in writing poetry, 198
Addison, Joseph, 18
Adolescents, 193–200, 212–227
  emotionally disturbed, poetry in communication with, 266–273
  music of, 233
Adults, emotionally disturbed, poetry in communication with, 266–273
African tribes, curative powers of song and, 48, 49
Aggression, disguised, wit as, 59
  in monsters of movies and nonsense poetry, 74
Alcoholics, poetry for, 168
Altschuler, Ira M., 153
American Indians, curative power of song and, 44–46
American Psychiatric Association, 176
Anxiety, management of poetry and insanity in, 36–37
Apache, shaman, 45–46
Aristotle, 151, 162
Aronov, B. M., 104
Art therapy(ies), 150, 175
Ashton-Warner, Sylvia, 247
Auden, W. H., 28–29, 31, 35, 38
Australian aborigines, 50
Autism, rhythmic sign language in, 9

B

Bambi, 73
Beatles, The, 233, 241
Behavior, development of, 228,
  rhythmic, embryonic, 5–6
Bell, George, xxi
Bentham, Jeremy, 32
Berger, Milton M., 163, 168
Berne, Eric, 147, 154
Blues, *See* Music, blues
Bonime, Walter, 105, 113
Bortz, E. L., 163
Bowra, C. M., 43, 51
Breast-feeding, rhythm in, 7
Brown, Rosalie, xxi
Bruner, Jerome, 229
Burnshaw, Stanley, 35
Bussolati, Beverly, xxi
Buryat tribe, Shamans of, 47
Byron, George Gordon, 36

C

Cahn, Meyer, 129
Carkhuff, R. R., 118
Carlyle, Thomas, 83
Carrier, W., 173
Carroll, Lewis, 57–58, 61–62, 71, 73, 74, 76
Case histories and examples, 170–172; of adolescents, 213–227; of patient Barbara, 215–218; Esther, 172; Francisco, 218–223; Glenda, 96–100; H., 189; Mrs. H., 179–183; Harold R., 172; Katina, 223–227; Lewis, 92–96; Lorene, 213–215; M., 189; Mollie, 172; R., 187–188; Richard N., 175; S., 188–189; Sam, 172; Sybil, 90–92; V., 191

Catharsis, 14–16, 22, 151, 190
Caudwell, Christopher, 36–37
Center for Creative Living, 89
Ceylon, Songs in healing in, 49–50
Chaucer, Geoffrey, 151
Cheyenne, Shaman, 46
Child, autistic, rhythmic sign language for, 231–232
Child(ren), American middle class deaf, poetry in communication with, 258, 266
  emotionally disturbed, poetry in communication with, 273, 284
  imagination of, 228, 230
  listening to, Montessori on, 231
  observation of reality, 230
  metaphorical thought of, 229, 230–231
  spontaneity and, 229
  and teacher, self-discovery for, 228, 247–248
  threatening elements in movies and, 73
  visions of utopias in poetry by, 232
Children, The, 231
Chippewa, curative power of song and, 46
Choctaw, Shaman, 46
Ciardi, John, 113
Clare, John, 87–88
Clark, Robert A., 104
Clock, biologic, 50
Clough, Arthur Hugh, 87
Coates, Samuel, 175
Coleman, J. C., 28, 31
Coleridge, Samuel Taylor, 32
College, group therapy at, 102–106
Commotion, 6
Communication, between minds, 60
  poetry as, 1, 118
  in psychotherapy, 115–116
  symbolic exchange in, 116–117, 118–119

types of, 117
using only sign modalities, 117–118
with deaf children, 258–266
written, 128
with emotionally disturbed adolescents and adults, 152–160
with emotionally disturbed children, 273–284
Compassion, in poem by prison inmate, 144
Cooscillation, 11
Correctional institution, poetry therapy in, 135–149
Counseling Center, poetry therapy in, 253–256
Cousins, Norman, xix
Cowper, William, 83
Creative process, poetic, *See* Poetry, creation of
Creativity, awareness as factor in, 136
Creedmore State Hospital, 152
Creek Indians, rituals of Shamans of, 46
Crootof, Charles, 150
Ctesias, 72
Cumberland Hospital, 82, 152
Curandera, poetic incantation of, 47

D

Dahlstrom, W. G., 113
Dakota Indians, medicine man of, 46
Dance, rhythm in, 212
DAP, *See* Draw-A-Person test
Darwin, Charles, 5
Davie, Donald, 29, 38
Deaf children, poetry in communication with, 258–266
Dean, Stanley, R., 40
Death, aggression expressed as, in

nonsense poetry, 76
  preoccupation with, in poem by prison inmate, 140
Decision making by emotionally fragile persons, 177–178
Defense mechanisms, 21–22
Densen-Gerber, Judianne, 287
Dependency needs, 95
Depression, 82–83
Diamond, Edwin, 157, 162
  Poetry therapy working out, 142, 143
Dickinson, Emily, 157, 187, 188, 214, 215
Dirty Dozens, 246
Discussion, of poetry, 190
Diseases, periodic, 5
Disney, Walt, 73
Dixmont State Hospital, 85, 184, 188, 189
Donne, John, 87
Doodling, 223
Doors, The, 239
Dostoevski, F. M., 167, 174
Dragon story, classic elements of, 62, 63
Draw-A-Person test, 104, 108
Dreams, displacement in, 45, 58, 105, 110
  interpretation of, Freud on 58
  poetry and, 59
  therapeutic value of, 58
  and wit, Freud on, 59
Drew Elizabeth, 227
Drug abuse, poetry therapy in, 287–293
  enthusiasm for, 291–292
  guest writers and, 292
  guidelines for, 289
  initial response to, 288
  institution of, 288
  scope of poetry in, 292
  value of, 292–293
Dryden, John, 83, 88
Dylan, Bob, 151, 193, 196
Dysrhythmia, 10

E

Edgar, Kenneth, xvi, 83, 102, 184, 191
Eichmann, Adolf, 195
El Camino Hospital, xxi
Eliot, T. S., xxii, 101, 152, 166, 174, 212
Emotion(s), definition, 12
  expression through poetry, 100
Emotionally disturbed adolescents and adults, poetry in communication with, 152–160
Emotionally disturbed children, poetry in communication with, 273, 284
  in poem by prison inmate, 147–148
Enemies of a Bishop, The, 29
Engle, P., 173
Environment, concern for, creation of, 230
  imagery, stimulated by, 243–244
Erotic feelings, breathing rhythm and, 14
Eskimo(s), Greenland, dispelling of anger by, 47, 48
  polar, shamans of, 48
  shaman, 45
Ethiopia, Zar cult of, healing by, 49
Externalization, 156, 186, 190, 191, 218

F

Fantasies, "writing out" of, in poetry therapy, 289–291
Fantasy, 252
Feelings, expression of, 190
Fetterman, David, 195, 196
FitzHerbert, J., 16

Fleischl, Maria, 150
Fontaine, Eliza., 13
Fowler, H. W., 157
Frank, Anne, 203
Franklin, Benjamin, 175
Free association, 251
Free association poems, 291
Freud, Sigmund, xix, 21, 22, 28, 30, 35, 58, 59, 118
Frost Robert, 22, 84, 87, 88, 151, 213
Frustration, youthful, in poem by prison inmate, 146–147

G

Gabriel, Sister Paul, 6, 16
Galt, John M., 176
Gangs, Street, 221–222
Gardner, Martin, 61
Gibran, Kahlil, 166, 168, 169, 174
Gide, André, 29
Ginsberg, Allen, 196, 289
Ginsberg, Louis, 159, 162, 216
Gleason, R. J., 200
Goffman, Erving, 198
Goldenson, Robert M., 28
Graves, Robert, 29–31
Greenacre, Phyllis, 60, 62, 65
Greenwald, Harold, xvi, 89
Greifer, Eli, xx, 82, 87, 102, 103, 152, 162, 189, 192
Grotjahn, Martin, 60, 63
Group poetry therapy, cohesiveness in, 190
 elimination of warm-up in, 156, 190
 in college students, 106–107
 poem selection in, 87, 103, 107
 problems, 203–207
 validation, 102–114
Group recitation, 85
Guthiel, Emil A., 105, 113, 192

H

Habits, rhythms and, 11
Hallucinations, 189
Hammer, Emanuel, 113
Happiness, search for, 97–98, 169
Harrower, Molly, 36
Hathaway, S., 113
Hazley, Richard, xvi, 83, 102, 184, 192
Headbanging, 8, 9
Hendrix, Jimi, 239
Henley, W. E., 87, 153, 189
Herrick, Robert, 87
Hillel, Rabbi, 164, 174
Hillside Hospital, 201–211
Hippocrates, 4
Hitler, Adolf, 8
Hogan, P., 101
Holmes, O. W., 83
Homer, 151, 222
Homosexuality, problem of, in poem by prison inmate, 144–145
Hooker, D., 16
Hooker, John Lee, 234
Hopelessness, in patient's poem, 98
Hopkins, Gerard Manley, 87
Hopkins, Lightning, 234
Horney, Karen, 107, 113, 164
Hospitalized Veterans Writing Project, Inc., 13
Hostility, in patient's poem, 97
Housman, A. E., 168
Hughes, Langston, 288
Hunting of the Snark, The, 62
Hypnotherapy, by Negritos, 50
Hypnotic effects, 9, 10, 85

I

I Am a Rock, 239
Identification, 111

I Heard My Children Crying, 234
Imagery, of rock music, 240
  of street culture, 243–244
  of TV commercials, 244
Imagination, of children, 229, 230
  observation of reality and, 230
Indiana State University of Pennsylvania, 83
Individual poetry therapy, 179–180
Infantilism, 110
Inman, W. S., 16
Insanity, and poetry, in management of anxieties, 36–37
Institute of the Pennsylvania Hospital, 11, 17, 175, 176, 179, 193, 195
Institutions, poetry therapy in, xxi
Intellectual defense, 94
Interaction, postnatal, rhythm in, 7
Isherwood, Christopher, 28, 29
Isoprinciple, 82–83, 103, 153

J

Jabberwock, descriptions of by subjects of study, 66–68
  drawing(s) of, by John Tenniel, 66
Jabberwocky, 63–64
  as classic dragon story, 62
  choice of, in poetry therapy, 61–62, 71
  effect of, on imagination, study of, 63–66
  imagery suggested by, 68–69
  meaning of, 63–67
  nonsense words in, 69–70
  subjects of study defining, 70–71
Jazz, rhythm in, 7
Jeffers, Robinson, 83
Johnson, Julia, 197–198
Johnson, Thomas H., 214

Jones, Robert, xvi, 175, 193
Jung, Karl, 105, 110, 113

K

Keats, John, 9, 85, 172, 199, 200, 205, 224
Keble, John, 35, 36, 37, 42
Kennedy, John F., 102
Kenneth E. Appel Award, 177
Kenny, Nick, 210
Kerouac, Jack, 216
King, B. B., 234
Kirkbride, Thomas, S., 176–177
Klages, L., 16
Kobak, Dorothy, xvi, 249
Kohl, Herbert R., 41
Kramer, Aaron, xvi, 201
Krauss, Robert, 118
Kris, E., 21
Kronmeyer, Robert, 174
Kunitz, Stanley, 288

L

Laing, R. D., 228
Landor, Walter Savage, 83
Lane, Homer, 29
Langer, S. K., 16
Langley Porter Inst., 11
Language, in communication, 58–59
  conversation modes, types of, 117
  of school and streets, 245, 246, 247
Laski, Harold J., 32
Lawrence, D. H., 29
Lear, E., 16, 75
Ledwith, Nettie H., 104, 113
Leedy, Jack J., iii, xi, xvii, 82, 102, 103, 113, 153, 162, 192
Lerner, Art, xx
Levertov, Denise, 288

Levit, Herbert, xvii, 184
Lewis, C. Day, 280
Logic, in communication with unconscious, 60
Loneliness, poem, 83, 85, 87, 88, 151, 153
Longfellow, Henry W., 83, 85, 87, 88, 151, 153
Lundlin, W. H., 104, 113

M

Machover, Karen, 113
MacLeish, Archibald, 28
Malaya, curative incantation in, 50
Malinowski, Bronislaw, 44
Mallarmé, Stéphane, 216
Manic-depression dysrhythmia, 10
Marmontel, 33
Married couples, poetry for, 168
Marti-Ibanez, Felix, 43–44
Masefield, John, 87
Masserman, J. H., 9, 16
Masturbation, compulsive, 8
Masturbation, frustration with, poem by prison inmate revealing, 144–145
McGinley, Phyllis, 24
Meerloo, Joost A. M., xvii, 3, 16
Memorization, of poems, 84, 103, 189–190
Menninger, Karl, 105, 113
Mental contagion, 12–14
Mental health center, poetry therapy in, 150–162
Mental hospital, newsletter in, 18; poetry therapy and workshop in, 201–211; recital at, 201–203
Mental retardation, 85
Metaphor, 198–199
Metaphors, in rock music, 239
Metropolitan Institute for Psychoanalytic Studies and Community Guidance Service, 89
Mid-Way Counseling Center, 249
Milieu therapy, 176
Milk dance, 7
Mill, John Stuart, 32–35
Millay, Edna St. Vincent, 26, 214
Miller, Joaquin, 153
Milton, John, 87
Minkowski, M., 15
Mintz, Eliza., E., 107, 113
Mittleman, B., 8, 16
MMPI, 104, 108
Moluches, healing ceremony of, 47
Monster(s), and calamities, in movies, children and, 73
fabled, of children, 62
classic elements of stories of, 63
fascination for, 74
frightening quality of, 74
healing powers of, beliefs of, 71
origin of, 72
therapeutic value of, 74
Monsters as Healers, 71
Montessori, Maria, 229, 230, 231
Moreno, J. L., xix
Morrison, Morris R., xvii, xx, 212
Mowbray, Jean K., xviii, 17
Mowrer, O. Hobart, 113
Murray, H. A., 113
Music, blues, authors concerned with, 234
blueslets inspired by, 234–236
in healing, 42–50
metaphors in, 239–240
oral sounds in, mood conveyed by, 237–238
origin of, 234
pop, as literature of youth, 234
rock, imagery of, 240
subjects of, 234
Music, rhythm in, 7, 14, 15
therapy, 153

Index

N

Nash, Ogden, 24
National Association for P. T., 83
Navajo, curative power of song and, 44–45
Negritos, curative power of song and, 50
Neruda, Pablo, 288
Neurosis, poetry as substitute for, 21
Newman, Cardinal, 35, 42
Newsletter, in mental hospital, 18
Nigeria, Yoniba tribe of, curative incantation of, 48
Nonsense, in communication with unconscious, 60
  definition of, 60
Nonsense language, development of, 59–60
Nonsense poetry, aggression in, expressed as annihilation, 75–76
  expressed as death, 75–76
  expressed as irreverence, 76–79
  expressed as mutilation, 75–76
  exploring unconscious through, 57–81
  of Lewis Carroll, 76–77
  liberties with language in, 78–79
  in poetry therapy, 58, 60–61
  therapeutic function of, 79
Northampton County Asylum, 88
Novalis, 3
Nowhere Man, 241
Nuer, poetry sung by, 48
Nursery rhymes, hidden meanings in, 61

O

Objectification of feelings, 190
Odyssey House, 287
Order, from chaos, 15, 164
Overprotectiveness, 168

P

Packe, Michael St. John, 32
Pan Tadeusz, 202
Paranoid schizophrenic reaction, 179–183
Parapathy, personification of, 105
Patient(s), desire to write poetry, 20, 21
  poems by, 175, 176, 216, 218–223, 224–227, 250, 251, 253–256
Personality, integration of, 20
Personification of the parapathy, 105
Piersol, G. M., 162
Pobble, The, 75, 81
Poe, Edgar A., 85
Poem(s), as defense, 128–129
  by deaf children, 261, 262, 265–266
  by emotionally disturbed child(ren), 279, 280, 281, 282, 283
  by mental patients, 175, 176, 216, 218–223, 224–227
  by patient(s), as catalyst, 128
  by school children, need for free expression in, 247
  by teacher, to stimulate imagination of youngsters, 234
  by therapist, to help patient face unexpressed problem, 148–149
  child's, in poetry therapy, 54–56
  choice of, criteria for, 82, 87, 105, 107, 153, 155
  compassion, 144, 147–148
  drug abuse, 288, 289–290, 291–292
  emotional theme of, 155
  for depression, 83
  free association, 290–291
  homosexuality as problem in, 144–145

Poem(s) (*cont.*)
 humor in, 139
 loneliness in, 143–144
 memorization of, 84, 103, 189–190
 on masturbation, 145–146
 prison, chronic hebephrenic schizophrenic, 136–138
 problems of society in, 232, 235–240, 241
 psychodynamics of, 115–131
 question of identity in, 241–243
 self-searching, 239–240
 sung, in healing, 42–50
 symbolization of self in, 127
 youthful frustration in, 146–147
Poet(s), defense mechanisms used by, 21, 22
 emulation of, 211
Poetic Mind, The, 35
Poetry, as catalyst and defense, 128–129
 as mode of communication, 118–119
 as substitute for neurosis, 21
 as therapy, 37, 163–174
 Auden and, 28–29, 31, 38
 Bentham and, 32–34
 by patients, psychodynamics of, 115–131, 136
 Byron and, 36
 communication through, 85, 89–101, 150, 190
 "correctional", 148
 creativity in, awareness as factor in, 136
 "dissecting" of, 136
 dreams, compared, 58
 dreams vs., 157
 effects of, 151, 213
 evaluation of, 284–285
 expression and, 101
 for alcoholics, 168
 for married couples, 168–169
 for non-fulfillment in family life, 167
 goal of, 257
 Graves and, 30–31
 healing, Navajo, 44–45
 insanity and, in management anxieties, 36–37
 Keble and, 35, 36, 37
 Mill and, 32–35
 Newman and, 35
 nonsense, *See* Nonsense poetry
 primitive societies, 40–51
 self-discovery for teacher and youngster through, 228–248
 sense of well-being from, 158
 success of, 207–211
 symbolic fulcrum of, 119
 symbolization of self in, 118–119
 therapeutic value of, 86–88
 writing of, 21
Poetry therapy, appreciation for, poems by prison patients revealing, 138–140
 in drug abuse, *See* Drug abuse, poetry therapy in
 introduction of patient to, 136
 nonsense poetry in, 58, 60
 verbalization of emotions in, 288, 293
 "writing it out" in, 289, 291
Poetry therapy group, xxi, 85
Poetry workshop, in mental hospital, 203–211
 poetry selected for, 210–211
Prelude, 37–38
Prescott, Frederick C., 35, 36, 38, 41
Psychoanalytic Therapy, Theory of, 115

Q

Quesalid, training in shamanism of, 134—135

R

Rankouts, 246–247
Read, Herbert, 16
Reality testing, suspension of, 158
Redding, Otis, 234
Regression, definition of, 74
  in rhythm, 68
  therapeutic, nonsense poetry and, 70
Reik, Theodor, 103, 106, 109, 114
Reiman, H. A., 16
Rhythm, 5–16
  abnormal expression of, 8–9
  biologic, 4–5
  catharsis and, 14–15
  communicative function of, 4, 9–10
  in dance, 212
  in poetry, 12–14
  in mental contagion, 12–14
  transfer from person to person, 11
Rimbaud, J. N. A., 216
Robbins, B. S., 101
Robinson, S. Sue, xviii, 17
Rorschach, Hermann, 114
Rosenblatt, Lousie, 212, 227
Rush, Benjamin, 175

S

Sandburg, Carl, 151
Schizophrenia, 184–192
Schizophrenic, chronic hebephrenic, poems by, 136–139
School, 600
  poetry therapy in, 249–253
Self-realization, 190–191
Senryu poetry, 50–51
Service, Robert, 154
Sexton, Anne, 289
Shakespeare, William, 87, 151, 153, 166, 204, 208
Shaman(s), American Indian, rituals of, 44–46
  of Bali, 40
  descriptions of, 44–45
  Eskimo, 45
Shamanism, 40–41
Sharpe, E. F., 162
Shelley, Percy B., 79
Shieman, Joy, xxi
Slippery Rock State College, 86, 102, 191
Smart, Christopher, 88
Smith, L. H., 152, 162
Song(s), to stimulate poetry therapy group, 84
  in healing, 42–50
Sonne, John C., 198–200
Spender, Stephen, 28
Steele, Richard, 18
Stekel, Wilhelm, 105, 114
Suicidal tendencies, 83
Symbolic parallelism, 105

T

Talmud, 164
Tatler, The, 17–21, 27, 196
Tate, Allen, 29
Teacher, as "middle-man", 229
  and child(ren), self-discovery for, through poetry, 228–248
  spontaneity and, 229
  responsibilities of, 228, 229
  structural, in poetry session, 233
Television commericals, imagery stimulated by, 244–245
Tenniel, John, illustration of Jabberwock by, 66
Tennyson, Alfred, 87, 151
Therapy, as poetry, 163–174
  definitions of, 163
Thinking, ways of, 61
Thompson, Francis, 14, 83
Through the Looking Glass, 71

Timing, in psychotherapy, 165
Togetherness, 251
Transference, 188–189
  breaking through, 254
  in patient's poems, 94, 98–99
  in poem by prison inmate, 140–141
  weaning process in, 141–142
Trask, Willard R., 42, 51
Two Old Bachelors, The, 75
Twyeffort, L. H., 152, 162

U

Unconscious, communicating with, 198
  effect on poetry of, 158
  nonsense in, 60
  exploring of, through nonsense poetry, 57–81

V

Van Der Post, L., 16
Verbalization, 156, 190

W

Wallawalla Indians, curative power of song and, 47

Ward, Aileen, 199, 200
Welch, Jennifer Groce, xxi
Weaning from transference, 141–142
Well-being, sense of, 158
Welsh, G. S., 113
White, Ann, xxi
Whitman, Walt, 151
Whittier, John G., 83
Williams, William Carlos, 289
Wit, as disguised aggression, 58
  and dreams, Freud on, 58

W

Words, meaning of, Humpty Dumpty and, 65, 71
Wordsworth, William, 34–35, 37–38, 41

Y

Yeats, W. B., *In Memory Of*, 31

Z

Zar cult, of Ethiopia, 49